FLOWER TYPES

SPIKE RACEME CORY UMBEL CYME

COROLLA SHAPES

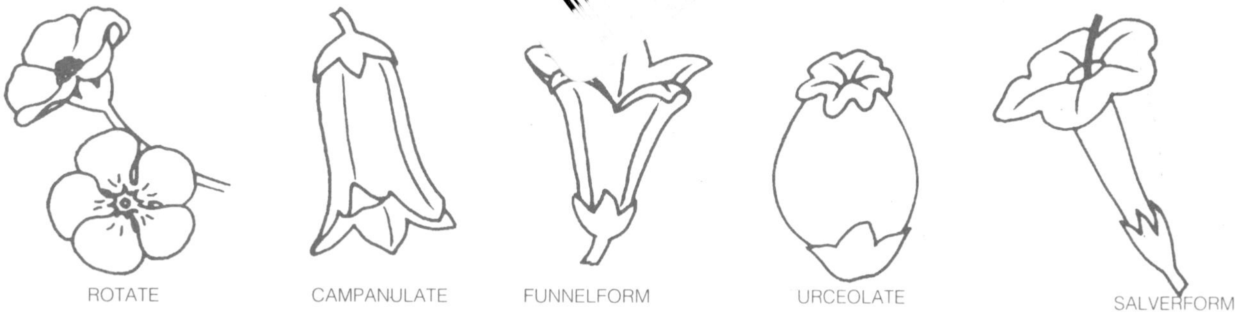

ROTATE CAMPANULATE FUNNELFORM URCEOLATE SALVERFORM

TREE AND SHRUB SHAPES

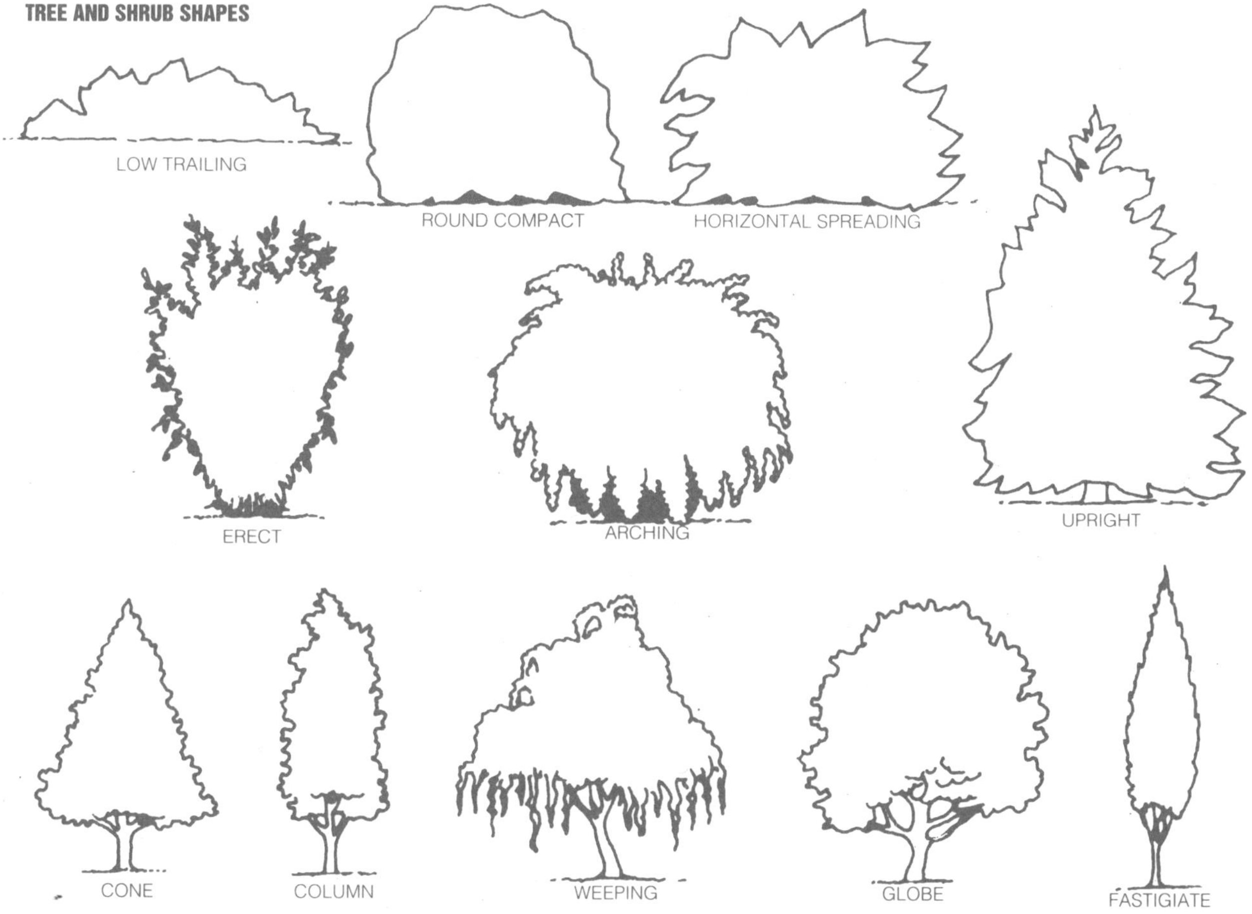

LOW TRAILING ROUND COMPACT HORIZONTAL SPREADING

ERECT ARCHING UPRIGHT

CONE COLUMN WEEPING GLOBE FASTIGIATE

D J Doads
February 1996

rose
gardening

Consultants
Daryl Johnson, Portland, Oregon
Clair Martin, The Huntington Botanical Garden
Nancy Rose, Minnesota Landscape Arboretum
Michael Ruggiero, The New York Botanical Garden
David Sattizahn, Hershey Gardens

Enabling Garden Consultant: Eugene Rothert, Chicago Botanic
Garden

Botany Consultant: Dr. Lucile McCook

rose
gardening

Boerner Botanical Gardens
Memphis Botanic Garden
Old Westbury Gardens

By Jim Browne
ACTING DIRECTOR, MEMPHIS BOTANIC GARDEN

William J. Radler
DIRECTOR, BOERNER BOTANICAL GARDENS

Nelson W. Sterner
DIRECTOR OF HORTICULTURE, OLD WESTBURY GARDENS

with Kathy Sammis

Series Editor Elvin McDonald
Principal Photography by Ralph Antczyk and
Albert Squillace

Pantheon Books, Knopf Publishing Group
New York
1995

Acknowledgments
This book was created with the help, expertise, and encouragement of a great many people. We would like to thank all the consultants who contributed so much to it, and entire staff of Boerner Botanical Garden, Memphis Botanic Gardens, and Old Westbury Gardens. We also appreciate the efforts of Kathy Grasso, Susan Ralston, Amanda Gordon, Altie Karper, Alan Kellock, David Prior, Annie Goh, May Low, Susan Kilpatrick, Marlin Hardeo, Doug Jensen, Jaime Gutierrez, Esther Jasek, Sadie Sammis, Patrick Markham, Jay Hyams, Eliraz and Yonatan Stein, Chani Yammer, Etti Yammer, Michelle Stein, and Deena Stein.

Project Director: Lori Stein
Book Design Consultant: Albert Squillace
Editorial Director: Jay Hyams
Associate Art Director: Chani Yammer

Library of Congress Cataloging-in-Publication Data
Sammis, Kathy.
Rose gardening / Kathy Sammis, writer
p.   cm. –(The American garden guides)
"Boerner Botanical Gardens, Memphis Botanic Garden, Old Westbury Gardens."
Includes index.
ISBN 0-679-75830-5
    1. Rose culture. 2. Roses. 3. Rose culture–United States.
4. Rose culture–Canada. 5. Roses–United States. 6. Roses-Canada.
    I. Boerner Botanical Gardens. II. Memphis Botanic Garden. III. Old Westbury Gardens. IV. Title. V. Series.
SB411.S24 1995   94.32985
635.9'3332–dc20   CIP

Manufactured in Singapore

First Edition

9 8 7 6 5 4 3 2 1

Opposite: 'Swarthmore', a Hybrid Tea Rose.

contents

Old Garden Roses with annuals and perennials.

'Secret', a Hybrid Tea .

'Veilchenblau', a Multiflora Rambler.

the american garden guides

The network of botanical gardens and arboreta in the United States and Canada constitutes a great treasure chest of knowledge about plants and what they need. Some of the most talented, experienced, and dedicated plantspeople in the world work full-time at these institutions; they are the people who actually grow plants, make gardens, and teach others about the process. They are the gardeners who are responsible for the gardens in which millions of visitors exclaim, "Why won't that plant grow that way for me?"

Over thirty of the most respected and beautiful gardens on the continent are participating in the creation of The American Garden Guides. The books in the series originate with manuscripts generated by gardeners in one or several of the gardens. Drawing on their decades of experience, these originating gardeners write down the techniques they use in their own gardens, recommend and describe the plants that grow best for them, and discuss their successes and failures. The manuscripts are then passed to several other participating gardens; in each, the specialist in that area adds recommended plants and other suggestions based on regional differences and different opinions.

The series has three major philosophical points carried throughout:

1) Successful gardens are by nature user-friendly toward the gardener and the environment. We advocate water conservation through the precepts of Xeriscaping and garden health care through Integrated Pest Management (IPM). Simply put, one does not set into motion any garden that is going to require undue irrigation during normal levels of rainfall, nor apply any pesticide or other treatment without first assessing its impact on all other life—plant, animal, and soil.

2) Gardening is an inexact science, learned by observation and by doing. Even the most experienced gardeners often develop markedly dissimilar ways of doing the same thing, or have completely divergent views of what any plant requires in order to thrive. Gardeners are an opinionated lot, and we have encouraged all participants to air and share their differences—and so, to make it clear that everyone who gardens will find his or her own way of dealing with plants. Although it is important to know the rules and the most accepted practices, it is also important to recognize that whatever works in the long run for you is the right way.

3) Part of the fun of gardening lies in finding new plants, not necessarily using over and over the same ones in the same old color schemes. In this book and others in the series, we have purposely included some lesser-known or underused plants, many of them native to our vast and wonderful continent. Wherever we can, we call attention to endangered species and suggest ways to nurture them back to their natural state of plenty.

This volume was originated by the staff at three botanic gardens: William Radler at Boerner Botanical Gardens in Hales Corners, Wisconsin (a suburb of Milwaukee), Nelson Sterner at Old Westbury Gardens on New York's Long Island, and Jim Browne at Memphis Botanic Garden. It was reviewed by Clair Martin of Huntington Botanical Gardens in San Marino, California, Nancy Rose of the Minnesota Landscape Arboretum near Minneapolis, David Sattizahn of Hershey Gardens in Hershey, Pennsylvania, Mike Ruggiero of The New York Botanical Garden, and Daryl Johnson, former rosarian at the International Rose Test Garden in Portland, Oregon. Material was added on enabling gardens by Gene Rothert and on botany by Lucile McCook.

Elvin McDonald
Houston, Texas

Preface: Roses of the Future

The rose we have come to know is far removed from what was originally provided by Mother Nature. And, if there has been substantial visual and performance change in the last hundred years, what is to be the fate of the rose in the next hundred? It is my opinion that a new class of landscape roses is just beginning to evolve.

Many gardeners would grow roses if they needed less care, an idea supported by the growing popular movement against the use of pesticides. The world is waiting for good, low-maintenance roses, and I predict that this new class of landscape roses will fill this need.

The new roses will exhibit a variety of forms that will grow equally well in all areas of the country; they will be vigorous but have compact habits that need little pruning. Some will have short stems for garden display, others will have longer stems for cutting, and cluster-flowering forms will also be represented. The plant will be winter hardy, resist such maladies as canker diseases, and tolerate low and fluctuating winter temperatures, heat, and humidity. It will have canes that are handsome even without leaves; thorniness will be acceptable only if it is decorative. The new rose will flower prolifically, and will quickly repeat; flowers will be long-lasting and resistant to sun-scorch and botrytis. The most popular cultivars will have clear bright colors, and striped, bicolored, and novel colors will also be available. All will have an assortment of fascinating and persistant fragrances. Leaves will be dense, thick, large and handsome, and some plants will provide beautiful color in autumn, as well as large and useful hips.

Above all, the plants will resist the most troublesome pests (such as spring budworm, leaf skeletonizer, rose curculio, gypsy moth, and potato leafhopper) and diseases such as blackspot, powdery mildew, and rose rust.

It is my belief that this new type of rose will not evolve, or will evolve painfully slowly if not aided by widespread testing and heavy promotion. This is best done in a variety of non-biased loaction that can often be found in botanical gardens or universities; commercial nurseries lack the objectivity as well as the variety of locations. It will take considerable foresight and planning to develop test programs for disease resistance. Roses are often marketed as disease resistant if they remain disease free in an area where the disease is not rampant, or if they are sprayed regularly. True resistance would mean that the problem is inconsequential to the plant's health even if the disease is present in the area and no pesticides are used.

I have been doing my own evaluation, testing, and breeding for about fifteen years and have had quite a bit of success. I encourage other to step on the bandwagon and join the fun of creating a flowering workhorse. While my goals for landscape roses are very high, I think that in the forseeable future we will have everblooming roses that will bring much joy for very little work.

William Radler,
Boerner Botanical Gardens

Enchanting beauty, delicious fragrance, entrancing colors, a multitude of shapes and textures—no wonder the rose has been the world's favorite flower for thousands of years. Early civilizations, from China to Crete to Greece and Rome, loved and cultivated roses. The Greek poetess Sappho declared the rose the "queen of flowers" more than twenty-five hundred years ago. Europeans enthusiastically embraced rose culture from the Middle Ages on, and the earliest English colonists brought their cherished specimens with them to the New World, where they were also delighted to be greeted by native species. Americans' continuing love of roses culminated in the 1986 designation by Congress of the rose as the official national flower of the United States.

   Why have roses been so universally loved? Beauty and fragrance must be the leading reasons. From bud to gradually unfurling bloom to individual petal, in colors ranging from delicate to vibrant, a rose flower in all its aspects is truly lovely. Many roses also fill the air with a heady, sweet fragrance, considered by many to be unmatched by that of any other flower. Fragrant rose oil, or attar of roses, has been used for centuries to scent perfume, and dried rose petals and leaves have likewise added their scent to potpourri and sachets. Herbalists traditionally valued the rose for its medicinal uses, and rose hips

From bud to bloom to individual petal to the garden in its entirety, roses are truly lovely. *Right:* Memphis Botanic Garden. *Opposite top*: 'New Dawn'. *Opposite bottom:* Old Westbury Gardens Formal Rose Garden. *Previous pages:* Boerner Botanical Gardens.

today are an important source of vitamin C. Roses, with all their beauty and fragrance, are also versatile. Many varieties are now available, with an array of growth habits and flower types, so that roses can fit into any landscape.

Definition As a member of the rose family, Rosaceae, roses are related to a number of ornamental and fruit-bearing trees, shrubs, and herbs, including strawberries, apples, and pears. Within this family, roses belong to the genus *Rosa*, which in turn includes about two hundred Species (wild) Roses and thousands of hybrids developed through the years from the species through chance or deliberate cross-pollination. Cultivated roses are further grouped into a number of classes based on ancestry and common characteristics. The classes themselves are divided into two broad categories: Old Garden Roses, cultivated before the introduction of the first Hybrid Tea in 1867, and modern roses, dating from that introduction.

NOTE: Further information about each category appears in Chapter 2.

SPECIES ROSES These are the wild, naturally occurring roses from which all other rose varieties have developed. They have simple, usually five-petaled and very fragrant blossoms, borne singly or in clusters once a year. Belying the common concept of roses as delicate, Species Roses are found throughout the northern hemisphere, including arctic and tropical regions. They produce masses of

Above: Rosa bracteata, a Species Rose.
Right: 'Highdownensis', a Hybrid
Moyesii.

bloom, followed by brightly colored, fleshy fruit called hips that attract birds.
Species Roses are vigorous, bushy, early bloomers that don't require the fertilizing and spraying demanded by their more refined cousins, and most are very winter hardy.

OLD GARDEN ROSES Within this category are two general groups. The pre-China Old Garden Roses, mostly one-time extremely fragrant bloomers with white or pink flowers, are the roses cultivated in Europe before everblooming roses from China were introduced around 1800. This group includes Gallicas, Damasks, Albas, Centifolias, and Moss Roses, all of which grow best in colder climates with a period of dormancy. The second group includes the repeat-blooming China roses and those associated with them: the Tea roses, Bourbons, Noisettes, Damask Perpetuals, and Hybrid Perpetuals.

Gallicas Gallicas are the forerunners of all later cultivated garden roses. They originated from *Rosa gallica,* the French rose, an ancient wild rose cultivated by the Romans and spread by them throughout their empire. Gallicas are extremely hardy (often surviving temperatures of -10° F. without injury), and free-spreading. Because they cross-breed readily and were once extensively cultivated, many varieties now exist, with five- to multi-petaled flowers, usually very fragrant, ranging from the original deep pink to red, purple, and even white, set off by striking yellow stamens. The lush dark green foliage, compact growth habit, and abundant hips add to the Gallica's appeal.

Damasks Damask roses are closely related to and nearly as ancient as the Gallicas. Although their ancestry is uncertain, they may have come from around Damascus, Syria; hence their name. Damasks are among the most fra-

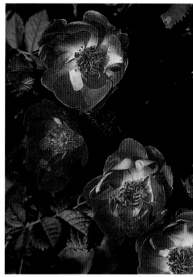

Left: 'Rosa Mundi', a Gallica-type rose.
Above: 'Magnifica', a Hybrid Rugosa.

grant of roses and have been grown for centuries for attar of roses. Damasks
have pink or white double or semidouble flowers, borne in clusters of three or
five. Most bloom only once a year, although 'Autumn Damask' (formerly *R.
damascena semperflorens)* blooms a second time in the fall—the first rose in the
West to do so. Damasks are generally fuller and taller than Gallicas, are exceptionally prickly, and hardy to 0° F.

Albas The ancestry of Albas, like Damasks, is uncertain, but it is thought to be
a cross between the Species Rose *R. canina* and either a Damask or a Gallica. It
was grown by the Romans and introduced to England sometime before the
second century AD. Albas are very upright, tall, and vigorous, with distinctive
bluish green foliage. Flowers are mostly double, white or pink-tinged, borne
abundantly in clusters and usually extremely fragrant. Albas are pest- and disease-resistant (though susceptible to rose rust), very hardy (to -15° F.), and
once-blooming.

Centifolias *Centifolia* in Latin means "hundred petals," and the way in which *R.
centifolia*'s many petals pack together and overlap makes the flower resemble a
cabbage—hence this plant's other name of the cabbage rose. Centifolias may be
ancient, or they may have been developed by Dutch hybridizers in the seventeenth century. The very full, heavy Centifolia flowers are highly fragrant,
white to rose, and once-blooming. Centifolias are much taller and more prickly
than Gallicas. Centifolias are not disease resistant, but they are hardy.

HISTORICAL NOTES

For a great percentage of its history, roses lived without the intervention of humans. Evidence from fossils indicates that roses have existed for about thirty million years, give or take several centuries. Wild roses have been found in many areas of the world. Europe is home to *R. canina, R. eglanteria, R. villosa,* and *R. spinosissima,* as well as *R. gallica.* The wild roses of the Americas include *R. virginiana, R. carolina, R. palustris,* and *R. setigera.* Some of our most important roses arose in Asia, including *R. rugosa, R. wichuriana, R. laevigata, R. bracteata,* and *R. multiflora.* The only yellow species rose, *R. foetida,* is from the Middle East.

People have appreciated and used roses for at least five thousand years; among the earliest records of use is on decoration found on jewelry from the Minoan civilization that flourished on Crete between 2800 and 2100 BC. Most experts agree that the first cultivation of roses was by the Chinese, who grew roses in the Imperial Gardens of the Chou Dynasty; they are mentioned in the writings of Confucius, who lived in the fifth century BC. During the empires of the Greeks and Romans, roses took on great importance and played a part in many myths and religious functions, as well as medicinally. Among the first mentions of the rose in literature was in Homer's *Iliad,* where Aphrodite used rose oil to annoint the Hector after he had fallen in battle; Sappho called the rose "Queen of Flowers." Other ancient civilizations used them as well: rose water was distilled by the Persians and other societies, for use in cooking, cosmetics and medicines.

The Romans had a passion for roses, and brought them from the Orient in great quantities. Thousands of petals carpeted floors in noblemens' mansions, and were sometimes dropped from above during parties; Romans ate the candied petals, steeped them in wines, and used them in their baths and perfumes. Eventually, they created greenhouses so that they could grow the precious flowers at home, and developed methods of transporting heated water to help them grow. The rose became politically significant as well: the term *sub rosa* was coined to describe the practice of hanging a rose in a room where confidential meetings were taking place.

For the first several thousand years that Westerners used roses, they used them as they found them; until the Middle Ages, roses remained as nature created them. (There is evidence that hybridization was practiced in China as early as the tenth century.) After the wane of the Roman Empire, roses became less important in the world, although they were used by monks, apothecaries, and other medicine people all over the world. But the crusaders of the twelfth and thirteenth centuries brought back exotic new species from the Middle East, particularly the Damask, reigniting interest in these more fragrant and hardy plants. By the fourteenth and fifteenth centuries, the practice of rose hybridization had begun in Holland, where hybridizers worked with Centifolias, introducing up to two hundred new strains between 1580 and 1710 (though Peter Beales, author of *Roses,* suggests that some of these might have been imported from warmer climates). Among the classes that became important were the Albas, significant for the role they played in the War of the Roses (see page 64).

The next major breakthrough in rose culture was the introduction of China Roses in Europe in the late eighteenth century, bringing new colors and the possibility of repeat bloom. Again, the first recorded planting of a China Rose in Europe–the pink 'Old Blush' in 1781– was in Holland, brought back by traders for the Dutch East India company. Within less than a decade, British East India traders were bringing pink and red China roses back, notably 'Bengal Rose' and 'Slater's Crimson'. These were followed by Teas, Bourbons, and Portlands, probably created by earlier hybridization in the Far East. Hybridization continued, crossing these roses with other Species and Old Garden Roses to create hardier and more profusely-blooming cultivars, as well as yellow roses. In the Victorian age, roses were often worn in buttonholes, and were the subjects of elaborate formal gardens, particularly in England and France.

Perhaps the world's most famous garden was created in the 1800s by the Empress Josphine, Napoleon's wife, at La Malmaison, her estate near Paris. She was determined to grow all of the then-known varieties of roses, some 250 of them. The British nurseryman who helped Josephine create her rose garden, John Kennedy, held a special passport that allowed him to travel between England and France even though the two countries were at war. Josephine's garden helped spark the rose's popularity throughout Europe.

The year 1867 was a watershed in the history of the rose. A few years earlier, nurseryman Jean-Baptiste Guillot found a rose that he considered"different" among the seedlings in his Lyons, France nursery. This rose, named 'La France', is considered the first Hybrid Tea rose, and the first of the modern roses. It took several years for the rose societies in France and England to accept this classification, but once they did a new era began. Several firms joined in creating excellent varieties, and soon they were winning prizes at rose competitions throughout Europe. They became enormously popular as garden plants as well. Other classes of modern roses, including Polyanthas, Floribundas, and Grandifloras followed. For many years, modern roses dominated the field to the exclusion of all others; more recently, Old Garden Roses have been rediscovered as gardeners seek more traditional forms and fragrance.

The history of the rose in the United States began with the first settlers. Colonists brought roses–Albas, Centifolias, Gallicas, Damasks, and Eglantines–with them from Europe and used them for medicines and cooking in their first gardens, as well as for ornament. Several early American artists depicted settlers adorned with roses. Colonists quickly found new Species Roses and sent them back to Europe. The earliest garden catalogs printed in the New World list several species of roses; by 1846, the *Prince Manual Roses* listed 1,630. In 1844, Robert Buist published *The Rose Manual,* the first volume in America devoted entirely to the rose; in 1882 nurseryman H.B. Ellwanger published The Rose, classifying and rating roses for use in America. The American Rose Society was founded in 1899 and grew quickly. The first great municipal rose garden was was established in Elizabeth Park in Hartford, Connecticut, in 1904, designed and planted by Theodore Worth. Another major garden is The Brooklyn Botanic Garden's magnificent Cranford Rose Garden, begun in 1927, which today grows over five thousand rose bushes.

The name of Harold McFarland stands out in the history of roses in America. McFarland began as an amateur grower; a printer by trade, he published the first *American Rose Annual* in 1916 and became president of The American Rose Society in 1930. He promoted the use of roses in municipal gardens, in institutional gardens (he even helped the prisoners in Sing Sing establish a rose garden) and most of all in home gardens. His own garden in Harrisburg, Pennsylvania, called Breeze Hill, appeared in photographs in his many books and catalogs. McFarland combined two of his skills when he developed improved methods of color printing for these publications.

Rose growing in America was also furthered by several important nurseries, notably Jackson & Perkins, which was founded in 1872 and was responsible for many popular cultivars, including the Floribunda class.

In 1986, the rose was declared the official national flower of the United States.

ROSES IN LITERATURE

Roses have been celebrated in literature since people began to write. The ancient Greeks, and Romans all wrote of roses. The Koran described roses in Paradise, and the Bible speaks frequently of them. By the Middle Ages, roses figured prominently in poetry and have retained that position ever since.

Perhaps the best-known mentions of roses in literature are in the poems and plays of Shakespeare. Who is not familiar with Juliet's plaintive query, "What's in a name? that which we call a rose/By any other name would smell as sweet." Describing Cleopatra, Geoffrey Chaucer wrote, "And she was as fair as is the rose in May." Robert Burns rhapsodized, "O, my Luve's like a red red rose/That's newly sprung in June." Irish poet William Butler Yeats often sang of the rose: 'Rose of all Roses, Rose of all the World!" "Red Rose, Proud Rose, sad Rose of all my days!" Gertrude Stein mused on the flower's essential nature, writing in a circle, "Rose is a rose is a rose."

Writers have also been fond of using the flaws and thorns and brief blossoming that lurk behind the beauty of roses as a caution. Shakespeare wrote in one of his sonnets, "Roses have thorns, and silver fountains mud/...And loathsome canker lives in sweetest bud." Robert Herrick cautioned, "Ne'er the rose without the thorn." Edmund Spenser admonished, "Gather therefore the Rose, whilst yet it prime,/ For soon comes age, that will her pride deflower." And Edward Fitzgerald lamented, "Alas, that Spring should vanish with the Rose!/That Youth's sweet-scented Manuscript should close!" In a different vein, Robert Louis Stevenson warned, "marriage is like life in this--- that it is a field of battle, and not a bed of roses."

Left: Elizabeth Park, the first municipal rose garden in America.

Above: 'Hermes', a China rose.

Moss Roses These roses sported from the Centifolias, the Gallicas, and 'Autumn Damask'. Their calyxes, stems, and hips are covered with a sticky, mossy growth, either green or brown, that gives off a resinous, piney fragrance when touched. The large double flowers are extremely fragrant; on sports of 'Autumn Damask', they are twice-blooming.

China Roses The introduction of everblooming roses from China to the West by European explorers in the late 1700s and early 1800s began a revolution in rose cultivation. The Oriental imports, which were hardy to 0 to -10° F., were crossed with the more hardy European roses to produce all of the later repeat-blooming roses. The Chinas also introduced new colors to rose growers, including reds, yellows, and apricots; the small flowers, however, were not very fragrant. Chinas originally were low-growing, although many are now strongly spreading, and some produce long canes suitable for climbing.

Tea Roses Tea roses, originally known as tea-scented China roses, were also introduced to the West from China. Like the Chinas, Tea roses grow and bloom all season long, until stopped by cold; the small bushes are less hardy than the tender Chinas, usually only to 10 to 20° F. The double flowers are larger and fuller than those of the Chinas, come in a range of delicate colors, and have a delightful tealike fragrance.

Bourbons The Bourbon rose is the result of natural crossbreeding that took place on the Indian Ocean island of Bourbon (now Réunion), where fields were hedged with China and repeating Damask roses. New varieties were then developed in France from the original Bourbon rose. The flowers are much larger and more fragrant than the Chinas and more repeat-blooming than the Damask. They are also taller and hardier than their ancestors, and newer varieties offer a range of colors and shrubby to climbing growth habits.

Noisettes Noisettes were created in the early 1800s when a South Carolina rice planter crossed a pink China with a white Musk Rose, *R. moschata*. The result was a repeat-blooming pink climber. A French nurseryman in Charleston named Noisette sent seeds of this new rose to his brother in France, who developed more varieties and called them Noisettes. In warmer climates, the tender Noisettes are rampant climbers, with fragrant flower clusters often borne throughout the season.

Damask Perpetuals Also known as Portland roses after the Duchess of Portland in whose English garden they appeared around 1800, Damask Perpetuals are descended from 'Autumn Damask', and China and Gallica roses. In Victorian times, when they were popular, they were called hardy perpetual roses, recognizing the characteristics for which these roses were bred. They were soon outmoded by the new Hybrid Perpetuals, however. The few Damask Perpetual varieties that remain are fine repeat bloomers, with very fragrant double blooms borne on short stems and a sturdy, rounded growth pattern.

Hybrid Perpetuals Hybrid Perpetuals were the culmination of eighteenth- and nineteenth-century rose breeding, the immediate ancestors of the Hybrid Tea and thus the last of the Old Garden Roses. They were first developed in the 1830s from Portland roses, hybrid Chinas, Bourbons, and Gallicas and became known as Victorian roses because of their extreme popularity during that era. Hybrid Perpetuals are tall, very hardy, to -5 to -15° F., vigorous shrubs that produce large, double, very fragrant and upright flowers and short stems. Contrary to their name, they do not always bloom continually all season long, but they do rebloom after their major spring flowering.

MODERN ROSES The American Rose Society has established 1867 as the dividing date between "old-fashioned" (Old Garden) and "modern" roses. Modern roses consist of the Hybrid Teas and other roses created after them.

Hybrid Tea Roses Hybrid Teas resulted from a cross between Hybrid Perpetuals and Tea roses, a successful attempt to combine the large flowers and hardiness of the former with the repeat blooming of the latter. 'La France' is generally recognized as the first Hybrid Tea, introduced in France in 1867. In 1900, the first yellow rose, 'Soleil d'Or', was introduced, opening up a whole new range of color possibilities for rose breeders; unfortunately, it also passed along susceptibility to blackspot. Today, Hybrid Teas (which are usually three to five feet tall) are the most popular roses, with their high-centered flowers, beautifully and variably colored, blooming prolifically all season on long and strong stems. Although there are very hardy Hybrid Teas available—and the variance in hardiness throughout the class makes it difficult to generalize about the hardiness of Hybrid Teas as a group—the search continues for a Hybrid Tea that can survive extremely cold weather and is resistant to blackspot, mildew, and rust.

Polyanthas The Latin word *polyantha* means "many-flowered," which is an apt description of this low-growing, compact shrub that produces large clusters of small, everblooming flowers. Polyanthas were developed by the same breeder who introduced the Hybrid Tea, in the 1870s and 1880s, a cross between *R. multiflora* and a dwarf China rose. Polyanthas are very hardy (to -5° F .) but not very fragrant; they are excellent for edging and low hedges. Because of their limited color range, lack of fragrance, and hesitant repeat bloom, they were overshadowed by Floribundas. They were an important step in the development of the Floribundas.

Floribundas Floribundas were the crossbreeding outcome of a desire to produce a rose with Polyantha hardiness and profusion of repeat bloom but with the larger, better-shaped flowers of the Hybrid Tea. The first Floribunda was produced in 1909, but the class itself was not recognized until the 1940s. The name recognizes the abundant bloom of this class, which produces larger and shrubbier plants (two to four feet tall) than its Polyantha ancestors. Originally, their clusters were of single or semidouble blooms; today, many resemble cluster-flowering Teas and offer a wide range of colors. Floribundas are fairly hardy (about the same as Hybrid Teas) and make excellent low-maintenance borders and hedges.

Grandifloras This class was established in 1954 with the introduction of 'Queen Elizabeth', still the finest Grandiflora. These roses are a cross between Hybrid Teas and Floribundas, combining the fine qualities of each parent: the hardiness, clustering, and abundant bloom of the Floribunda and the larger, long-stemmed, high-centered blossoms of the Hybrid Tea. Grandifloras can be very

'Shalom', a Floribunda.

A BRIEF LESSON IN BOTANY

Plants are living things and share many traits with animals. Plants are composed of millions of individual cells that are organized into complex organ systems. Plants breathe (take in and expel gases) and extract energy from food; to do this they require water, nutrients, and atmospheric gases. Like animals, plants reproduce sexually, and their offspring inherit characteristics through a genetic code passed along as DNA.

Plants, however, can do one thing that no animal can do. Through a process called photosynthesis, plants can capture energy from the sun and convert that energy into compounds such as proteins, fats, and carbohydrates. These energy-rich compounds are the source of the energy for all animal life, including humans.

THE IMPORTANCE OF PLANTS

Because no living animals can produce the energy they need to live, all their energy comes from plants. Like other animals, we eat green plants directly, in the form of fruits, vegetables, and grains (breads and cereals), or we eat animals and animal products that were fed green plants.

The oxygen we need to live on Earth is constantly pumped out of green plants as a byproduct of photosynthesis. Plants prevent the erosion of our precious soils and hinder water loss to the atmosphere.

Plants are also an important source of drugs. Fully one-quarter of all prescriptions contain at least one plant-derived product. Aspirin, one of the most commonly used drugs, was originally isolated from the bark of the willow tree.

THE WHOLE PLANT

Basically, a plant is made up of leaves, stems, and roots; all these parts are connected by a vascular system, much like our circulatory system. The vascular system can be seen in the veins of a leaf, or in the rings in a tree.

LEAVES

Leaves are generally flattened and expanded tissues that are green due to the presence of chlorophyll, the pigment that is necessary for photosynthesis. Most leaves are connected to the stem by a stalk, or petiole, which allows the leaves to alter their position in relation to the sun and capture as much energy as possible.

Leaves come in an astounding variety of shapes, textures, and sizes. Some leaves are composed of a single structure, or blade, and are termed simple. Other leaves are made up of many units, or leaflets, and are called compound (see endpapers).

STEMS

Technically, a stem is the tissue that supports leaves and that connects the leaves with the roots via a vascular system. Stems also bear the flowers on a plant. Therefore, a stem can be identified by the presence of buds, which are the unexpanded leaves, stems, or flowers that will develop later.

A single plant can produce more than one kind of stem; the upright, above-ground stem produces leaves and flowers, while a horizontal, below-ground stem can swell and store food products from photosynthesis. Underground stems can overwinter and produce new plants when conditions are favorable.

The stem of a plant often changes as the plant matures. When a shrub is young, its stems are green and soft; as the shrub grows and ages, however, the stem may develop woody tissues. Woody stems on a shrub are like the wood of a tree trunk–just smaller. Wood is composed of hardened cells that provide strength to the stem and that allow water, gases, and nutrients to move both vertically and horizontally through the stem. Concentric circles inside a woody stem are called annual rings. The oldest wood is in the center of the rings, and the youngest wood is in the outer ring. Light-colored rings, or early wood, are composed of cells that were added early in the growing season of each year; these cells are larger and are less densely packed together. Late wood is darker in color because the cells are smaller and packed more closely. Each set of a light and dark ring represents one year in the life of the growing plant stem. When a plant grows under constant environmental conditions, with no changes in temperature or moisture during the year (like in some tropical rain forests), the wood is uniform in color and lacks annual rings.

Bark forms on the outside of woody stems and is made up mostly of dead cells. This corky tissue is very valuable to the stem because it protects the new wood, allows gas exchange into the stem, and lets the stem grow in diameter. All of the bark is not dead tissue, however; the innermost layer is living vascular tissue. If a stem is girdled or the bark is damaged, this vascular tissue, which moves the food products of photosynthesis around in the plant, will be destroyed, and the plant will die.

ROOTS

Although out of sight, roots are extremely important to the life of the plant. Roots anchor a plant in the soil, absorb water and nutrients, and store excess food, such as starches, for the plants' future use. Basically, there are two types of roots: taproots and fibrous roots. Taproots, such as the edible part of a carrot, are thick unbranched roots that grow straight down. A toproot takes advantage of moisture and nutrients far below the soil surface and is a storehouse for carbohydrates. Fibrous roots are fine, branching roots that often form dense mats, making them excellent agents of soil stabilization. Fibrous roots absorb moisture and nutrients from a shallow zone of soil and may be more susceptible to drought. Roots obviously need to come into contact with water, but they also need air in order to work properly. Except for those adapted to aquatic environments, plants require well-drained soils.

VASCULAR SYSTEMS

Plants have a well-developed vascular system that extends throughout the plant body and that allows movement of water and compounds from one part of a plant to another. Roots absorb water and minerals, and the vascular system funnels them to the leaves for use in photosynthesis.

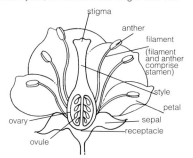

stigma
anther
filament
(filament and anther comprise stamen)
style
petal
sepal
receptacle
ovary
ovule

Likewise, energy-rich compounds that are produced in the leaves must travel to the stems and roots to provide nutrition for further growth. The vascular system also strengthens plant tissues.

PHOTOSYNTHESIS

A green plant is like a factory that takes raw materials from the environment and converts them into other forms of energy. In a complex series of energy transfer and chemical conversion events called photosynthesis, plants take energy from the sun, minerals and water from the soil, and gases from the atmosphere; these raw materials are converted into chemical forms of energy that are used for plant growth. These same energy-rich compounds (proteins, sugars and starches, fats and oils) can be utilized by animals as a source of food and nutrition. All this is possible because of a green pigment, chlorophyll.

Photosynthesis is an extremely complex series of reactions that takes place in the cells of leaves, the byproducts of which are connected to other reactions throughout the cell. The most basic reactions of photosynthesis occurs like this: Energy from the sun strikes the leaf surface, and electrons in the chlorophyll molecule become "excited" and are boosted to a higher energy level. Excited electrons are routed through a chain of reactions that extracts and stores energy in the form of sugars. As a byproduct of electron loss, water molecules (H_2O) are split; hydrogen moves in to replenish the electrons lost from chlorophyll, and oxygen is released, finding its way into our atmosphere. In another photosynthetic reaction, carbon dioxide from the atmosphere is "fixed," or converted into organic compounds within the plant cell. These first chemical compounds are the building blocks for more complex reactions and are the precursors for the formation of many elaborate chemical compounds.

PLANT NUTRITION

Plants require mineral nutrients from the soil, water, and the atmosphere in order to maintain healthy growth and reproduction. Macronutrients, those nutrients needed in large amounts, include hydrogen, oxygen, and carbon –all of which are abundant in our atmosphere. Other macronutrients are nitrogen, phosphorus, potassium, sulfur, and calcium. If macronutrients are in limited supply, growth and development in the plant will be strongly curtailed. Nitrogen is an important component of chlorophyll, DNA, and proteins and is therefore an essential element for leaf growth and photosynthesis. Adding nitrogen to garden soil will generally result in greener, more lush plant growth. But beware of too much of a good thing; too much nitrogen can burn tender plants. Or, you may have large and lovely azalea leaves, but with no flowers! Phosphorus is also used in building DNA and is important in cell development. Phosphorus is necessary for flowering and fruiting and is often added to garden soil. Potassium is important in the development of tubers, roots, and other storage organs.

LIFE CYCLE

Higher plants (except for ferns) begin life as a seed. Given the right set of conditions (temperature, moisture, light), a seed will germinate and develop its first roots and leaves using food stored in the seed (humans and other animals take advantage of the high-quality food in seeds when they eat wheat and corn, just to name a few). Because of the presence of chlorophyll in the leaves, the small plant is soon able to produce its own food, which is used immediately for further growth and development. As the seedling grows, it also grows in complexity. The first, simple root gives way to a complex root system that may include underground storage organs. The stem is transformed into an intricate system of vascular tissue that moves water from the ground up into the leafy part of the plant, while other tissues transport energy-rich compounds made in the leaves downward to be stored in stem and root systems.

Once the plant reaches maturity, flower initiation begins. Flowers hold the sexual apparatus for the plant; their brilliant colors and glorious odors are advertisements to attract pollinators such as insects or birds. In a basic, complete flower, there are four different parts, given below. However, many plants have incomplete flowers with one or more of these parts missing, or the parts may be highly modified.

1. Sepals. The outermost part of the flower, sepals cover the young floral buds. Although they are often green, they may be variously colored.

2. Petals. The next layer of parts in the flower, petals, are often colorful and play an important role in attracting pollinators.

3. Stamens. Stamens are located next to the petals, or may even be basally fused to the petals. The stamens are the "male" reproductive parts of the flower; they produce the pollen. Pollen grains are fine, dust-like particles that will divide to form sperm cells. The tissue at the end of the stamen that holds pollen is called the anther.

4. Pistil. The innermost part of the flower holds the plant's female reproductive apparatus. The stigma, located at the tip of the pistil, is often covered with a sticky substance and is the site where pollen is deposited. The stigma is held by a floral tube, call the style. At the base of the style, the ovary holds one to many ovules, which contain eggs that represent undeveloped seeds.

Pollination is the transfer of pollen from an anther to a stigma and is the first step in the production of seeds. Pollen can be transferred by an insect visiting the flower, by the wind, or even by the splashing of raindrops. After being deposited on a compatible stigma, the pollen grains grow into tubes that travel from the stigma, down the floral tube into the ovary, depositing sperm cells to the ovules. If all goes well, sperm cells unite with the eggs inside the ovules, and fertilization takes place.

After fertilization, the entire floral structure is transformed into a fruit–in the case of roses, this is represented by hips. Fruit can be fleshy, like an apple, or dry like a pea pod. Within each fruit, fertilized eggs develop into seeds, complete with a cache of storage tissue and a seed coat.

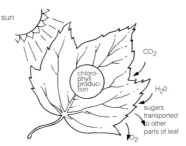

sun

CO_2

chloro-phyll produc-tion

H_2O

sugars transported to other parts of leaf

O_2

'The Fairy', a Polyantha, growing with annuals at The New York Botanical Garden.

tall, often reaching over six feet. Flowers are fine for cutting, but plants are only slightly more hardy than Hybrid Teas. As with other classes, hardiness varies from cultivar to cultivar; 'Queen Elizabeth', for example, is quite hardy in the New York area.

Shrub Roses This is a class created to encompass all bushy roses that don't fit into the other classes of modern roses. It includes hybrids of several Species Roses, Kordesii (created by hybridizer Wilhelm Kordes), Bucks (created by Professor Griffith Buck), and a catchall subclass called Shrub Roses. As a group, they are hardy (though hardiness varies within the group), with easy-to-grow, robust plants with a spreading growth habit. Flowers are single or double, of varying colors, often blooming over a long season. Some Shrub Roses work well as groundcovers, while others work well as bushes or hedges, and others can be trained as climbers.

Miniature Roses The origin of the Miniature Rose is uncertain; most believe it may have descended from 'Roulette' (formerly *R. chinensis minima),* coming to England from either China or Mauritius in the early 1800s. It faded from popularity but was rediscovered growing in Switzerland. Today, Miniatures are the subject of great interest among hybridizers, as their size makes them adaptable to all types of gardens and containers. Miniature Roses typically grow from ten to eighteen inches high, with all aspects of the plant–flowers, leaves, and stems–proportionately small. They are quite hardy (from -5 to 5° F.), and come in trailing, cascading, and climbing forms.

Climbing Roses Climbers are roses that have canes long enough to require support; they do not have tendrils that would allow them to climb on their own. Climbing Roses have a variety of origins. Many are sports of Hybrid Teas and Floribundas (these are less hardy than other Climbers), while many others originated from hardy Species Roses, especially *R. wichuraiana.* Climbers produce lateral branches, all along which flowers appear. Some Climbers are everblooming, while others bloom only in the spring.

Ramblers Ramblers derive mainly from *R. wichuraiana* and *R. multiflora.* Like Climbers, they have long, pliable canes that must be trained or tied to a support. Most Ramblers bloom only once in a season, in large, brightly colored clusters borne on second-year shoots. Ramblers have smaller leaves and more flexible canes than Climbers. They are large and hardy (from -5 to 5° F.), but are susceptible to disease.

Hybrid Musks Hybrid Musks are shrub-type roses (sometimes classed as Shrub Roses) more closely related to *R. multiflora* than to the Musk Rose, *R. moschata.* Developed in the early twentieth century, Hybrid Musks can be grown as large, free-standing bushes or hedges or trained as Climbers. Grown in the sun, these roses are good repeat bloomers. They vary in hardiness: some are more hardy than Hybrid Teas, some are less so.

Tree Roses Tree roses are created by a two- or threefold grafting process—a sturdy rootstock joined to a long, straight stem finished off by a flowering top. Tree roses may be upright and rounded, or weeping, or miniature. They are not very hardy. They are not a distinct class of roses, as Hybrid Teas or Gallicas;

roses from several classes may be used as tree roses.

English Roses This is a relatively new type of rose, developed by the English rose breeder David Austin and first introduced in 1969, though most are from the 1980s. Seeking to create a repeat-flowering and disease-resistant Shrub Rose with the beauty and fragrance of the old rose, Austin crossed Old Garden Roses with modern types, especially the Floribundas. The result is old-style roses with heady fragrance and fully double repeat blooms plus a range of old and modern colors. Plants vary in disease resistance and hardiness.

As hybridizers continue to create new roses, new types and classes of roses are sure to emerge.

Roses in Your Garden The fascinating variety of rose shapes, sizes, and growth habits means that a rose exists for every garden and landscape. In fact, nurseries now use the term "landscape roses" to denote roses that can be planted anywhere in the landscape, just like other flowering shrubs. Modern roses such as Hybrid Teas and Grandifloras, with their constant bloom, upright growth habit, but rather sparse foliage, are well suited for formal, geometric beds. Old Garden Roses, on the other hand, tend to spread and then droop when in full bloom; these are more suitable for informal gardens. Climbers and Ramblers call for and enhance structures in your garden, as they sprawl over rock walls, clamber up arches and trellises, droop along fences, twine around pillars. If you want a hedge or background, roses can provide that as well, from the tall and elegant Grandifloras to the low-growing Polyanthas to the bushy and free-growing Shrub Roses, Rugosas, and Species Roses. For large gardens, combine rose types, or roses and other plants (see Chapter 3); for small garden spaces, plant a few specimen roses such as Hybrid Teas, or choose Polyanthas or Miniatures, or enhance your limited outdoor areas with roses in containers.

In addition to type of garden or growing area for your roses, you'll want to consider how you want to use your roses and what degree of hardiness you require. If you want cut roses all season long, plant the long-stemmed Hybrid Teas and Grandifloras that bloom continuously. If you want fragrance, grow the Old Garden Roses and only those modern roses specifically noted for their scent. For good bedding effects, choose everblooming Floribundas, Teas, Chinas, English Roses, Polyanthas, and Miniatures. Remember that many roses bloom only once, at the beginning of the season. Single bloomers include the pre-China Old Garden Roses–the Gallicas, Damasks (except 'Autumn Damask'), Albas, and Centifolias–Species Roses, and some Climbers, Shrub Roses, and Ramblers. Nevertheless, many of these are valuable in the garden throughout the season for their interesting foliage, shape, texture, hips, and color.

Climate can be an important factor in choosing rose varieties for your garden. Many modern roses are not hardy in cold climates, even with protection (see Chapter 5 for more information on growing roses in cold regions). Species Roses are the hardiest, followed by most Shrub and pre-China Old Garden Roses; also quite hardy are Hybrid Perpetuals, Polyanthas, Miniatures, modern Shrub Roses, and old Climbers and Ramblers. Floribundas are often hardy to

When choosing roses for your garden, consider their growth habit–the size and shape of the entire bush–as well as the blossoms. *Above:* Blossom and bush of 'Belle Isis', a Gallica-type rose.

Foliage and hips add interest in the rose garden after the blossoms are spent.

Zone 6, while English Roses survive in Zone 5 and south. Hybrid Teas and Grandifloras will not in most cases make it through harsh winter temperatures. Note that even within classes, especially among the modern roses, hardiness varies considerably among varieties; most information about hardiness of a class is too general to be very useful; your best bet is to find someone in your area who has grown a particular cultivar.

A particular rose variety may grow quite differently in one area than another. For example Tea roses and Hybrid Teas that grow only moderately in the Northeast, with sparse foliage, become landscape shrubs and hedges in the Southwest. Some Old Garden Roses are repeat bloomers in warm climates but produce flowers only once in northern areas.

Seaside gardens, with their cool, moist air and sandy soil, call for Rugosas, Species Roses, and Old Garden Roses; Rugosas in particular are a common sight along the beaches of the East Coast. Many-petaled roses such as the Centifolias are not suited to the cool, damp, foggy climate of the Pacific Northwest; the flowers retain moisture and ball up. Although roses may seem delicate, they tolerate pollution quite well, and so are suited for urban gardens.

REQUIREMENTS FOR ROSE GROWING

Soil To get off to a good start, roses need deeply prepared soil generously enriched with organic matter such as compost, sphagnum, peat moss, or well-rotted manure. Addition of organic materials is especially important for clay and sandy soil. This will ensure good drainage and air circulation, critical for success, as roses will not tolerate wet feet. Ideally, soil where roses are to grow should be slightly acidic, with a pH of 6.0 to 6.6, but they will grow in somewhat more alkaline or acidic conditions as well. (For information on preparing and amending your soil, see Chapter 4.) Be sure your roses are planted well away from trees, shrubs, and large perennials that would compete for soil nutrients and water; roses do not like root competition from more aggressive plants.

Sun Roses need at least six hours of sunlight a day to do their best. If you have to choose between morning or afternoon sun, go for the morning, so disease-promoting moisture evaporates early in the day. Also, afternoon shade may protect plants in hot climates from burning and drying out. Over time, roses that once thrived in full sun may become weak and spindly from increased shade; if this happens, cut back interfering tree limbs that are causing the shade, or move the roses to a sunnier location. If this is not an option, plant Species and Old Garden Roses that will bloom early in the season before trees leaf out and shade the flowers. You can also plant Climbers whose base will be in the shade but whose tops will grow up into the sun.

Air Circulation This is very important for roses that are susceptible to foliar diseases, which are promoted by moist conditions. Adequate air circulation allows leaves wet from overnight dew or rainstorms to dry out thoroughly and quickly. It also keeps pockets of cold air from pooling around your roses in the winter. You can give your roses the circulation they need by choosing an appropriate site, allowing them plenty of space when you plant, and pruning when needed.

Water As with sunlight, roses need ample water–at least one inch per week–to produce the lavish flowers and growth they are capable of. This means you must have the means for convenient irrigating at hand near your roses for periods during the growing season when nature fails to deliver the one inch. Roses grown on a hillside must be terraced so they can retain the required amounts of water.

Protection Depending on the variety and climate, roses need varying amounts of protection from cold winter temperatures; see Chapter 4 for details. Roses in an otherwise acceptable site, such as a seaside garden, may need the protection of a fence or hedge from the buffeting of the wind; set the barrier well away so it will not shade the roses or increase the wind turbulence. Although roses can be bothered by pests and diseases, many varieties of roses are resistant, and even susceptible types that are healthy and growing in well-maintained beds will prove resistant. See Chapter 4 for details on dealing with rose diseases and pests.

ABOUT THE AUTHORS

Jim Browne's background is in taxonomy and plant genetics. As host of the most popular gardening radio show in Memphis, he realized that many of his listeners were rose enthusiasts and became one himself. He has lectured to Rose Societies throughout the Southeast. Browne is currently acting director of the Memphis Botanic Garden.

Nelson W. Sterner, director of horticulture for Old Westbury Gardens, became interested in growing roses because, after growing many other types of plants, he wanted a true challenge. What he found was not so much a challenge as a great garden plant. Sterner believes that with regular garden maintenance, roses provide dramatic rewards: color all season long, fragrance to fill the air, and cut flowers for the home that are difficult to beat. He states emphatically that roses are easy to grow, inexpensive to purchase, and a delight to have in the garden. He recommends that beginning gardeners follow the leads in this book and try few of the easier ones (like 'Carefree Wonder', 'Queen Elizabeth', and 'Touch of Class') to open themselves up to a new gardening world.

William Radler received a degree in landscape architecture from the University of Wisconsin-Madison in 1968 and has been employed with Milwaukee's County Park System ever since. In November, 1994, he began an early retirement to devote more time to breeding disease resistant and hardy roses, an avid interest since 1974. Growing roses has been his hobby since the age of twelve. He is especially interested in new information, whether it pertains to worthwhile plants, maintenance techniques and gadgets, or dispelling gardening myths. He also like to write, and is the author of "Rose Growing Simplified," published by Friends of Boerner Botanical Gardens. Radler is an Official Judge of the All America Rose Selections.

Roses in the cottage garden at Old Westbury Gardens.

PLANT SELECTOR

2

Though gardening is essentially a hands-on endeavor, some of its greatest pleasures are vicarious: for most gardeners, nothing surpasses the joy of discovering a new plant. And since more than five thousand different roses are currently under cultivation—and nurseries, botanists, and private gardeners the world over are dedicated to finding and introducing more—there will never be a shortage of horticultural treasures from which to choose.

This chapter is designed to help you sift through those treasures and make a choice. Our originating gardeners have selected more than 150 roses that they consider worthy of your attention, mixing common, easy-to-find varieties with others you might not know about, but should. Experts from other botanic gardens around the country then added plants that thrive in their own regions.

The first part of the Plant Selector lists the included varieties according to color. Following that is the main portion of the chapter—detailed "plant portraits" describing the best conditions of each class of roses, routine care, propagation, pest and disease tolerance, and uses in the landscape. Two hundred of the recommended plants are illustrated, with captions noting their size and main attributes.

There are only a few keys to successful gardening; choosing the right plant is among them. If a well-tended plant refuses to thrive or succumbs to disease, it probably doesn't belong in its present site. Before deciding to plant roses, you need to understand the special conditions of your own garden. Is it sunny, shady, or a combination of both? Is rainfall abundant, or nearly nonexistent? Is the soil sandy, loamy, heavy, well or poorly drained? What is your soil's natural pH? Information on how to answer these questions is located in Chapter 4; your local nursery, botanical garden, or agricultural extension can also help. But don't forget that your site is unique, with a microclimate of its own created by the contours of the landscape, shade, and natural barriers; it may be different from those next door, let alone at a nursery ten miles down the road. You might be able to find a small area within your site that can sustain roses even if the entire site is not suitable for them.

Most varieties of roses have similar requirements: several hours of sun each day (six hours per day is usually the minimum); well-drained, fertile soil; good air circulation; access to water; sufficient distance from competing plants. If you can't supply these elements, consider growing Species Roses, which are less particular. Roses are not low-maintenance plants and they will not adapt to conditions that aren't suited to them.

Hardiness Information on hardiness of roses varies from publication to publication; in many cases, this information is totally erroneous, repeating myths that have little basis in fact. For this volume, gardeners in cold regions—William Radler of The Boerner Botanical Gardens, near Milwaukee, and Nancy Rose of Minnesota Landscape Arboretum—have supplied more accurate data. However, be advised that most roses are called "hardy" if they survive in Zone 6; if you live in an area colder than that, follow advice from your local nursery, botanic garden, or country extension service. Many plants in the following chapter have been singled out for their hardiness in Milwaukee and Minnesota, and ongoing experimentation may very well yield more cold hardy varieties in the coming years. See pages 208-209 for more information on growing roses in cold regions.

Pests and diseases Many catalogs tout pest and disease resistance for particular plants. William Radler has spent much time observing and experimenting with pest and disease tolerance and resistance, and has come to the conclusion that few plants are truly pest- and disease-free; if the pest is rampant in a particular area, most varieties will suffer. This is particularly true of blackspot and powdery mildew. See pages 199-201 for more information about pests and diseases, and on current experiments on organic controls and new resistant varieties.

Providing accurate information on hardiness and pest and disease resistance is difficult for some rose enthusiasts because it can discourage new gardeners. Just remember: roses are not for everyone, but just about everyone who wants to grow roses can do so. With proper selection and care—and an acceptance of certain inherent problems—every gardener can enjoy the rewards of the effort it takes to grow roses well.

The map below was created by the United States Department of Agriculture. It divides the United States into climate zones. Most nurseries (and this book) use these classifications to advise where plants will be hardy. Although this is a useful system, it is not foolproof; it is based on average minimum temperature, and a particularly cold winter might destroy some plants that are listed as hardy in your climate zone. More often, you will be able to grow plants that are not listed as hardy in your zone, particularly if they are in a sheltered area. There are other climate-zones classifications; the Arnold Arboretum's is also used quite often. The climate zones referred to in this volume are those of the USDA.

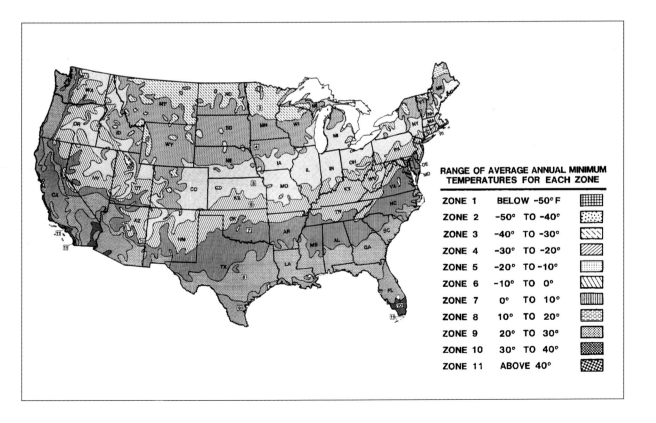

RANGE OF AVERAGE ANNUAL MINIMUM TEMPERATURES FOR EACH ZONE

ZONE 1	BELOW −50° F
ZONE 2	−50° TO −40°
ZONE 3	−40° TO −30°
ZONE 4	−30° TO −20°
ZONE 5	−20° TO −10°
ZONE 6	−10° TO 0°
ZONE 7	0° TO 10°
ZONE 8	10° TO 20°
ZONE 9	20° TO 30°
ZONE 10	30° TO 40°
ZONE 11	ABOVE 40°

'Belle Isis', Gallica, light pink

'First Prize', Hybrid Tea, pink blend.

'James Veitch' Moss, mauve.

'Lagerfeld', Grandiflora, mauve (lavender).

'Cherry Brandy', Hybrid Tea, orange blend.

R. foetida bicolor, Species, red blend.

Would Jove appoint some
    flower to reign
In matchless beauty
    on the plain
The Rose (mankind will
    all agree)
The Rose the queen of flowers
    should be.
SAPPHO, C. 600 BC

SPECIES ROSES

Species roses are the wild, naturally occurring roses; all other rose varieties have developed from them. Wild roses are found throughout the Northern Hemisphere; they can withstand all extremes of climate, from the bitterly cold arctic to the heat of North Africa, and can grow in all types of soil. Many originate in China and central Asia; some others are native to Europe and North America. Because many wild roses are freely suckering, very hardy, and adaptable, they have naturalized and spread widely, far from their ancestral homes. At least two hundred wild rose species exist.

There is much debate about which roses should be called true species roses. Over the years, the category has been refined several times, with some roses being reassigned when it was determined that they do not occur in nature. As recently as 1993 such plants as *R. ×hibernica* and *R. micrugosa* were considered to be species roses; they have now been reclassified in the catchall "shrub rose" group. The genus *Rosa* can be further divided into four subgenera: *Hulthemia, Hesperhodos, Platyrhodon,* and *Eurosa* (*Rosa*). Most of the roses in common cultivation are members of *Eurosa*, though one of the plants on the following list (*R. roxburghii,* Chestnut Rose) is in the *Platyrhodon* group. It is certain that further changes will take place in rose classification in the future.

Most species roses have simple, five-petaled flowers that resemble the blooms of relatives in the Rose family, such as the strawberry, apple, pear, and

R. bracteata, the Macartney Rose, shown growing with tobacco flower at the National Arboretum in Washington, D.C.

blackberry. Prolific bloom occurs once annually, in the spring; a few species, like *Rosa rugosa*, repeat. Most Species Roses set brightly colored hips in the fall, and many have very attractive fall foliage. Plants are vigorous and very bushy, making good background borders, hedges, and screens; those with sprawling growth are fine groundcovers. Many Species Roses that enjoy a good amount of sun in the spring during the blooming period can tolerate some shade for the rest of the season.

Species Roses are low-maintenance, easy-to-grow garden plants (for the most part). Many are extremely hardy and disease-resistant as well. Hybridizers have worked, and continue to do so, to combine these traits with the modern roses' ability to everbloom. Wild roses usually don't need fertilizer or spray, and pruning is required only to cut out dead and crowded wood and to control the size of the plant if necessary. Most Species Roses bloom on both old and new wood, so prune when plants are dormant, if possible. Many Species Roses have a place in the home landscape.

R. banksiae (Lady Banks Rose) Both single and double forms of this rose are native to China. The double white variety, *R. banksiae alba plena*, was brought back to England in 1807 by William Kerr and named after the wife of the director of Kew Gardens, who had supported Kerr's plant-gathering expedition. In 1824, John Parks brought the double yellow Lady Banks Rose, *R. banksiae lutea,* to England. Both varieties climb rampantly, twenty to thirty

Above: R. banksiae hips are large and showy, typical of the hips of many species roses. *Below:* 'Kiftsgate', a form of *R. filipes,* a vigorous, climbing Species Rose.

R. CANINA INERMIS (THORNLESS DOG ROSE) Species. Canes grow up to ten to twelve feet long. Hardy, vigorous, and coarse shrubs. One- to two-inch pinkish to white flowers. Abundance of orange-red hips in autumn. Few thorns, lightly fragrant.

R. CAROLINA (PASTURE ROSE) Species. Shrub three to six feet tall. Two-inch pink flowers, borne singly or in small clusters. Pairs of straight prickles on each node's stems. Orange and yellow foliage in the fall. Hardy and vigorous, but hip production is not good.

R. EGLANTERIA (SWEETBRIAR OR EGLANTINE ROSE) Species. Eight to ten feet. Foliage appears in early spring; spicy apple scent. Two-inch flowers, pink with white centers, borne individually or in clusters. Abundant bright red hips, especially effective in winter. Canes very thorny.

'GREENMANTLE' Hybrid eglantine. Often over eight feet, frequently reblooms in the fall. Fragrant foliage. Single, rose red flowers with white centers, lightly scented.

feet, producing profuse clusters of one-inch blossoms early in the season on the previous year's wood. Plants are hardy only to 20° F., but in mild climates like England, the Lady Banks Rose is known as a "house-eater," as it will grow up and over houses. The yellow form has little fragrance, while the white has a sweet violet scent. Plants are evergreen in the South.

R. bracteata (Macartney Rose) This five-petalled climbing rose, discovered by Lord Macartney in China in 1793, was brought to America in the early eighteenth century. According to some rumors, it was Thomas Jefferson who first introduced it. A tender rose, often harmed by frost, it spread rampantly through the southern part of the country, in some cases covering farmland and pasture with its thorny branches—it has also been called the "farmer's disaster rose." It is the parent of a popular climber, **'Mermaid'**.

R. canina (Dog Rose) Native to and widespread in England, now naturalized in North America, *R. canina* is an ancestor of many Old Garden Roses and has long been used in Europe as an understock for modern varieties. Its name derives from its supposed ability to cure the bite of a mad dog. Flowers are lightly fragrant, pinkish to white, one to two inches across, followed by oval scarlet hips high in vitamin C. Plants grow into hardy and vigorous shrubs, with canes up to ten to twelve feet long. The distinguishing characteristic of *R. canina* is the large numbers of sizable hooked prickles.

R. canina inermis (Thornless Dog Rose) is a common understock in Europe, but is rare in North America. Identical to *R. canina,* except that it has few thorns, it is one of the most attractive fruit-bearing winter shrubs in the northern United States.

R. carolina (Pasture Rose) Native to eastern and central North America, this generally short bush spreads rapidly through underground suckers. Fragrant pink two-inch flowers are borne singly or in small clusters, midseason. Pairs of straight prickles appear on stems at each node. Hardy, vigorous plants grow to three feet in the wild, up to six feet under cultivation. Foliage turns orange and yellow in the fall, but hip production is not good.

R. davurica (introduced 1910) Fragile-looking flowers on this North Asian species are wonderfully fragrant, purple-pink, appearing later than blooms of most other species roses. Light green foliage turns yellow in fall, accompanied by small orange hips. Plants are extremely vigorous and hardy, freely suckering, with dark canes; they make a fine hedge. Cut back after bloom and while dormant to control size.

R. eglanteria (Sweetbriar or Eglantine Rose) Native to Europe, now widely naturalized; brought to North America and to Australia by early settlers. Eglantines begin the sweetly scented rose season when their foliage appears in early spring: the leaves release a spicy apple scent when moist with dew or after a rain, or when brushed against (and sometimes under other weather conditions). New growth gives off the strongest apple scent. The sweetly fragrant two-inch flowers are pink with white centers, borne individually or in clusters. Bright red hips appear abundantly in clusters, and are quite effective in winter. Plants are very vigorous, growing eight to ten feet, with very

R. canina inermis, a nearly thornless rose. Other thornless or nearly thornless roses include China roses like *R. chinensis viridiflora* (the Green Rose) and 'Slater's Crimson China"; Hybrid Perpetuals like 'Reine des Violettes' and 'Paul Neyron'; 'Mrs. Dudley Cross', a Tea tose; 'Queen Elizabeth', a Grandiflora; 'Faint Heart', a Hybrid Tea; 'Marie Pavie', a Polyantha.

R. FOETIDA BICOLOR (AUSTRIAN COPPER BRIER) Hybrid foetida. Vigorous shrubs growing five to ten feet. Rich coppery orange-red flowers with yellow centers, one-and-one-half to two-and-one-half inches across, occasionally reverting to the original yellow. Prone to black spot.

R. FOETIDA PERSIANA (PERSIAN YELLOW ROSE) Hybrid foetida. Plants grow to ten feet. Firm bright green foliage. Very double flowers, medium to deep yellow. Has definite odor some find objectionable.

R. HUGONIS (FATHER HUGO'S ROSE) Species. Vigorous shrubs six to eight feet. Graceful, arching, prickly branches. Ferny leaves turn bronze in autumn. Masses of deep yellow two-inch flowers. Slight fragrance, small and few hips. Suitable as climbers. Hardy. Plants prefer poor soil.

R. xKORDESII Species. Hardy climber or shrub. Dark green foliage on shrub five feet tall. Pinkish-red double flowers in small clusters. Disease resistant.

thorny canes, so the Eglantines make excellent intruder-proof hedges—but are a nightmare for pruners.

HYBRID EGLANTINES Many crosses have been made between Eglantines and other roses, notably the Penzance hybrids, created in the 1890s by Lord Penzance, an English judge. Four are listed below.

    'Anne of Geierstein' (Penzance, 1894) Flowers are single, deep crimson, very fragrant. Blooms in summer, then sets bright red hips. Vigorous plants make handsome shrubs.

    'Greenmantle' (Penzance, 1895) Produces single, rosy red flowers with white centers, lightly scented. Vigorous plants often over eight feet frequently rebloom in the fall.

    'Julia Mannering' (Penzance, 1895) Single (sometimes semidouble) flowers are light pearly pink, with darker pink veins. Both foliage and flowers of this vigorous plant are fragrant.

    'Lady Penzance' (Penzance, 1894) A cross between *R. eglanteria* and *R. foetida bicolor.* Single, fragrant flowers are coppery salmon with bright yellow centers. Plants are very vigorous, with drooping branches and deliciously apple-scented foliage.

R. foetida (Austrian Yellow or Austrian Brier) Native to southwestern Asia, in spite of its popular name. As implied by its Latin name, roses in this species have a definite odor that some people find objectionable and others pleasant. This was the first yellow rose to reach Europe. The bright yellow, two- to two-and-one-half-inch flowers bloom early, followed by round, deep red hips. Hardy plants grow to ten feet, with rich brown and prickly canes. *R. foetida* is highly susceptible to blackspot. It does thrive in poor soil without much care.

HYBRID FOETIDAS

    R. foetida bicolor (Austrian Copper Brier) is a sport of *R. foetida.* The striking flowers are coppery orange-red on the face with yellow centers and yellow on the back of the petals, one-and-one-half to two-and-one-half inches across; they occasionally sport back to pure yellow and intermediate forms. The short-lived blooms share the odor of *R. foetida,* while the leaves have a pleasant fragrance when crushed. Plants are large, growing five to ten feet.

    R. foetida persiana (Persian Yellow Rose) is a double form with medium to deep yellow flowers that contributed tones of yellow and orange to modern roses.

R. gallica (see Gallica roses, page 56)

R. hugonis (Father Hugo's Rose) Discovered in China in 1899 by the Reverend Hugh Scallan (Pater Hugo), who sent seeds back to England, this is also known and marketed commercially as the Golden Rose of China and has become quite popular. One of the first roses to bloom in spring, it produces masses of deep yellow two-inch flowers on graceful, arching, prickly branches. Fragrance and production of dark red hips are slight. Plants prefer poor soil; growing up to eight feet (though usually up to only six feet and vase-shaped), they are suitable as climbers. Hardy everywhere in the United States.

R. eglanteria.

plant selector

R. x kordesii This is a modern Species Rose created by the German rose breeder Wilhelm Kordes in 1952 resulting from seed from *R. rugosa* hybrid 'Max Graf'. The result was a new, artificially created species named *R.* x *kordesii*, which was then crossed with modern floribundas and hybrid teas to produce a breed of very hardy climbers and shrubs.

R. laevigata (Cherokee Rose) Native to China, but well established in North America by colonial times. This plant is not winter hardy and will thrive and bloom only in southern regions. Flowers are large (two-and-one-half to three-and-one-half inches across), open, and fragrant, usually white, with fluffy golden stamens. Blooms appear early in the season and are followed by large, oblong to round, densely prickled red hips. Leaves are bright green and glossy. Plants are vigorous, with a trailing or climbing growth habit and thorny canes that grow fifteen to twenty feet long.

R. macrantha This species closely resembles *R. eglanteria,* growing as a vigorous shrub. Its pale pink flowers, however, are much smaller than those of *R. eglanteria,* so it is also called the Small-Flowered Rose. It grows all through Europe and is naturalized in the United States.

HYBRID MACRANTHA

'Raubritter' (Kordes, 1936) produces silvery pink semidouble blossoms, similar to Bourbon roses, covering the length of its thorny branches. It is very susceptible to mildew in late summer, but it has usually finished flowering by that time. A spreading/sprawling shrub, it blooms heavily for a short period in summer and does not rebloom.

R. minutifolia, a native of Baja California, is adapted to dry climates. A small rose with simple pink flowers, it blooms in winter and sets seeds before the extremely hot, dry summers of its native environment begin. This rose is being researched in the Southwest for use in landscaping.

R. moschata (Musk Rose) Known since ancient times and native to Asia, this rose derives its name from its musklike fragrance, especially noticeable in the evening. It grows as a rampant climber in warm, humid climates, but only to about ten feet in cooler regions. Medium-sized ivory-white flowers appear in midseason, followed by small red hips. *R. moschata* is most notable as the parent of the Noisettes and the Hybrid Musks.

R. moyesii Native to China and named for the Reverend E. J. Moyes of the China Inland Mission, this was the first truly red wild rose species discovered. Deep blood-red flowers are one-and-one-half to two-and-one-half inches wide, borne singly or in small clusters, early to midseason. The eye-catching flowers are succeeded by equally arresting bottle-shaped hips, two to two-and-one-half inches long and brilliant orange-red. Upright plants have an awkward growth pattern, reaching ten feet tall or more, with slightly thorny canes and delicate fernlike foliage. **'Nevada'** is a fine hybrid, with masses of single, white, three-inch flowers borne on short stems, repeating through the season. This can be a large plant; its dark, plum-colored canes are attractive left to arch naturally or trained or wrapped around posts and pillars.

R. multiflora (Japanese Rose) Native to Asia. This rose is the ancestor of the

R. LAEVIGATA (CHEROKEE ROSE) Species. Vigorous plants; thorny canes grow fifteen to twenty feet. Bright green and glossy leaves. Large, open, and fragrant flowers, usually white. Early blooms, followed by large, densely prickled red hips. Not winter hardy; blooms only in Southern regions.

'RAUBRITTER' Hybrid macrantha. Spreading, sprawling shrub. Clear, silvery pink semidouble cupped blossoms. Blooms heavily for short period in summer and does not rebloom. Susceptible to mildew in late summer, when it has finished flowering. Thorny.

R. MOYESII Species. Ten feet tall or more. Delicate fernlike foliage. Blood-red flowers, one-and-one-half to two-and-one-half inches wide, borne singly or in small clusters. Two- to two-and-one-half-inch orange-red hips.

R. MULTIFLORA (JAPANESE ROSE) Species. Vigorous, dense shrub; grows rampantly. Smooth light green leaves. Masses of single, white, three-quarter-inch blossoms appear in early to midseason, followed by small round red hips that remain into winter. Sweet fragrance. Arching canes grow ten to more than twelve feet. Virtually thorn free.

Above: R. multiflora. Above right:
'Veilchenblau'.

Multiflora Ramblers as well as many Polyanthas and Floribundas and is also widely used as an understock. It is a vigorous, dense shrub whose rampant growth has become a major weed-control problem in some areas. Masses of single, white, three-quarter-inch sweetly scented blossoms appear in pyramid-shaped clusters in early to midseason, followed by small round red hips that remain into the winter. Arching canes grow ten to twelve feet or more.

HYBRID MULTIFLORAS

'Seven Sisters Rose' (formerly *R. multiflora platyphylla*) is a hybrid with pink to mauve-purple flowers, more tender than *R. multiflora*.

'Trier' is a tall shrub, growing up to six feet with clusters of creamy yellow single or near-single flowers and was used in the development of Hybrid Musk roses.

'Veilchenblau' is a fast-growing Rambler that bears abundant fragrant lavender flowers and is sometimes called "The Blue Rose."

R. palustris (Swamp Rose) Native to swampy areas of North America and sent to Europe in the eighteenth century. Medium pink two-inch flowers are sweetly fragrant, with bold gold stamens, blooming singly or in small clusters late in the season. In wet, swampy soil, plants grow eight feet tall or more in dense thickets; cultivated on dry ground, plants grow to about six feet. Canes are not very thorny.

R. pendulina (Alpine Rose) A very hardy native of the Alps. Medium to deep pink flowers are lightly and sweetly scented, borne singly or in clusters in mid to late season. These are followed by bottle-shaped one-inch-long orange-red hips that hang from the reddish stems. Plants have a graceful, arching growth habit, three to four feet high, and are nearly thornless. They readily accept

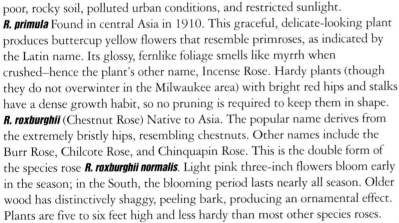

These photographs of growth habits of three Species Roses demonstrate the fact that generalizations cannot be made. From left to right, *R. palustris, R. setigera, R. xanthina.*

poor, rocky soil, polluted urban conditions, and restricted sunlight.

R. primula Found in central Asia in 1910. This graceful, delicate-looking plant produces buttercup yellow flowers that resemble primroses, as indicated by the Latin name. Its glossy, fernlike foliage smells like myrrh when crushed–hence the plant's other name, Incense Rose. Hardy plants (though they do not overwinter in the Milwaukee area) with bright red hips and stalks have a dense growth habit, so no pruning is required to keep them in shape.

R. roxburghii (Chestnut Rose) Native to Asia. The popular name derives from the extremely bristly hips, resembling chestnuts. Other names include the Burr Rose, Chilcote Rose, and Chinquapin Rose. This is the double form of the species rose **R. roxburghii normalis**. Light pink three-inch flowers bloom early in the season; in the South, the blooming period lasts nearly all season. Older wood has distinctively shaggy, peeling bark, producing an ornamental effect. Plants are five to six feet high and less hardy than most other species roses.

R. rugosa (see rugosa roses, p. 48)

R. sericea (Himalayan Rose) Native to the Himalayas, this species rose is unusual in that it usually has only four petals. Flowers are creamy white, one-and-one-half to two inches wide. Most prominent features are the huge, broad, glimmering red prickles. The large plants covered with the impressive prickles make a fine, impenetrable hedge. Prune to encourage new growth with abundant prickles, but leave plenty of old wood, on which the blossoms are borne.

R. setigera (Prairie Rose) Native to the United States and southern Ontario, this is also known as the Bramble-Leaved Rose because its leaves and canes resemble those of the blackberry plant. Scentless, deep pink flowers are borne

'TRIER' Hybrid multiflora. Tall shrub or climber, up to six feet. Small, almost dainty, foliage. Creamy yellow single or near-single flowers. Slightly fragrant.

R. PALUSTRIS (SWAMP ROSE) Species. Grows eight feet tall or more in wet areas; to two feet in dry ground. Mid to dark green foliage. Medium pink two-inch flowers, blooming singly or in clusters late in season, followed by oval hips in autumn. Fragrant. Not very thorny.

R. PENDULINA (ALPINE ROSE) Species. Three to four feet high. Dark green foliage. Medium to deep pink flowers, borne singly or in clusters, mid to late season. Lightly and sweetly scented. One-inch-long orange-red hips hanging from reddish-purple stems. Nearly thornless. Accepts poor, rocky soil, polluted urban conditions, and restricted sunlight.

R. PRIMULA (INCENSE ROSE) Species. Graceful shrub with arching stems to five feet long. Glossy, fernlike foliage. Buttercup yellow flowers. Bright red hips. Smells like myrrh when crushed. Hardy. Dense growth habit; no pruning required.

in clusters late in the season. Red foliage and clustered orange hips add beauty to the fall garden. This is the only climbing rose native to North America, with canes that can grow sixteen to twenty feet; use as a groundcover or train as a climber. Samuel and John Feast, Baltimore florists, used *R. setigera* as a parent to produce hybrid climbers. One of these is **'Baltimore Belle'** (1843), which produces large clusters of very double, pale pink and fragrant flowers. It is not as hardy as *R. setigera,* so its other parent is believed to be a noisette.

R. spinosissima (Scotch Rose or Burnet Rose) Native to Europe and Asia and early naturalized in North America. This species is aptly described by its Latin name, "most thorny," as spinosissimas are the most heavily bristled and prickled of all rose groups. Flowers are creamy white, pink, or yellow (occasionally red or purple), one to two inches across, and not very fragrant, produced freely early in the season. The small, round hips are deep purple or black. Spinosissimas grow to only three to four feet, are very hardy, and thrive in any type of soil, so they make good covers for banks and semiwild areas. They also are effective as borders and hedges. Plants sucker freely.

SPINOSISSIMA HYBRIDS

R. spinosissma altaica, discovered in the Altai Mountains of Russia, is much more vigorous than *R. spinosissima,* growing to six feet high and across, making it an ideal hedge plant. Its larger and fragrant flowers are creamy white, borne on large stalks. The fernlike foliage turns yellow in the fall; hips are purple or maroon. An enduringly popular Spinosissima hybrid is **'Stanwell Perpetual',** first introduced by Lee in 1838. It is probably a cross between *R. spinosissima* and *R. damascena semperflorens,* now 'Autumn Damask'; true to that heritage, it is the only repeat-blooming Spinosissima hybrid. Double blush pink three- to three-and-one-half-inch flowers are fragrant and repeat reliably after their initial early to midseason bloom. Color deepens in cool fall weather. Vigorous plants grow three to five feet tall and wide, with attractive fernlike foliage, and thrive on neglect.

'Golden Wings' is another useful and easy to find Spinosissima hybrid, with good foliage and a light pleasant scent. A hardy shrub (to Zone 6) introduced in 1956 by Shepherd, it bears abundant soft yellow flowers in spring, followed by fewer but constant blooms throughout the summer.

The renowned German rose hybridizer, Wilhelm Kordes Sons, developed a series of hardy, early-blooming Spinosissima hybrids. **'Frülingsgold'** ("spring gold") (1937) was created from *R. spinosissima hispida* and a hybrid tea. Its scarlet-tinted buds open to enormous (three-and-one-half to five inches wide) sweetly scented, single yellow flowers. Vigorous, arching, heavily thorned canes grow six to eight feet high and wide, making a good hedge. **'Frülingsmorgen'** ("spring morning") (1942) is a cross between *R. spinosissima altaica* and a Hybrid Tea. Its large (three- to three-and-one-half-inch) flowers are lavender pink with yellow centers and maroon stamens; the blooms are fragrant and borne profusely and are followed by exceptionally large red hips. The six-foot-high shrubs can

Everywhere the rose is met, and reminds us of cultivated gardens and civilization. It is scattered ovet the prairies in small bouquets and when glittering in the dew and swaying in the pleasant breeze of the early morning, it is the most beautiful of all prairie flowers.
CAPTAIN JOHN CHARLES FREMAN, SEVENTEENTH CENTURY AMERICAN EXPLORER

be trained as pillar roses. Neither of the hybrids forms suckers. To prevent top-heaviness, prune each back every two years (after an initial growth period of four to five years) to promote new growth from the base.

'Harison's Yellow' (1830) This rose is now widely distributed across North America, because pioneers carried it with them on their way West, but its exact parentage remains a mystery. One parent is *R. spinosissima;* the other may be *R. hugonis* or *R. foetida persiana*. Although it is also called the Yellow Rose of Texas, it was discovered by George Harison in his New York City garden in 1830; he gave it to a nurseryman who traded it to another nurseryman, William Prince, who introduced it to the market. Flowers are bright yellow, double, two to two-and-one-half inches across, appearing profusely along arching canes early in the season. Upright, spreading plants grow five to seven feet and are freely suckering, with thorny canes and ferny green leaves. This is an extremely vigorous, hardy, rose.

R. virginiana Native to and widely distributed over eastern North America, this became one of the first native American roses cultivated in Europe after

'Harison's Yellow', shown planted with *Deutzia gracilis;* both flower in mid to late spring, and the arching, profusely flowering yellow rose is a fine background for the more refined white *Deutzia gracilis.*

R. ROXBURGHII (CHESTNUT ROSE) Species. Five to six feet tall. Light green foliage, distinctive bark. Light pink three-inch single flowers; blooms nearly all season in South, early in season elsewhere. Spherical, bristly orange-yellow fruit. Moderately fragrant. Not hardy.

R. RUBRIFOLIA (now called *R. glauca*) Species. Shrub to six feet tall. Often grown for its glaucous purple foliage, which provides interest in autumn. Small, soft mauve-pink flowers in clusters. Oval reddish-purple hips in autumn. Slightly fragrant.

R. SERICEA (HIMALAYAN ROSE) Species. Vigorous shrub to ten feet tall. Creamy white, one-and-one-half- to two-inch-wide flowers with only four petals; huge red prickles. Bright-red, oval fruit.

R. SETIGERA (PRAIRIE ROSE) Species. Canes grow sixteen to twenty feet, forming bramblelike mat. Red foliage; clustered orange hips. Deep pink flowers borne in clusters late in the season. Scentless.

R. SPINOSSISSIMA ALTAICA Spinosissima hybrid. Six feet high and across. Fernlike foliage turns yellow in the fall; hips are purple or maroon. Large creamy white flowers. Fragrant. More vigorous than *R. spinossissima*; useful as hedge.

'FRUHLINGSGOLD' ("SPRING GOLD") Spinosissima hybrid. Canes six to eight feet high and wide. Vigorous upright plant with dark green foliage. Scarlet-tinted buds open to enormous (three-and-one-half to five-inch-wide) single yellow flowers. Sweetly scented. Heavily thorned.

R. VIRGINIANA Species. Upright shrub to five feet tall. Glossy, bright green leaves turn rich colors in the fall, accompanied by round, ruby-red hips. Bright pink two- to three-inch flowers, borne singly or in small clusters. Freely suckering.

R. XANTHINA (MANCHU ROSE) Species. Angular shrubs, ten feet tall and six feet wide. Dark green, fernlike foliage. Small, rich yellow semidouble flowers in clusters produced early in season. Moderately fragrant.

colonists sent plants from Virginia to England in 1724. Bright pink two- to three-inch flowers are borne singly or in small clusters. The glossy, bright green leaves turn color richly in the fall, accompanied by round, ruby red hips. Upright plants grow to five feet and are freely suckering.

R. wichuraiana Native to Asia, this trailing plant was named after Dr. Max Ernst Wichura, a German botanist, who discovered it in Japan in 1861. It became known as the Memorial Rose in the United States after it became popular as a groundcover for graves. *R. wichuraiana* has passed on its vigor and disease resistance to many subsequent climbing hybrids. Flowers are single, white, one to one-and-one-half inches across, late blooming, and very fragrant, followed by small, oval, red hips. The shiny, bright green leaves turn yellow in fall. Trailing shoots grow ten to twenty feet and can be trained to climb, in which case they may be harmed by extreme winter cold.

R. xanthina Discovered in China in 1906, the Manchu Rose produces small, rich yellow semidouble flowers in clusters. It forms an angular shrub, to ten feet tall and six feet wide, that is suitable for hedging. The flowers, which appear in spring, are moderately fragrant. A hybrid, **'Canary Bird'** has single flowers that sometimes reappear in autumn.

Above: R. xanthina.
Left: R. wichuraiana.

Above: 'Agnes'. *Below: R. rugosa* grow-ing near the shore on Long Island.

RUGOSA ROSES

The rugosa rose, *R. rugosa,* is one of the hardiest of all roses. Masses of natural-ized rugosas are common sights along the seacoast of the northeastern United States, rugged bushes covered with bright mauve-pink blossoms and striking orange-red hips resembling cherry tomatoes. Because rugosas dwell happily in salt spray, wind, and dry, sandy soil, they are often called Beach Roses. (In Japan, they are called *hama nashi,* or "Shore Pear.") They originated in north central to northeastern Asia and were brought to the United States in the nineteenth century, where they quickly adapted and spread in the wild.

Rugosas make excellent low-maintenance landscape shrubs and hedges. They are vigorous growers, extremely hardy, and virtually disease-free. They thrive on neglect, and do well in the polluted air of cities. Their freely pro-duced, large mauve-pink or white flowers are very fragrant and long-lasting. Bloom often continues even after formation of the beautiful, large, and bright hips, which are an excellent source of vitamin C and attract birds as well. The handsome rugosa foliage is distinctive—dark green, leathery, and wrinkled (*R. rugosa* translates as the "rose with wrinkled leaves"), and it turns yellow, red, and orange in the fall. Canes are extremely prickly. Little pruning is needed,

R. RUGOSA RUBRA Rugosa. Dense, rounded shrub. Leathery foliage, which turns colors in fall. Deep mauve pink flowers. Very fragrant, blooms all summer and long-lasting. Large red hips. Prickly canes. Vigorous, hardy, and virtually disease free.

R. RUGOSA ALBA Rugosa. Dense, rounded shrub. Leathery foliage, which turns colors in fall. White flowers. Very fragrant, blooms all summer and long-lasting. Large red hips. Prickly canes. Vigorous, hardy, and virtually disease free.

'AGNES' Rugosa hybrid. Four- to six-foot-tall dense, upright plants with dark green, crinkled foliage. Blooms early to midseason, occasionally reblooming later in season. Full double light yellow flowers, three inches across. Very fragrant, very thorny canes. Disease resistant, winter hardy.

'BLANC DOUBLE DE COUBERT' Rugosa hybrid. Four to seven feet tall and wide. Dense and bushy plant. Dark green, leathery, and wrinkled foliage. Two- to three-inch snowy white flowers, semidouble, bloom all season. Very fragrant. Remove spent petals to allow formation of the large bright orange-red hips. Vigorous, hardy, and disease resistant.

The discovery, protection, and preservation of our old roses constitutes a challenge to all rose lovers. No one person can do justice to it. It is a duty resting upon all who love the rose, its history, its romance, its usefulness as an agency of human happiness, to save our disappearing old roses for the benefit of present and future generations and to make known their manifold advantages to all who love gardening.
FRANCIS E. LESTER, *AMERICAN ROSE ANNUAL,* 1931

except to trim back overly dense or leggy plants. The new canes that grow up from the base of the plant produce the following year's flowers; removing up to one-third of old wood—on plants at least three years old—after the first burst of growth in the spring will stimulate production of more new canes.

In areas subject to the rose stem girdler, Rugosas require removal of all wood greater than two years old; where the rose stem girdler is not a problem, this is not needed. If chlorosis is a problem—as it is in the Milwaukee area with some established plants—a light sprinkling of manganese sulfate on the soil surface will usually correct it. Minnesota Landscape Arboretum reports problems with the mossy rose gall wasp, which makes ugly galls that can weaken and eventually kill canes; galls should be pruned yearly for this reason. Breeders have created many hybrid forms of Rugosas. Some of these may not be as hardy or disease resistant as the species Rugosas.

R. rugosa Single, mauve-pink flowers, two-and-one-half to three-and-one-half inches across, with five to twelve petals, bloom continuously all summer on three- to five-foot-tall bushes.

R. rugosa alba A white sport of *R. rugosa,* identical in all respects except for the color. **R. rugosa albo-plena** is a double white form, a good ground-hugging hybrid.

R. rugosa rubra A deep mauve-pink sport of *R. rugosa,* again identical to the parent except for the color.

RUGOSA HYBRIDS

'Agnes' (Saunders, 1900) *R. rugosa* and *R. foetida persiana,* the Persian Yellow, were crossed to produce this unusual yellow Rugosa. The light yellow flowers are fully double, three inches across, with twenty-four to thirty delightfully fragrant petals. Blooms early to midseason, with occasional rebloom later in the season (it rarely reblooms in the Milwaukee area). Its exceptionally thorny canes are subject to canker and rose stem girdler; renewal pruning keeps these in check. Vigorous four- to six-foot-tall plants are upright and bushy, disease resistant, and completely winter hardy.

'Arnold' (Dawson, 1893) One of the first hybrid rugosas developed. Single, deep red flowers rebloom sparsely throughout the season. Inherited color from its Hybrid Perpetual parent but the foliage and growth habit of *R. rugosa.*

'Belle Poitevine' (1894) Exceptionally vigorous, hardy, disease-resistant, and carefree hybrid Rugosa. Double lilac-pink four-inch flowers are very fragrant and recur, followed by numerous edible hips high in vitamin C.

'Blanc Double de Coubert' (Cochet-Cochet, 1892) A very popular Shrub Rose, widely considered the best of the white Rugosas. Very fragrant two- to three-inch snowy white flowers are semidouble, with eighteen to twenty-four petals, and are among the first roses to bloom in the garden and continue all season. Spent blooms are unattractive; removing petals allows formation of the large bright orange-red hips. Vigorous, bushy plants grow four to seven feet tall and nearly as wide, with typical

'HENRY HUDSON' Rugosa hybrid. Low and bushy. Large (to three inches) double flowers with yellow stamens. recur. Very fragrant. Hardy and fairly disease free.

'PINK GROOTENDORST' Rugosa hybrid. Four to six feet tall and wide. Rough-textured foliage. Large clusters of small, one-to-two-inch double medium pink flowers, tending to revert to red. Lightly fragrant blooms borne profusely in midseason and continue until fall. Vigorous, winter hardy.

'SARA VAN FLEET' Rugosa hybrid. Six to eight feet. Leathery, wrinkled dark green foliage. Rosy pink semidouble flowers, three to three-and-one-half inches across. Blooms continuously. Very fragrant. Disease resistant and winter hardy.

'TOPAZ JEWEL' Rugosa hybrid. First repeat-blooming hybrid rugosa. Three to four-foot mound of semidouble soft yellow flowers. Susceptible to blackspot and less hardy than the species.

GROWING ROSES FOR HIPS

Some roses produce decorative red or orange hips in the fall and winter after flowers have gone by. Even small hips are a colorful and attractive addition to the late-season landscape. The larger, succulent hips make tasty jelly, jam, and tea.

Roses that flower only once a season and single-flowered roses are most likely to produce ornamental hips.

Many Shrub Roses have bright red hips, including 'Bonica' and 'Carefree Wonder', (with exceptionally large ones). Species Roses frequently produce attractive hips; the rugosas are especially noted for their large, bright, abundantly produced orange to red hips prized for jams and jellies. Note, however, that many of the new Hybrid Rugosas do not produce the characteristic large hips; 'Blanc Double de Coubert', 'Hansa', 'Schneezwerg', and 'Max Graf' are ones that do. Species Roses with ornamental hips include:

R. canina: scarlet; oval
R. eglanteria: bright red; small, oval, abundant; remain over the winter
R. foetida: deep red; round
R. gallica: red; medium, round
R. glauca: dark burgundy ripening to bright orange; small, round
R. laevigata: red; large, bristly
R. moschata: red; tiny; flagon-shaped, in clusters
R. moyesii: bright orange-red; large, bottled-shaped, dramatic.

Above: 'Frau Dagmar Hastrup' hips
Right: Red and white 'Max Graf'

Rugosa foliage, disease resistance, and hardiness; propagates easily from runners.

'Conrad Ferdinand Meyer' (Muller, 1899) The influence of the Hybrid Tea parent shows in the exhibition-type buds opening to large, intensely fragrant, many-petaled pink flowers three-and-one-half to four-and-one-half inches across. Blooms abundantly early to midseason, and will repeat well if plant is deadheaded. Exceptionally vigorous plants grow nine to twelve feet tall and are well suited for growing around a pillar. Foliage is more like Hybrid Teas than Rugosas; plants are disease resistant (though susceptible to blackspot and powdery mildew in the Milwaukee area) but not reliably winter hardy.

'Dr. Eckener' (Berger, 1930) Huge, fragrant semidouble flowers, pale yellow with hints of pink and copper as they age, make this a useful plant despite its wicked thorns.

'F.J. Grootendorst' (de Goey, 1918) Like its Polyantha parent, this Rugosa Hybrid bears its flowers in large clusters of small, one- to two-inch double flowers, bright red and serrated like carnations. The blooms are

borne profusely in midseason and continue until fall. Vigorous, compact plants grow four to six feet tall and wide, making a fine hedge or border, with small, dark green leaves that turn dull as the summer progresses. Disease resistant and winter hardy.

'Flamingo' (Howard, 1956) Five-petaled lightly fragrant pink flowers have strong yellow stamens and bloom throughout the season. Bushy plants grow four feet tall and wide and are excellent for the border. It is not very hardy and prone to blackspot in the Milwaukee area. Foliage shows the influence of the Hybrid Tea parent.

'Frau Dagmar Hastrup' (unknown, 1914) Also known as 'Frau Dagmar Hartopp'. Extremely fragrant, clove-scented silvery pink flowers are single, with five petals, three inches across, and bloom repeatedly from early/midseason until frost. Spent flowers are followed by large red hips. Vigorous, spreading plants grow three to four feet tall and wide, with typical Rugosa foliage; bushes are very hardy and disease free. Nancy Rose at Minnesota Landscape Arboretum considers 'Frau Dagmar Hastrup' to be the best Hybrid Rugosa for its beautiful fragrant flowers, clean green foliage, and showy hips.

'Henry Hudson' Part of the Canadian "Explorer" series, this low, bushy variety bears pink buds that open to very fragrant white flowers with yellow stamens. The blossoms, which recur, are large (to three inches) and double (to twenty-five petals). It is very hardy and fairly disease free, though it is susceptible to rose stem borer. It should be deadheaded regularly.

'Max Graf' (Bowditch, 1919) A natural cross between *R. rugosa* and *R. wichuraiana,* discovered in a private garden in Connecticut, this is a trailing rose with flowers like species rugosas but the vigorous procumbent growth habit of the wichuraianas, so it makes a fine ground and bank cover. It also became a parent of *R.* x*kordesii.* Five-petaled single bright pink flowers are three inches across with golden-stamened centers, borne profusely once per season and followed by red hips. Small, shiny leaves turn red in the fall; disease-resistant plants have fierce prickles.

'Mme. Charles Frederic Worth' (Schwartz, 1889) A very early Hybrid Rugosa, no longer in commerce. Semidouble, extremely fragrant, rosy carmine flowers appear in late spring and continue through the season. Low-growing plants reach three feet, with Rugosa-type foliage that turns yellow in the fall.

'Pink Grootendorst' (Grootendorst, 1923) A medium pink sport of F. J. Grootendorst, which it resembles in all other ways.

'Nova Zembla' A pure white sport of 'Conrad F. Meyer'.

'Rotes Meer' (Oswald Bauer, 1984) Most Hybrid Rugosas are marred by spent bloom that remain on the plant like a wad of discolored tissue paper. 'Rotes Meer' (synonym 'Purple Pavement') is the exception. Its semidouble clusters of deep fuschia flowers self-clean when spent, dropping neatly from the plant. The bush, which grows to about three feet tall and wide has strong erect canes, and the foliage turns yellow and gold in the fall, highlighted by colorful hips.

'Rugosa Magnifica' (Van Fleet, 1905) Carmine red, strongly fragrant, double flowers are three inches across, with golden stamens, borne repeatedly and followed by numerous orange-red hips. Vigorous, spreading, very hardy plants grow four to five feet tall, with rugosa-type foliage.

'Sarah Van Fleet' (Van Fleet, 1926) Named for the wife of famous American hybridizer Dr. Walter Van Fleet. Rosy pink semidouble flowers are very fragrant, three to three-and-one-half inches across, with eighteen to twenty-four petals and prominent yellow stamens. Blooms continuously on vigorous, bushy six- to eight-foot plants that make good background shrubs, with typical rugosa foliage; its growth tends to be loose and floppy. Usually disease resistant and winter hardy, it will experience dieback and is susceptible to blackspot in the Milwaukee area.

'Schneezwerg' (Lambert, 1912) Also called 'Snow Dwarf'. Delicate, semidouble, pure white flowers are three to three-and-one-half inches across, with eighteen to twenty-four petals and prominent yellow stamens, borne in clusters early to midseason with good repeat. Orange-red hips follow. Plants are slow to transplant, but when established prove to be vigorous, spreading plants growing five feet tall and wide, with medium to dark green, small rugosa-type foliage and thorny canes. Disease free and winter hardy, bushy plants make a fine hedge.

'Topaz Jewel' (Moore, 1987) The first repeat-blooming hybrid rugosa, this makes a three- to four-foot mound of semidouble soft yellow flowers. It is somewhat susceptible to blackspot and is considered less hardy than the species.

Right: 'Blanc Double de Coubert'.
Far right: 'Belle Poitevine'.

'Schneezwerg'.

'Nova Zembla'.

'Dr. Eckener'.

'Conrad Ferdinand Meyer'.

'F. J. Grootendorst'.

SPORTS

A sport is a sudden, spontaneous change from botanical type–a mutation. The change can be an alteration like change in growth habit–for example, a climbing form of a bush variety––or flower color. The new characteristic can be passed on from one sport to its progeny. Some well-known examples of sports include:

'Chicago Peace'–a more intensely colored sport of 'Peace'.

'Climbing Charlotte Armstrong'–a climbing sport of a hybrid tea.

'Climbing Queen Elizabeth'–a climbing sport of a grandiflora.

'Climbing Cecile Brunner'–a climbing sport of a polyantha.

'New Dawn'–everblooming sport of 'Dr. W. Van Fleet.'

'Summer Snow'–a floribunda sport of 'Climbing Summer Snow'.

The conserve of Roses . . . strengtheneth the heart and taketh away the shaking and trembling thereof, and in a word is the most familiar thing to be used for the purpose aforesaid, and is thus made: Take Roses at your pleasure, put them to boyle in faire water, having regard to the quantity; for if you have many Roses you may take more water; if fewer, the lesse water will serve: the which you shall boyle at the least three or foure houres, even as you would boyle a piece of meate, untill in the eating they be very tender, at which time the Roses will lose their colour, you would think your labour lost, and the thing spoiled. But proceed, for though the Roses have lost their colour, the water hath gotten the tincture there-of; then shall you adde unto one pound of Roses, foure pounds of fine sugar in pure powder, and also according to the rest of the Roses. Thus shall you let them boyle gently after the sugar is put thereto, continually stirring it with a woodden Spatula untill it be cold, where-of one pound weight is worth six pound of the raw or crude conserve, as well for the vertues and goodnesse in taste, as also for the beautiful colour.
From John Gerard's *Herball*, 1597.

Opposite: 'La Belle Sultane'.

OLD GARDEN ROSES: PRE-CHINAS

Old garden roses are those cultivated (as opposed to occurring in the wild) prior to 1867, the date established by the American Rose Society as the introduction of the hybrid tea, the first modern rose. Old garden roses are divided into two groups, again separated by the introduction of a new type of rose. The pre-China old garden roses are those that were cultivated in Europe before the ever-blooming roses were introduced from China in the late 1700s and early 1800s. The second group comprises the repeat-blooming Chinas and those that came after them, up to the advent of the hybrid tea.

The pre-China old garden roses are the gallicas, damasks, albas, centifolias, and moss roses. Almost all of these are one-time bloomers with white or pink wonderfully scented flowers. Especially fragrant are the gallicas and damasks. For best growth, the pre-Chinas need a colder climate that produces a period of dormancy. They bloom better on old than new wood.

GALLICAS

Gallicas are generally considered to be the forerunners of all later cultivated garden roses. Gallicas originate from *R. gallica,* the wild French rose, so named because–although it is native to Europe and western Asia–it was especially widely grown in France. It has also been known as *R. rubra,* or the Red Rose, although the flowers might more accurately be described as very deep pink. The Roman writer Pliny described *R. gallica* in his *Natural History* of the first century AD, calling it the Rose of Miletus, and the Romans used it extravagantly at their feasts and festivals. They also used it medicinally, so they carried it with their armies and planted it throughout their empire. Medieval monks continued to cultivate *R. gallica,* and early settlers brought it with them to North America. During the eighteenth century, *R. gallica* was so extensively cultivated commercially near the town of Provins, France, that it became known as the Rose of Provins–not to be confused with the name Rose of Provence for Cabbage Rose (formerly *R. centifolia*).

Several characteristics allowed *R. gallica* to spread rapidly throughout its range: its free production of long underground runners, its extreme hardiness, its toleration of both very cold and very hot climates, its disease resistance, and its copious production of easily germinating seeds. *R. gallica* also cross-breeds readily, so now there are many different kinds of gallicas, in a range of colors from blush white through the pinks to red, mauve, and purple, with anywhere from five to many petals. Blooms may also be spotted or variegated. Foliage is generally dark green, lush, and coarse; growth habit is moderate and upright. As a group, gallicas are noted for their scent. Single- and semi-double-flowering varieties produce an abundance of hips. Gallicas do not need much pruning; simply thin out old wood as it accumulates. Prune after blooming to encourage new growth, which will produce flowers in the following seasons.

Apothecary's Rose (formerly *R. gallica officinalis*) The name of this gallica refers to its widespread medicinal use from medieval to more recent times. The

'APOTHECARY'S ROSE' (formerly *R. gallica officinalis*) Gallica. Three to four feet tall. Erect, bushy growth. Slightly coarse dark grayish green leaves. Large, rounded, deep red hips. Semidouble flowers, two to three inches across. Very fragrant, few thorns.

'ROSA MUNDI' (formerly *R. gallica versicolor*) Gallica. Three to four feet high, erect unless weighed down by flowers. Slightly coarse dark grayish green leaves. Flowers are three to four inches across, semidouble, pinkish white petals with deep pink and red stripes.

'ALAIN BLANCHARD' Gallica-centifolia hybrid. Dense, bushy mound, four feet by four feet. Dark green foliage. Large, semidouble light red flowers with lighter spots. Very fragrant.

'ANTONIA D'ORMOIS' Gallica. Five feet high and three feet wide. Pale pink double cupped flowers fade to nearly white. Moderately fragrant.

Pilgrims brought the Apothecary's Rose to America for its beauty as well as its medicinal and household uses. Other common names are the Red or Damask Gallica. In Virginia and neighboring states it is also called the Offley Rose, because it was supposed to have been grown in the Yorktown garden of General Nelson; when British troops under Cornwallis approached during the Revolution, Mrs. Nelson supposedly withdrew to the family estate of Offley, near Richmond, bringing the rose with her. This may also be the Red Rose of Lancaster, from the fifteenth-century Wars of the Roses. The very fragrant flowers are two to three inches across, semidouble, with twelve to eighteen rose red petals. Flowers open in the sun to show prominent yellow stamens. Plants are three to four feet tall and have few thorns. The large hips are rounded and deep red.

'Rosa Mundi' (formerly *R. gallica versicolor*) The name of this famous and very old gallica is supposed to derive from Fair Rosamond, the twelfth-century mistress of King Henry II of England. It's a sport of *R. gallica officinalis* and the first striped rose. Its semidouble pinkish white petals are striped heavily with deep pink and red, centered by a cluster of yellow stamens. Each uniquely marked and fragrant flower is three to four inches across, with eighteen to twenty-four petals. Bushes are three to four feet high; although the bush is upright, it often sprawls when weighed down with blossoms.

'Alain Blanchard' A gallica-centifolia hybrid, with large semidouble light red flowers with lighter spots and dark green foliage. It forms a dense, bushy mound, usually four feet by four feet and has a lovely scent.

'Antonia d'Ormois' This gallica flowers later than most others; its pale pink double cupped flowers fade to nearly white. Bushes grow to about five feet high and three feet wide.

'Belle Isis' (Parmentier, 1845) Fragrant, double, cupped light pink flowers are two-and-one-half to three inches across, with forty-five to fifty-five petals; the flowers look flat when open. Blooms once only, in midseason. Rounded three-

R. gallica.

'Charles de Mills'.

to four-foot plants are bushy, with bristly canes and small gray-green leaves. Some sources list this as a centifolia hybrid.

'Cardinal de Richelieu' (Laffay, 1840) This rose does not have a stable flower color, but when it is right, it is a rich, velvety deep purple and sweetly fragrant, three to four inches across and double, with thirty-five to forty-five petals, blooming once in midseason. Compact plants grow three to four feet high, with glossy dark green foliage; tiny thorns pepper the canes, as with most gallicas. Neat shrubs are good for hedging.

'Charles de Mills' (Date unknown) Very double flowers have swirled deep red petals with tinges of purple and a lavender reverse; they are intensely fragrant. Blooms are cupped and quartered, three to three-and-one-half inches across, packed with up to two hundred petals, borne in clusters in midseason for an extended period. Vigorous upright plants grow to four to five feet high and wide, with few thorns.

'Complicata' (Origin and date unknown) Single, five-petaled bright pink flowers are four to five inches across, with white to pale pink centers and prominent gold stamens. Fragrant blooms are borne freely once in the summer. Dense, vigorous plants will grow to ten feet treated as a climber, or the arching canes can be pruned to form an attractive five-foot shrub, well suited for an informal garden. Plants have few thorns and light gray-green leaves; colorful round orange hips. Tolerates poor soil and partial shade.

'Désirée Parmentier' (Prior to 1848, Origin unknown) Flowers are bright cerise pink, darkening with age, with open golden-stamened centers.

'James Mason' (Beales, 1982) A modern gallica. Abundant large, semidouble velvety red flowers with prominent yellow stamens appear in mid June. Tall, spreading shrubs with heavy dark green foliage that sometimes hides the blossoms are good landscape plants.

'La Belle Sultane' (1795) Also known as 'Violacea'. Fragrant, vivid pink (mottled with lighter pink) flowers have brilliant yellow stamens in the open center, followed by dark plum and orange hips. Spreading plants have fine dark green foliage. Strong, upright new canes grow up to six feet, then arch over and flower the following year. Pruning out some old wood in the fall encourages production of new canes.

'Président de Sèze' (Prior to 1836) A gallica with interesting coloration—magenta and lilac edged in paler tones—with petals that fold inward. Thornier than most gallicas, it grows to four feet tall and three feet wide.

'Sissinghurst Castle' (reintroduced 1947) Vita Sackville-West found this old gallica in the famous gardens at Sissinghurst Castle in 1947. Velvety deep plum flowers are small and very fragrant, borne once in the season. Moderately vigorous bushes have small but abundant foliage, growing up to three feet tall and wide, and will tolerate shade.

'Superb Tuscan' (also known as 'Superb Tuscany' and 'Tuscany Superb') (prior to 1848) Frilly semidouble velvety maroon flowers are four inches across and very fragrant, with thirty-four to forty petals curled around a center of golden stamens, borne once in midseason. Upright, rounded plants grow three to four feet tall, with few thorns and lush dark green foliage.

'BELLE ISIS' Gallica. Three to four feet tall. Small gray-green leaves. Double, cupped light pink flowers are two-and-one-half to three inches across; flowers look flat when open. Blooms only once, in midseason. Very fragrant. Bristly canes.

'CARDINAL DE RICHELIEU' Gallica. Three to four feet tall. Abundant dark green foliage. No stable flower color; usually a rich, velvety deep purple, three to four inches across and double, blooming once in midseason. Sweetly fragrant. Tiny thorns.

'DÉSIRÉE PARMENTIER' Gallica. Dense shrub three to four feet tall. Bright cerise pink flowers, darkening with age, with open golden-stamened centers. Medium green foliage, small prickles.

'SUPERB TUSCAN' Gallica. Three to four feet tall. Lush dark green foliage. Frilly, semidouble velvety maroon flowers, four inches across, with curled around a center of golden stamens, borne once in midseason. Very fragrant. Few thorns.

'KAZANLIK' (formerly known as *R. damascena trigintipetala*) Damask . Three- to four-foot-tall bushes that flower once. Pink flowers, with about thirty petals; colors fade as bloom ages. Very fragrant.

'MADAME ZÖETMANS' Damask. Upright, spreading bushes. Darkish green foliage, though new foliage is reddish. Blush white flowers with pale peach-pink centers, very double blooms with prominent green eye.

'CELSIANA' Damask. Contained shrub, to five feet tall by four feet wide. Nodding clusters of clear pink semidouble flowers with yellow anthers fade to white in heat. Very fragrant. Light gray-green foliage.

'BLUSH DAMASK' Damask. Tall and vigorous bushes. Slightly cupped, double medium-sized blush pink flowers with deeper pink centers. Very fragrant. Not as thorny as other Damasks. Very floriferous in bloom, but with fleeting effect.

DAMASKS

Damask roses have an important place in the history of rose culture, as they gave rise to the Damask Perpetuals and then the Hybrid Perpetuals, which became the forerunners of the Hybrid Teas. Damasks are nearly as ancient as the Gallicas and are probably hybrids with both *R. gallica* and *R. canina* in their ancestry, plus perhaps *R. phoenicia*. Their origin is uncertain, but the belief that they came from around Damascus, Syria, gave the rose its Latin name, *R. damascena*. They are supposed to have been introduced to Europe by physicians returning from the Crusades, but they were known throughout the region long before that time, cultivated for both their exceptional fragrance and their medicinal properties.

There are two types of Damasks: Summer Damask, which blooms once, and Autumn Damask, the first twice-blooming rose known in the West.

Damask roses have very fragrant medium-sized semidouble or double flowers, pink or white, borne in clusters of three or five. They are fiercely armed with multitudes of very strong curved prickles and glandular bristles. Plants are generally fuller and taller than the Gallicas. Damasks are very hardy (though not recommended in Zone 5 and colder) and require little care, other than routine pruning to remove dead and cluttered canes. Occasional hard pruning immediately after bloom has ended will encourage new growth for the following years' flowers. Pegging of long-caned varieties will encourage the production of flowering laterals.

'York and Lancaster' (formerly *R. damascena versicolor*) This rose is supposedly named to commemorate the union of the feuding houses of York (whose emblem was a white rose) and Lancaster (red rose) at the conclusion of the fifteenth-century Wars of the Roses. The semidouble two- to three-inch flowers are uniquely varied in color; blooms on a single branch may have all white, all pink, or both white and pink petals. The fragrant flowers bloom only once, in midseason. Bushy plants usually grow three to four feet tall; it grew like a climber at Boerner Botanical Gardens in Milwaukee.

'Kazanlik' (formerly *R. damascena trigintipetala*) This is the Damask rose widely grown for attar of roses (the fragrant oil used in making perfume), named for the Kazanlik Valley in the Balkan Mountains of Bulgaria where it has long been cultivated. Flowers are pink, extremely fragrant, with about thirty petals; the color fades as the bloom ages. The three- to four-foot-high bushes flower once and have an awkward growth habit.

'Autumn Damask' (*R. damascena semperflorens*, 'Rose of Castile') Also called *R. damascena bifera* and known as the Rose of Four Seasons (*Rose des Quatre-Saisons*) in France and the Damask Monthly in England. This was the first rose in the West to flower a second time and was a hybridizers' only source of that characteristic until the Chinas were introduced. It has many-petaled, fragrant, clear pink flowers, three-and-one-half inches wide, appearing in clusters in early summer and again in the fall. Bushes are three to four feet high.

'Madame Zöetmans' (Marest, 1830) For years, this variety was the most admired pale rose. Flowers are blush white with pale peach-pink centers; the very dou-

ATTAR OF ROSES

Attar of roses is a volatile oil extracted from the petals of roses, mostly Damasks and Gallicas, and used in making perfume. It is an intensely concentrated essence of the classic rose fragrance, worth two to three times its weight in gold, since it takes two tons of petals to produce a single pound of attar of roses, over thirty thousand rose flowers to yield a single ounce of attar. Think of that the next time you enjoy the heady aroma of one of your old garden roses!

The Damask rose 'Kazanlik' (formerly *R. damascena trigintipetala*) has for many years been one of the main sources of attar of roses. This rose was named for the Kazanlik Valley in the Balkan Mountains of Bulgaria, where it was first found and is still widely grown. Most attar today is produced in Bulgaria and Turkish Anatolia.

You can extract a few drops of your own attar of roses as the ancient Persians did: Steep fresh, very fragrant rose petals in water (preferably in the sun during the day), and when the water's surface becomes speckled with drops of greenish yellow oil, skim the droplets of attar off with a bit of cotton or tissue.

THE WARS OF THE ROSES

Perhaps the only war named for a flower, the Wars of the Roses were a thirty-year series of battles between two noble families, York and Lancaster, battling for the throne of England. The struggle began in 1455, just two years after the Hundred Years' War came to an end, and concluded in 1485 with the defeat of the last Yorkist king, Richard III, by the first Tudor king, Henry VII, a member of the house of Lancaster. Henry defused further opposition by promptly marrying the daughter of one of the earlier Yorkist kings. During the thirty years of this civil war, the English throne changed hands repeatedly between the two families, and many great nobles on both sides were killed.

The York-Lancaster struggle became known as the Wars of the Roses because of the symbols of the two warring families. The badge of the house of Lancaster was a red rose, while the badge of the house of York was a white rose. The York rose was an Alba–formerly known as *Rosa xalba semi-plena,* the 'White Rose of York', noted for its fragrance. The Lancaster rose was a Gallica–probably *Rosa gallica officinalis,* now called the 'Apothecary's Rose'. Nobles supposedly signaled where their loyalties lay by the color of the flower they would pluck from a rose garden.

According to legend, the white and pink Damask rose, formerly called *Rosa damascena versicolor,* inspired the union of the feuding Lancaster and York families–hence its popular name of 'York and Lancaster'. However, this rose must have been named in memory of the two families and their conflict, since it has been known to exist only since 1551.

ble blooms resemble snowballs. Bushes are upright and spreading. The bristles, young prickles, and new foliage are reddish.

'Madame Hardy' (Hardy, 1832) Named for the wife of its creator, the curator of Paris's Luxembourg Gardens, this variety is one of the purest white roses, a cross between a Damask and either an Alba or a Centifolia. The large, fragrant, creamy white flowers (three- to three-and-one-half inches across) are very double, with up to two hundred sometimes pink-tinged petals and a green center, or pip, borne profusely in clusters. Bushy plants are upright and vigorous, growing four to six feet tall and wide, with abundant dark green foliage; they can be trained on a pillar or fence. It is probably the hardiest Damask.

'Blush Damask' (Dates to 1759) Its fragrant flowers are slightly cupped, blush pink with deeper pink centers. Bushes are vigorous and tall, but not as thorny as other Damasks.

ALBAS

Like the Gallicas and Damasks, the Albas are ancient old garden roses, cultivated by the Romans and perhaps introduced by them to England before AD 100. They are probably native to southern or central Europe, natural hybrids between either a Gallica or a Damask and a form of *R. canina*. Albas are very upright, tall, and vigorous; original single-flowered varieties grew five feet high, but the often double-flowered hybrids may reach to over ten feet in warm climates. The usually fragrant flowers range in color from white to blush to pale pink, borne in clusters once a year. Foliage is a distinctive bluish green. The large, scarlet, pitcher-shaped hips are produced best by varieties with fewer petals. Many Albas are less prickly than the Gallicas and Damasks. They are resistant to powdery mildew and dependably hardy through Zone 5A; they are grown in Zone 4 with some dieback. They are sometimes highly susceptible to rose rust and moderately susceptible to blackspot.

Because of their height, easy-to-grow Albas are best placed toward the back of the garden, as large shrubs, or trained as climbers or around pillars; many can also be pegged. Albas will tolerate some shade. Pruning consists mainly of cutting out dead and crowded wood, soon after blooming. Occasional hard pruning will encourage new growth that will produce the next season's blooms.

'Alba semi-plena' is also known as the White Rose of York, supposedly the emblem of the house of York in the fifteenth-century Wars of the Roses. The pure white, three-inch, fragrant flowers have eight to twelve petals, opening to reveal yellow stamens. The tall, spreading bush is free-flowering and often grows ten feet tall, with long, arching canes.

'Great Maiden's Blush' (formerly *R. alba incarnata*) originated sometime before 1797 and was also known as 'La Cuisse de Nymphe Emué', or 'Thigh of a Passionate Nymph'. Flowers are a pale blush pink, two to three inches across, very double and fragrant, produced abundantly from early to midseason. Plants grow into large, arching shrubs five to six feet tall, with bristly and

WHITE ROSE OF YORK Alba. Shrub to six feet tall, four feet wide. Pure white single flowers, light green stems. Smooth matt gray foliage. Sweetly scented.

'ALBA SEMI-PLENA' Alba. Upright, graceful bush to eight feet tall. Matt, gray-green leaves. Semidouble, pure white flowers with distinctive anthers. Good autumn fruit. Sweetly scented.

'CELESTIAL' Alba. Early blooming plants grow five to six feet tall. Leaden gray foliage. Semidouble light blush pink flowers moderately full, three-and-one-half inches wide. Sweetly fragrant. Lightly prickled.

'KÖNIGEN VON DANEMARK' Alba. Five to six feet tall. Grayish green, coarse foliage. Very double, quartered, pink flowers shading toward light pink on outer petals; three-and-one-half inches wide; appears very early in season. Flowers slightly smaller than most other Albas. Very fragrant.

Above: 'Alba semi-plena'.
Top: 'Celestial'.

Opposite: 'Fantin-Latour'.

prickly canes. Another variety called **'Small Maiden's Blush'** is identical, except that the bush is smaller. Flowers of both varieties tend to ball.

'Celestial' (before 1848) Double flowers are moderately full, three-and-one-half inches wide, and sweetly fragrant, in a light blush pink. Plants are early blooming and attractively shaped, growing five to six feet high and fairly wide, with lightly prickled canes.

'Königin von Danemark' (1826) has very double, quartered, pink flowers shading toward light pink on the outer petals. The very fragrant blooms are three-and-one-half inches wide and appear late in the season. Spent flowers tend to stay on the bush and should be deadheaded; this variety does not set hips. Plants grow five to six feet tall, with very prickly canes that can be pegged or trained to climb.

'Madame Legras de St. Germain' (1846) Probably a cross between an Alba and a Damask, this rose produces very double three-inch white flowers with a lemony center, early blooming and very fragrant. Foliage is darker than on most other Albas. The six- to seven-foot shrub with nearly thornless canes has a spreading growth habit well suited to pegging.

'Madame Plantier' (Plantier, 1835) was one of the most popular white roses of the 1890s, often used then as a hedge in formal gardens and for cemetery plantings. It is probably a hybrid between *R. alba* and *R. moschata,* an Alba and a Musk. Its very double, creamy white, one-and-one-half- to three-inch flowers bloom profusely in fragrant clusters in midseason. Canes have few thorns. Plants are dense and bushy, growing to five feet, and are very hardy and long-lived.

CENTIFOLIAS

Centifolias are familiarly known as cabbage roses because the many petals of this rose pack together and overlap like the leaves of a cabbage. The Latin name, *centifolia,* means "hundred petals," derived from the many (although not necessarily one hundred) petals on each flower. The Centifolia is also known as the Provence Rose, after the area of France where it was once extensively grown—a name sometimes confused with the Provins Rose, which is *R. gallica.* It became very popular in the Netherlands during the seventeenth century among painters and hybridizers, and so gained the name the Holland Rose. The origins of 'Cabbage Rose' (formerly *R. centifolia)* are obscure; the many-petaled roses described by ancient Greek and Roman writers may well have been Centifolias, in which case the plant probably originated in the Mediterranean region. Or Dutch hybridizers may have developed it, perhaps as a cross between an Alba and an Autumn Damask.

Centifolias have very full, heavy, nodding flowers, white to deep rose, intensely fragrant and borne on clusters once a year. The coarsely toothed leaflets also tend to droop. Most Centifolias don't set hips. Plants are much taller and more prickly than the Gallicas, with upright canes that arch over in their second season. Tall-growing Centifolias can be grown on pillars. Pruning consists mainly of cutting out dead and crowded old wood after flowering. An

'FANTIN-LATOUR' Centifolia. Bushy, vigorously-growing plants four to five feet tall. Large, dark green leaves. Two- to three-inch very double somewhat flat flowers borne profusely in midseason. Very fragrant. Few prickles. Winter hardy, slightly susceptible to blackspot and mildew.

'LAURA' Centifolia. Vigorous shrub to five feet tall. Medium pink very double flowers borne profusely in midseason. Very fragrant. Few prickles. Dark green foliage.

'PETITE DE HOLLANDE' Centifolia. Three to four feet. Vigorous production of many small, double, very full half-inch globular rose-pink flowers borne on single stems over long midseason. Very fragrant. Thorny. Susceptible to blackspot and mildew; winter hardy.

'ROSE DE MEAUX' Centifolia. Two to three feet tall. Short, erect, well-foliated bush; twiggy growth. Double, light or medium rose flowers, one to one-and-one-half inches across; borne in profusion. Moderately fragrant. Straight prickles.

occasional hard pruning will promote vigorous new growth. Centifolias are susceptible to blackspot and mildew; be sure to plant in full sun so moisture will evaporate from the many-petaled flowers as quickly as possible. Plants are dependably hardy to Zone 6B.

'Bullata' (1815) Also called the Lettuce-Leafed and the Cabbage-Leafed Rose because of its exceptionally large and crinkled leaves. Flowers are clear blush, darkening toward the center.

'Fantin-Latour' (origin and date unknown) Named for the French artist who painted "Roses in a Bowl," this Centifolia has two- to three-inch very double flowers with up to two hundred pale blush petals. The very fragrant, somewhat flat flowers are borne profusely in midseason. Bushy plants grow vigorously, four to five feet tall, with large, dark green, smooth leaves and canes with few prickles. More hardy, and less susceptible to blackspot and mildew than 'Cabbage Rose'.

'Petite de Hollande' (before 1838) A small-flowered Centifolia, although not as diminutive as 'Rose de Meaux'; both need to be cut back hard to about eighteen inches in spring, before growth, to make the plants look dwarf. Very full and fragrant half-inch globular rose-pink flowers are borne on single stems over a long midseason period. Bushy plants grow three to four feet, with vigorous and spreading new growth. The thorny canes can be pegged, and flowers are excellent for cutting. Susceptible to blackspot and mildew and winter hardy.

'Rose de Meaux' (Sweet, prior to 1789) Also known as the Pompon Rose. Double, very fragrant, light or medium rose flowers, only one- to one-and-one-half inches across but borne in profusion. This delightful dwarf grows two to three feet tall and is excellent for beds and borders. Growth is twiggy, and canes are covered with straight prickles. Miniature Cabbage Roses like this one were very popular until the Polyanthas were developed.

MOSS ROSES

Moss roses originated as sports (mutations) of the Centifolias, Damasks, Autumn Damasks, and Gallicas (which explains their repeat bloom) and first became known in the eighteenth century. A sticky growth covers their calyx lobes, hips, and flower stalks, giving plants the appearance of being covered in moss. When rubbed, the mossy growth exudes a piney, resinous fragrance. The moss is red or green. On sports of Centifolias, the moss is soft, abundant, and bright green; on Damask sports, it is brownish, fairly sparse, and bristly. Flowers are intensely fragrant, very double, and range in color from white to deep maroon. Most bloom only once a season, but a few, like the 'Damask Moss', flower again lightly in the fall.

Prune mosses as for Centifolias and Damasks. Hips that form if spent blooms are not deadheaded are also covered with the mossy growth. The drooping foliage tends to mildew, and flowers are susceptible to botrytis blight, so be sure to plant moss roses in full sun to minimize dampness. Plants vary in hardiness depending on their origin.

The essential points of difference in the rose are the number of petals, the comparative number of thorns on the stem, the color, and the smell. The number of petals, which is never less than five, goes on increasing in amount till we find one variety with as many as one hundred, thence known as Centifolia.

PLINY, DIED AD 67

'Communis' (formerly *R. centifolia muscosa*) (about 1700) The original Moss Rose, this is also known as 'Common Moss' and 'Old Pink Moss' and has been well-loved for many years. Flowers are very double and intensely fragrant, rose-pink, two-and-one-half to three inches across, with long, lacy sepals; they are produced once a year, in midseason. Plants are heavily mossed in green, with very prickly canes; growth of the four- to six-foot bushes is vigorous, upright, and arching.

'James Veitch' (Verdier, 1865) Moss-covered buds are deep red, opening to small starburst-shaped magenta flowers tinted white at the petals' base, borne in clusters at the ends of canes. Bloom occasionally repeats. Foliage is red-edged and bright green when young. Moderately tall plants are vigorous, with very prickly and bristly canes. Does not set hips.

'Laneii' (Laffay, 1854) Also called 'Lane's Moss'. Flowers are large, very double, mossy, and crimson-magenta, borne in clusters on the ends of plum-colored canes. Tall, vigorous plants have prickly canes and bristly petioles and leaves. 'Laneii' does not set hips.

'Old Red Moss' (origin unknown) Flowers are deep carmine red, starburst-shaped. The reddish moss is dense and bristly. Older canes are plum colored. Bushes are tall, vigorous, and spreading, and orange-red hips appear after flowers are spent.

'Salet' (Lacharme, 1854) The best twice-bloomer of the Mosses, but the mossiness is weak; flowers well in midseason and repeats its bloom in the fall, most reliably in the South. Rosy pink two-and-one-half- to three-inch flowers are double, sweetly fragrant, and slightly quartered. Vigorous plants grow three to four feet tall, with bristly canes.

Old roses usually lend a more informal, less rigid atmosphere to a rose garden.

'JAMES VEITCH' Moss. Vigorous, moderately tall plants. Red-edged bright green foliage when young. Deep red moss-covered buds, opening to small starburst-shaped magenta flowers tinted white at petal's base, borne in clusters; bloom sometimes repeats. Very prickly.

'LANEII' Moss. Tall and vigorous. Deep green foliage. Bristly petioles and leaves. Large, very double, mossy, and crimson-magenta flowers, borne in clusters, initially cupped, but opening flat exposing a large green eye. Prickly.

'MOUSSELINE' ('Alfred de Dalmas') Moss. Foliage lush, growth tidy and manageable. Semidouble, creamy pink flowers, continuously from mid June to November. Green moss, tinted pink, turning to russet on older shoots. Moderately fragrant.

'SALET' Moss. Vigorous plants, three to four feet tall. Leaves bright green, especially when young. Rosy pink two-and-one-half- to three-inch flowers; double and slightly quartered. Flowers well in midseason and repeats bloom in fall. Sweetly fragrant. Bristly canes.

OLD GARDEN ROSES: CHINAS AND CHINA-INFLUENCED ROSES

This second group of old garden (pre-1867) roses is distinguished from the first group by one outstanding characteristic: repeat bloom. The ability to bloom well throughout the growing season came from the China roses and was passed on by them to the succeeding classes–the Teas, Bourbons, Noisettes, Damask Perpetuals, and Hybrid Perpetuals, a succession that culminated in the first modern rose, the Hybrid Tea.

CHINAS

Along with teas and silks, European traders of the late 1700s and early 1800s brought another treasure home with them: *R. chinensis*, the China rose, which the Chinese had cultivated for centuries, creating many hybrids from their native wild roses. These hybrids possessed a special characteristic unknown to European roses–they were everblooming, putting out new flowers all through the growing season. Breeders immediately seized on this attribute, crossing the repeat-blooming Chinas with the hardier but once-blooming Western roses and revolutionizing rose growing in the process. The Chinas (and the related Teas) became the ancestors of all modern roses.

Because of the nearly continual bloom of the Chinas, they were called Monthly Roses in England and Daily Roses in the United States. Some Chinas are almost as hardy as other European classes, despite their class's reputation for tenderness. Chinas are generally small, low-growing plants, especially in northern climates; they can be grown in containers and brought indoors in winter. Some survive northern winters outdoors if given adequate protection. China flowers are small to medium, single or loosely double, borne in clusters, and they brought exciting colors to the Western rose world–a true scarlet red, plus shades of apricot and yellow. Other China flowers are white or pink; they are not particularly fragrant. Leaves are glossy and pointed. Hips will form on most if spent flowers are not deadheaded.

Chinas require little pruning in most cases; simply remove dead, diseased, and crowded wood, and trim bushes to shape as needed, especially in the South, where Chinas grow quite large. Flowers are produced on both old and new wood, so pruning isn't needed for new flower production, although light pruning does stimulate new blooming growth. Prune between blooming periods to make the plants tidy and encourage repeat bloom. In colder climates, prune during winter dormancy, cutting back by about one-third.

'Old Blush' The first China rose introduced in the West, brought to Sweden in 1752 and to the rest of Europe around 1789. It is also called 'Parson's Pink China', because it was grown in Mr. Parson's garden in England in the late 1700s. Deep pink buds open to clear medium pink semidouble flowers, two-and-one-half inches across and loosely formed, with little or no fragrance, borne in clusters. Outer petals are darker than inner ones, and flowers darken in sunshine and as they age. Upright, bushy plants grow three to five feet tall and flower reliably all season.

'Slater's Crimson China' (*R. chinensis semperflorens*) Although not discovered grow-

'Slater's Crimson China'.

'SERRATIPETALA' (formerly *R. chinensis serratipetala*) China. Small, carnationlike flowers with fringed or serrated petals, outer ones crimson and inner ones light pink. Good all-season bloom with tea fragrance. Nearly thornless plants.

'GLOIRE DES ROSOMANES' ('Ragged Robin', 'Red Robin') China. Vigorous, upright plants flower continuously, growing three-and-one-half to four feet tall. Bright red, semidouble cupped three-inch flowers in large clusters. Tea-rose fragrance. Few thorns.

'MADAME LAURETTE MESSIMY' China. Bushy, upright shrub, two feet by two feet. Large, nodding, double flowers are pink, darker at the edges and yellow in the center. Blooms are free-form, borne singly or in clusters of two or three. Tea-scented.

'SOPHIE'S PERPETUAL' ('Dresden China') China. Tall shrub, up to eight feet in height; sometimes grown as a small climber. Globular blush pink flowers with deeper pink and cerise shadings; flowers throughout the summer. Very fragrant. Lush dark green foliage. Nearly thornless.

'Green Rose'.

ing wild in its native China until the 1800s, this rose was introduced to England in 1789. It had been given to Gilbert Slater, a director of the East India Company, by a sea captain who had found the plants in Calcutta. Flowers are double, with red petals touched with white at the base, borne singly or in pairs, with a light tea scent. Plants are small and nearly thornless. This is the rose that brought true red to Western roses, but it had virtually disappeared from the West by the mid-twentieth century. Fortunately, the 'Belfield Rose', discovered in Bermuda in 1953 although it had been growing there since the late 1700s, turned out to be a naturalized specimen of 'Slater's Crimson China'.

'Roulette' (also called *R. chinensis minima,* 'Fairy Rose') (Introduced 1818) Small, light pink one-inch flowers have sixteen pointed petals and are borne singly or sometimes in clusters. Strongly prickled bushes can be kept to one foot high, with tiny pointed leaves. In warm climates, plants will grow much larger as they build on themselves year after year.

'Mutabilis' ('Butterfly Rose', *R. chinensis mutabilis*) As its Latin name suggests, the two- to three-inch single flowers of this rose change as they mature, beginning creamy yellow and then transforming to pale orange, pink, and finally a dull deep pink. Clusters of flowers are borne on twiggy, rounded three- to five-foot plants with reddish stems.

'Green Rose' (*R. chinensis viridiflora*) (Cultivated before 1855) A distinctively odd plant, this rose has sterile, scentless flowers made up of multiple sepals rather than petals, bright green with reddish bronze touches, to one-and-one-half inches across. Plants are three to five feet tall, thornless. Considered by some to be an eyesore in the garden, flowers are attractive in arrangements.

'Serratipetala' (formerly *R. chinensis serratipetala*) (Vilfray, 1912) Interesting, small, carnationlike flowers have fringed or serrated petals, outer ones crimson and inner ones light pink. One-inch buds are crimson flushed with pink. Good all-season bloom with tea fragrance. Nearly thornless plants have an erratic growth habit.

'Eugene de Beauharnais' (Hardy, 1838) Sometimes referred to as a hybrid Bourbon China. Its leaves are less pointed than other Chinas, its growth habit more compact. The very fragrant flowers are deep purple-red, three to four inches across, with thirty-five or more velvety petals. Plants have straight, bristly prickles.

'Hermosa' (Marcheseau, 1840) The name of this rose, a hybrid China, means "beautiful" in Spanish, a reference to its lightly tea-scented lilac-pink flowers, one to two inches across, cupped and globular with twenty-five to thirty petals, borne constantly in clusters. Bushy plants grow three to four feet high and are suitable for containers. Foliage is gray-green.

'Madame Laurette Messimy' (Guillot, 1887) A hybrid China. Large, nodding, double flowers are pink, darker at the edges and yellow in the center, with fifteen petals. Tea-scented blooms are free-form, borne singly or in clusters of two or three.

'Gloire des Rosomanes' (Vibert, 1825) A hybrid China. Bright red, semidouble three-inch flowers have twenty-five to thirty petals, with cupped form, borne in large clusters and a Tea-rose fragrance. Vigorous, upright plants flower continuously, growing three-and-one-half to four feet tall with few thorns; suitable for hedges.

TEA ROSES

The Tea rose, *R. x odorata,* was introduced to the West from its native China in the early 1800s, not long after its relatives the Chinas found their way west. Like the Chinas, the Teas are an ancient Chinese rose, apparently a cross between *R. chinensis* and *R. gigantea,* a rampant evergreen white climber native to the Himalayas of China and Burma. The name refers either to the tealike scent of the flowers and foliage or to the tea fragrance the plants picked up during shipping from the Orient in the tea chests and cargo holds of the East India Company. They quickly became quite popular in England and Europe, appreciated for their abundant everblooming, their delightful fragrance, their refined and delicate foliage and stems, and their suitability as cut flowers.

Tea rose blooms are slightly larger than those of the Chinas, double or semidouble, in a wide range of delicate colors from white, cream, yellow, and buff to salmon, apricot, and pink. Buds are long and tapered, and the flowers are high-centered. The delicate, graceful appearance of all parts of the plant led to the Tea roses being called the "aristocrats of the rose world." Many of the Tea rose's qualities were passed on to modern roses—flower form and color, bountiful all-season rebloom. Unfortunately, the Tea roses are even less hardy than the Chinas, and they passed this characteristic on to modern roses as well. In southern climates, though, Tea roses make fine landscape shrubs, and some—true to their heritage—are rampant climbers. In northern areas, they can be grown as container plants and moved indoors during harsh winter months; they may survive outdoors if given adequate protection. Tea roses are pruned just as Chinas are.

'Duchesse de Brabant' (Bernède, 1857) This gained fame as the rose Theodore Roosevelt always wore in his buttonhole. Cupped two- to three-inch tulip-shaped flowers are shades of soft pink, with forty or more petals, very fragrant. Blooms early in the season and prolifically from then on, especially in warm climates. Disease-resistant plants are vigorous and bushy, growing three to five feet tall, with fairly thorny canes. This is one of the hardier Tea roses.

'Mrs. B. R. Cant' (Cant, 1901) Nonstop, full, nodding flowers are very double, silvery pink suffused with buff, with a delicate light scent. Compact but vigorous plants have hooked prickles.

'Mrs. Dudley Cross' (William Paul & Sons, 1907) Very full, many-petaled pale yellow flowers are pleasantly scented and sometimes develop a flush of red in cooler weather. Blooms are borne in clusters of two or three on single stems throughout the summer. Canes are nearly thornless. Plants are best grown in drier climates because the many-petaled flowers don't open well in damp conditions.

Tea roses, which are the cream of the dwarf old roses, after all is said, require more careful handling that any others and reward it gallantly. Teas are best in beds, so they will never be forgotten throughout the season; so they may have their doses of liquid manure; so they may have their hips snipped off; so they will surely be hilled up in winter if need be. The more delicate the rose, the nearer we want it our center of outdoor living, for its sake and ours. With Tea roses, we should plan to live intimately and on a high plane of pleasure.
ETHELYN EMERY KEAN,
OLD ROSES, 1935

'MRS. DUDLEY CROSS' Tea. Vigorous open shrub, grows four feet tall, three feet wide. Fully double pale yellow flowers flush red in cool weather. Blooms in clusters of two or three on single stems throughout the summer. Nearly thornless. Best in dry climates.

'SOMBREUIL' Tea. A climbing Tea rose, grows to eight feet. Very double creamy white flowers, tinted blush at the center, three-and-one-half to four inches across. Excellent repeat bloom. Very thorny. Very hardy for a Tea rose.

'BOULE DE NEIGE' Bourbon. Compact, upright shrub, four feet tall, three feet wide. Pure white, round double flowers, tinged with scarlet, with yellow stamens, borne singly or in clusters from midseason on. Strongly fragrant. Hardy. Dark green foliage not subject to blackspot.

'COQUETTE DES BLANCHES' Bourbon. Vigorous and bushy, grows to five feet tall, four feet wide. White lightly washed with pink, fully reflexed flowers, borne singly or in pairs. Lightly scented. Abundant mid green foliage. Very hardy, good fall rebloom.

'Park's Yellow Tea-Scented China' According to some records, this was the first Tea rose; it is difficult to find today. It has an unusual scent, typically large foliage, few thorns, and double cupped flowers in a soft, deep yellow. A climber, it reaches six feet.

'Sombreuil' (Robert, 1850) A climbing Tea rose. Creamy white flowers, tinted blush at the center, are three-and-one-half to four inches across, cupped, very double, and fragrant. Excellent repeat bloom. Thorny plants are disease resistant (though sometimes show mildew) and will grow ten feet tall or more; they train well as climbers or around pillars. This is one of the hardiest Tea roses and may survive northern winters in a sheltered site with added protective materials.

BOURBONS

Hybridizers deliberately used the China roses to produce new and improved types of roses, but nature created the Bourbons. This class of rose was the result of natural cross-breeding on the French Ile de Bourbon (now Réunion) in the Indian Ocean off Madagascar in 1817. Fields on the island were commonly fenced with hedges of mixed roses. One was a China, generally 'Parson's Pink China' or 'Old Blush', and the other was the Autumn Damask. An estate owner discovered the new rose in his hedge and transplanted it to his garden, where a visiting French botanist noticed it, sending seeds back to France in 1817. These new Bourbon roses became very popular in Europe, as they were very repeat-blooming, with fragrant flowers larger than the China parents. Blooms were semidouble and bright pink, in clusters; plants were vigorous and much more hardy than the Chinas, with glossy green foliage. Soon the Bourbons were crossed with Gallica and Damask hybrids, creating many new colors—including red, white, and striped—and growth habits.

Today's Bourbons are moderately hardy, vigorous, bushy shrubs that grow five to six feet tall. Some are climbers. Flowers are exceptional for their fragrance, lovely colors, and excellent repeat bloom on most. Pruning depends on the particular variety's ancestry, as Bourbons have been heavily hybridized. Bloom is on old wood, so don't start pruning until the plant is two to three years old. Prune while the plant is dormant, before new growth starts; trim back main shoots by one-third and others by two-thirds. After blooming, cut laterals back again by one-third. Bourbons are more susceptible to blackspot than other old garden roses.

'Boule de Neige' (Lacharme, 1867) The French name translates as "snowball," which aptly describes the pure white, round double flowers, borne singly or in clusters from midseason on. The tight, round buds are touched with scarlet. Strongly fragrant blooms have sixty petals and prominent yellow stamens. Compact plants grow four feet tall and wide (up to eight feet in southern California) and are winter hardy and also suitable for container growing. The dark green foliage is not subject to blackspot. Repeats well.

'Coquette des Blanches' (Lacharme, 1871) A very hardy Bourbon with good fall rebloom. Lightly scented, white lightly washed with pink, fully reflexed flow-

CUTTING FOR FRAGRANCE

The best time to cut rose flowers for fragrance is on a warm, sunny morning after the gentle warmth of the early sun has released droplets of richly scented oil but before wind or excess sun has dissipated these fragrant oils. This timing is especially needed for the white and yellow roses, whose light scent is particularly apt to evaporate and vanish as the day goes on. Even the heavy Damask odor of red and pink roses is held in by cool, damp weather. Fragrance is noticeably diminished on mildewed roses. Handle fragrant roses gently, as their petals are prone to bruising. Old garden roses, such as those in the basket picture below, make beautiful cut flowers, although they don't last as long as many modern roses, which have been bred for sturdiness.

ers resemble small white snowballs; they are borne singly or in pairs. Petals may be edged with red tinges. Plants are vigorous and bushy.

'Eugene E. Marlitt' (Geschwind, 1900) Bright carmine-red flowers have reflexed petals and cupped centers; they are lightly fragrant and fully double. Nodding blooms are borne in groups of three to four. In colder climates, grows as a shrub; in warm regions, the vigorous plants can be grown as climbers. Very popular when introduced, now rare.

'La Reine Victoria' (Schwartz, 1872) Globe-shaped, cupped, and deliciously fragrant rich pink flowers have shell-like petals. The three- to four-inch flowers bloom abundantly in small clusters in midseason and repeat well in the fall; they are long-lasting and excellent for cutting. Slender plants grow four to six feet tall, with mostly smooth canes and soft green foliage. Disease resistant; survives winter only with protection and difficulty at Boerner Botanical Gardens.

'Mme. Ernst Calvat' (Schwartz, 1881) A lighter pink sport of 'Mme. Isaac Pereire'.

'Mme. Isaac Pereire' (Garcon, 1881) A large plant with large flowers, renowned for its intense fragrance. Deep magenta-pink saucer-shaped blooms are three to four inches across and fully double, borne all summer, set off effectively by large, bold foliage. Vigorous, spreading plants grow four to six feet tall, are moderately thorny, and can be used as small climbers.

'EUGENE E. MARLITT' Bourbon. Grows as a shrub (to four feet tall) in cool climates, can be grown as climber in warm regions. Very double bright carmine-red flowers with reflexed petals and cupped centers; borne in groups of three to four. Lightly fragrant. Few thorns.

'HONORINE DE BRABANT' Bourbon. Vigorous shrub, to six feet tall; sometimes grown as a climber in warm regions. Large, cupped lilac flowers, delicately striped with purple. Large, lush foliage, few thorns.

'LA REINE VICTORIA' Bourbon. Slender erect plants grow four to six feet tall, Globe-shaped, cupped rich pink flowers, three to four inches across bloom abundantly in small clusters in midseason, repeating in the fall. Soft green foliage. Winter hardy, disease resistant.

'MME. ERNST CALVAT' Bourbon. A lighter pink sport of 'Mme. Isaac Pereire'; slightly less vigorous. Sometimes grown as a small climber. Saucer-shaped blooms, three to four inches across and fully double, borne all summer; large, bold foliage. Intense fragrance. Moderately thorny.

'MME. ISAAC PEREIRE' Bourbon. A large plant, to seven feet tall, sometimes grown as a small climber. Deep magenta-pink saucer-shaped blooms, three to four inches across and fully double, borne all summer; large, bold foliage. Intense fragrance. Moderately thorny.

'MME. PIERRE OGER' Bourbon. A sport of 'La Reine Victoria', similar to its parent in all respects except for the color of its flowers, which are creamy pink with a rosy blush. Pale flower color deepens with exposure to the sun. Vigorous plants may produce canes long enough to be pegged.

'QUEEN OF THE BOURBONS' ('Bourbon Queen', 'Reine des Iles Bourbon', Souvenir de la Princesse de Lamballe') Bourbon. Thick-branched shrub, to six feet tall, with abundant foliage. Large, semidouble cupped flowers, rose pink. Rarely repeats. Strongly scented.

'ALISTER STELLA GRAY' (Golden Rambler) Noisette. Vigorous shrub with spindly branches that can be trained on arches and trellises. Small, double yellow flowers with darker centers, fading to almost white at the edges, cascade in clusters. Some repeat bloom. Strong scent. Relatively thornless.

'Mme. Pierre Oger' (Oger, 1878) A sport of 'La Reine Victoria', similar to its parent in all respects except for the color of its flowers, which are creamy pink with a rosy blush. Pale flower color deepens with exposure to the sun. Vigorous plants may produce canes long enough to be pegged.

'Souvenir de la Malmaison' (Béluze, 1843) Named for the famous rose garden created by the Empress Josephine at La Malmaison, her estate near Paris. Spicily fragrant, creamy flesh-pink flowers are three to four inches across, opening from large, urn-shaped, soft pink buds. Very double, full blooms have more than fifty pointed and reflexed petals; flowers may not open fully in damp weather. Vigorous two- to four-foot bushy plants have hooked prickles and rebloom well. A climbing form grows to six to eight feet. Particularly winter tender in cold regions.

'Zéphirine Drouhin' (Bizot, 1868) A popular, thornless Bourbon grown (and pruned) as a climber. Very fragrant, cerise pink flowers are three to four inches across, semidouble and high-centered, borne abundantly during the summer. Canes grow ten to twelve feet and are excellent for training on a wall or trellis, around a pillar, or up a tree. Young canes and leaves are burgundy-purple, and young growth in particular is susceptible to mildew.

NOISETTES

Noisettes were the first class of hybrid roses created in the United States. John Champneys, a rice planter in Charleston, South Carolina, crossed 'Parson's Pink China' with the white Musk rose, *R. moschata*. The resulting rose, 'Champneys' Pink Cluster', had the color of its China parent and the climbing character of the Musk, along with repeat blooming. These roses were sold in America with the Champneys' name. Champneys' neighbor, the French nurseryman Philippe Noisette, grew some of these roses and sent seed to his brother Louis in France, who introduced the 'Blush Noisette' to the market in 1817. The new roses were very popular in France, so the class became known as Noisettes rather than Champney's. Ultimately Noisettes lost favor to hardier roses.

The original Noisettes had clusters of small flowers, but hybridizers soon crossed them with larger-flowered Teas, Bourbons, and Chinas, increasing both flower size and color range—from white, pink, red, and purple to buff, yellow, and cream. Noisettes are vigorous, bushy climbers in southern regions but are not hardy or vigorous growers in the North. They don't require much pruning; simply cut spent flowers back to the next set of leaves and keep old and dead wood cut out. When grown like climbers, Noisettes should be pruned like climbers, with the flower-producing laterals cut back by two thirds after blooms are spent.

'Blush Noisette' (Noisette, 1817) The first Noisette, this is a seedling of 'Champneys' Pink Cluster', to which it is similar in all respects except that the flowers are blush to white. Plants will tolerate some shade and a northern exposure.

'Champneys' Pink Cluster' (Champneys, 1811/12) Vigorous climber that pro-

'FELLENBERG' ('Fellemberg') Noisette. Short, vigorous climber to seven feet long, with pointed, glossy, dark green leaves. Bright crimson cupped flowers, one-and-one-half to two inches across, produced in clusters of twelve to fifteen. Tea scent. Thorny.

'MME. ALFRED CARRIERE' Noisette. Rampant climber, may grow to fifteen feet or more in warm climates. Abundant light green leaves. Large, nodding, double white flowers, three inches across, good repeat bloom. Disease resistant and moderately thorny. Hardier than most Noisettes.

'COMTE DE CHAMBORD' Damask Perpetual. Upright plants grow three-and-one-half to four feet. Very double rich pink flowers with densely packed petals. Dense prickles, light green foliage. Heady fragrance. Susceptible to mildew and blackspot.

'QUATRES SAISONS D'ITALIE' Damask Perpetual. Tall, vigorous shrub. Many-petaled magenta-pink flowers, borne on long, bristly stems. Very fragrant. Plants bloom in early summer and again, but less profusely, in fall. Dark green foliage. Very thorny.

duces large clusters of two-inch, double pink flowers, fragrant and repeat-blooming. The ancestor of all Noisettes. Canes have few thorns and grow eight to twelve feet in warmer climates, but only about three feet in regions with cold winters. Plants are disease resistant.

'Fellenberg' (before 1835) A vigorous climber suitable for growing around a pillar. Bright crimson cupped flowers, one-and-one-half to two inches across, with pointed and reflexed petals and a tea scent, are produced in clusters of twelve to fifteen. Dark green leaves are long, pointed, and glossy.

'Maréchal Niel' (Pradel, 1864) Considered by many to be one of the most beautiful yellow roses. Long, pointed buds open to large, double golden-yellow blooms, three to four inches across, on nodding stems. The very fragrant blooms are produced abundantly throughout the season. Vigorous climbing plants are very tender, but thrive in southern climates, growing to ten feet.

'Mme. Alfred Carrière' (Schwartz, 1879) A beautiful Noisette, this is a rampant climber, especially in warmer climates, where it may grow to fifteen feet or more. Large, nodding, double white flowers are very fragrant and globular, three inches across. Plants have good repeat bloom and are disease resistant and moderately thorny. More hardy than other Noisettes.

DAMASK PERPETUALS (PORTLANDS)

The ancestry of this class of roses is somewhat confusing, and types within the class are called both Damask Perpetuals and Portlands. All seem to have the repeat-blooming 'Autumn Damask' in their heritage, along with Chinas. The Portland rose was first grown around 1800 in the garden of the second Duchess of Portland at Balstrode Park in England, a reblooming cross of Autumn Damask, a China, and *R. gallica.* The objective of creating these new hybrids by crossing European with Chinese roses was to produce reliable repeat bloom. This effort was successful, and the new class became very popular for about fifty years under the name Hardy Perpetual Roses, until they were displaced in favor of their larger-flowered and more vigorous descendants, the Hybrid Perpetuals.

Damask Perpetuals, or Portlands, are neat, rounded shrubs, with richly fragrant, fully double flowers in shades of pink and red, borne on short stems. Prune as for Damasks, thinning occasionally as needed and removing dead wood, with a hard pruning every two or three years to encourage better flower production on new wood. Since these are not vigorous growers, canes should not be removed during the growing season, though deadheading should be done regularly. In some areas they seem to resent hard pruning; at Boerner Botanical Gardens, Milwaukee, they usually die back to near ground level. When an unusual winter allows them more saved wood, they respond with greater vigor.

'Duchess of Portland' *(R.* x *portlandica,* the Portland Rose) (c. 1800) The first Portland rose, as noted above, with bright red, repeat-blooming flowers.

'Comte de Chambord' (Robert & Moreau, 1860) Very double and very fragrant rich pink flowers have up to two hundred petals, the larger outer ones cup-

'Sombreuil', trained as a climber.

In the fifty years from 1840 until 1890, Hybrid Perpetuals attained complete dominance of the rose gardening of Europe and America; and if we may trust the writers of that period, they developed into marvels of incredible beauty. The pictures in their quaintly illustrated books are not entirely convincing, and the few actual roses which have come down to us are not the paragons of beauty we might expect; but, in spite of all, the Hybrid Perpetuals are impressive roses of noble stature and dignified bearing, and almost all of them possess that ineffable perfume which we associate with old-fashioned roses.

G.A. Stevens, *Roses in the Little Garden*, 1911

ping the many folded inner ones. Upright plants grow three-and-one-half to four feet, with dense Damasklike prickles and light green foliage. It is susceptible to mildew and blackspot, and the densely packed petals tend to ball up in cool, damp weather.

'Jacques Cartier' ('Marchesa Boccella') (Moreau-Robert, 1868) Similar to 'Comte de Chambord', but much flatter. Uneven-sized petals on the deep pink flowers give this rose an appealing ragged look. The three-foot by two-foot shrub has leathery dark green foliage. There has been some confusion over the name of this rose, and it is now shown as 'Marchesa Boccella'.

'Quatres Saisons d'Italie' ('Rose of the Four Seasons') (origin and date unknown) Many-petaled magenta-pink flowers are very fragrant, borne on long, bristly stems. Plants bloom in early summer and again, but less profusely, in fall, and have dark green foliage.

'Rose du Roi' (Lelieur, 1815) Striking bright crimson flowers have shadings of purple, and the center petals curl to reveal light red shades on their reverse side. Blooms are double, two-and-one-half to three inches across, very fragrant, and appear throughout the midseason and again in the fall. Upright, bushy plants grow three to four feet tall, with bright green leaves. Plants will tolerate some shade, but don't grow vigorously in colder regions, and are susceptible to blackspot late in the season. Flowers are produced on both old and new wood, so prune back by one-third after the first spurt of growth to encourage best fall repeat bloom. This rose became the parent of the first Hybrid Perpetual.

'Yolande d'Aragon' (Vibert, 1843) A strong, upright bush, four feet tall by three feet wide, produces large, flat, fully double scented flowers in rich pink to bright purplish, amid light green foliage.

HYBRID PERPETUALS

The Hybrid Perpetuals were the culmination of eighteenth- and nineteenth-century rose breeding, a complex hybrid cross of most of the old garden roses that had gone before them, including Portland roses, Hybrid Chinas, Teas, Bourbons, and perhaps others. As a parent of the Hybrid Tea, the Hybrid Perpetuals were also the last of the old garden roses. The first ones were created by the French breeder Jules Laffay in the 1830s, and their popularity grew and spread rapidly. They were so much the rage among rose gardeners from 1840 to 1880 that they became known also as the Victorian Rose. Breeders created over three thousand varieties of Hybrid Perpetuals, but they were ultimately completely overshadowed by their offspring, the Hybrid Tea, and only about fifty varieties remain today. Most are susceptible to blackspot, rust, and mildew in Zone 5.

Hybrid Perpetuals owed their popularity to the beauty and size of their very large, often deliciously fragrant flowers, and to the fact that many were hardier than their China and Tea ancestors. And while they don't bloom "perpetually" all season long, some do rebloom, though not as dependably as Chinas and Teas. Most carried the short neck and extreme doubleness and

'BARON GIROD DE L'AIN' Hybrid Perpetual. Sturdy upright plants, growing four to five feet tall. Very double cupped ruby red petals with ragged white edges, four inches across. Very fragrant. Good midseason and fair repeat fall bloom. Not very vigorous, but disease resistant. Strong thorns.

'BARONNE PRÉVOST' Hybrid Perpetual. Upright, vigorous plants grow four to five feet tall. Early-blooming, flat, open flowers, deep rose-pink, fully double, three to four inches across; silvery on reverse side. Good midseason and fall repeat bloom. Very fragrant. Strong prickles.

'CHAMPION OF THE WORLD' Hybrid Perpetual. Sprawly bush, four feet tall and three feet wide. Bristly, pointed buds open to clusters of cupped, deep pink flowers. Lightly fragrant. Plants tolerate partial shade but are less hardy than many other Hybrid Perpetuals.

'HUGH DICKSON' Hybrid Perpetual. Tall, vigorous plants with arching stems, to eight feet long. Full, high-centered clear crimson flowers. Dark green foliage. Can be pegged on pillars; needs support if grown as a shrub. Powerfully fragrant. Winter tender.

'MABEL MORRISON' Hybrid Perpetual. Bushy, upright plants are three to four feet tall. White, cupped, double flowers, sometimes blushed with very pale pink. Very fragrant. Profuse midseason and good repeat fall bloom. Blue-green disease-resistant foliage.

'MAGNA CHARTA' Hybrid Perpetual. Spreading plants, three feet tall and wide. Large, globe-shaped three- to four-inch flowers, clear pink with red shading. Dark green foliage. Very fragrant. Tolerant of some shade, but susceptible to blackspot and mildew.

'PAUL NEYRON' Hybrid Perpetual. Shrub three feet tall, two feet wide. Enormous peonylike flowers, very double and lilac pink, borne constantly from early midseason and then less profusely through frost. Flowers may reach six to seven inches. Highly susceptible to mildew; not very hardy.

'REINE DES VIOLETTES' Hybrid Perpetual. Bushy, rounded, upright shrubs grow five to eight feet tall. Carmine red or mauve flowers, three to four inches across, very double. Flowers profusely midseason and on into the fall if deadheaded. Very fragrant. Gray-green leaves, nearly thornless.

form of their European ancestors. Colors range from white through the pinks and reds to purple, and a few have traces of cream and pale yellow. Plants are upright and vigorous bushes, varying in hardiness, producing their many-petaled flowers on short, stiff stems. Many tend to grow like climbers after the first bloom period. The practice of pegging down these long canes results in low spreading plants with abundant blooms. When pegging is not practiced, prune to thin out older wood and cut canes back by two-thirds during dormancy and again after the first flowering. Larger-growing Hybrid Perpetuals can be treated as climbers and wrapped around pillars. Feed and water all Hybrid Perpetuals after the first blooming period to encourage good rebloom in the fall.

'Paul Neyron'.

'Baron Girod de l'Ain' (Reverchon, 1897) Unusual flowers have thirty-five to forty ruby red petals with ragged white edges. Blooms are cupped, very double, four inches across, and very fragrant. Plants are sturdy and upright, growing four to five feet tall, with good midseason and fair repeat fall bloom. It blooms only on canes that have gone through at least one winter; it does not bloom well in Zone 5A. Not as vigorous as other Hybrid Perpetuals, but disease resistant. This is a sport of 'Eugène Fürst'.

'Baronne Prévost' (Desprez, 1842) One of the oldest Hybrid Perpetuals still on the market; still one of the best and one of the first to bloom in the spring. Flat, open flowers are wonderfully fragrant, deep rose-pink, fully double, three to four inches across, with up to one hundred tightly packed petals that are silvery on the reverse. Good midseason and fall repeat bloom. Upright, vigorous plants grow four to five feet tall, with many strong prickles and tough, disease-resistant foliage. Benefits from pegging.

'Champion of the World' (Woodhouse, 1894) Bristly, pointed buds open to clusters of cupped, deep pink flowers with about thirty-five slightly ruffled petals, lightly fragrant. Plants tolerate partial shade but are less hardy than many other Hybrid Perpetuals, perhaps reflecting the China parentage of 'Hermosa'.

'Frau Karl Druschki' ('Snow Queen', 'Reine des Neiges', and 'White American Beauty') (Lambert, 1901) This white rose is very similar to Hybrid Teas in flower form, but has the short neck and repeat blooming flaw of the Hybrid Perpetual. Its tight buds are marked with pink. Blooms are double, three to four inches across, with thirty-five petals, and open well even in damp weather; occasionally has blush pink centers. Plants are very vigorous and hardy, growing five to seven feet tall. The late-season canes are usually bloomless and topheavy in Zone 5, for which reason some choose to train them on pillars or as climbers. Their distinctive green foliage is susceptible to mildew, however.

'Hugh Dickson' (Dickson, 1905) Full, powerfully fragrant clear crimson flowers are high-centered and cupped, with more than thirty-five petals and exposed centers. Tall, vigorous plants respond well to pegging. Winter tender.

'Mabel Morrison' (Broughton, 1878) White, cupped, double flowers with thirty fragrant petals sometimes blushed with very pale pink. Profuse midseason and good repeat fall bloom. Bushy, upright plants are thirty to forty feet tall, with

FALSE ROSES

A rose by any other name may smell as sweet, but (in spite of Gertrude Stein) a so-called rose may not be a rose at all. Here are a few "false roses."

Christmas or Lenten rose (*Helleborus niger* or *H. orientalis*) Perennial herb with flowers that resemble five-petaled roses; blooms in late winter or very early spring.

Moss rose (*Portulaca grandiflora*) The popular low-growing annual portulaca.

Mountain rose (*Antigonon leptopus*) Tendril-climbing vine that produces bright pink flowers.

Rock rose (*Cistus*) A genus of shrubs with showy flowers that resemble single roses.

Rose acacia (*Robinia hispida*) Attractive shrub with showy pink flowers in May and June.

Rose apple (*Eugenia jambos*) Tropical tree grown for its fruit.

Rose campion (*Lychnis coronaria*) Silver-foliaged annual more commonly known as dusty miller.

Rose of heaven (*Lychnis coeli-rosa*) Annual that produces flowers of various colors.

Rose mallow (*Hibiscus*) Common name for members of the showy-flowered *Hibiscus* genus.

Rose of Jericho (*Anastatica hierochuntica*) Small annual herb also called resurrection plant because the mature plant rolls up into a dry ball that will uncurl when moistened.

Rose of Sharon (*Hibiscus syriacus*) Also called rose of China and Chinese rose; an upright, summer-flowering hardy shrub.

Rose root (*Sedum roseum*) Fragrant-rooted succulent perennial.

Desert rose (*Adenium obesum*) Small succulent shrub with showy flowers, often grown indoors.

blue-green disease-resistant foliage. Requires winter protection in Zone 5. Does not resprout vigorously from hard pruning.

'Magna Charta' (Paul, 1876) Large, globe-shaped three- to four-inch flowers are clear pink with red shading. Large, spreading plants grow best in their natural, bushy shrub form. Dark green foliage is tolerant of some shade, but is susceptible to blackspot and mildew. This hybrid perpetual was used in the breeding of modern roses.

'Paul Neyron' (Levet, 1869) One of the most popular Hybrid Perpetuals, noted for its enormous peonylike flowers, borne constantly from early midseason and then less profusely through frost. Very double and very fragrant lilac-pink flowers are typically five inches across but may reach six to seven inches, with fifty or more petals, set against light green foliage. The sparse repeat bloom often has overly long, topheavy thornless arching canes up to five to six feet that respond very well to pegging. This is the best Hybrid Perpetual for repeat bloom in most areas; it reblooms poorly in Zone 5, probably due to its inability to resprout vigorously from hard pruning. It is highly susceptible to mildew and requires winter protection in Zone 5.

'Reine des Violettes' (Millet-Malet, 1860) The French name translates as "Queen of the Violets." Carmine red or mauve flowers fade to shades of lavender, violet, and magenta. Blooms are wonderfully fragrant, three to four inches across, very double, with seventy-five petals, borne profusely midseason and on into the fall if spent flowers are deadheaded to prevent hip formation. Bushy, rounded, upright shrubs grow five to eight feet tall, with gray-green leaves and nearly thornless canes. In wet weather, flowers may refuse to open.

'Vick's Caprice' (Vick, 1891) A sport found in the garden of a Mr. Vick in New York. Cupped three-inch rose-colored flowers are striped with white and carmine; they are very fragrant and repeat bloom well. Plants are extremely hardy, relatively thornless, vigorous, and disease resistant.

AYRSHIRE ROSES

This is a small group of single- and double-flowered varieties developed from *R. arvensis,* the Field Rose, found growing wild in Europe and especially in the hedgerows of the British Isles. From this parent, the Ayrshire roses inherited great vigor, an ability to thrive in almost any growing conditions, and a rampant growth habit–canes may grow as long as thirty feet in a single season. These trailing or climbing roses may not grow as rampantly in colder regions of the United States, and need some protection from harsh winter weather.

BOURSAULT ROSES

Boursault Rose was the popular name given to what was assumed to be a cross between the thornless Alpine Rose, *R. pendulina,* and a China rose; recent studies have placed the parentage of the Boursault Roses in question. The first of these hybrids was given to the renowned French horticulturist Henri Boursault in the early 1800s to grow and study in his garden, and his name then became attached to the entire class. Like its Alpine parent, the

Boursault will grow in almost any kind of soil and conditions, including partial shade. Blooms are borne in fairly large clusters early in the season, in shades of red and pink; they are usually nonfragrant. The thornless, supple shoots are long-jointed and in winter canes turn reddish purple; in favorable growing conditions, they may grow ten to twelve feet in a season. Most Boursaults are climbers.

'Drummond's Thornless' This large, mounding plant can grow twelve feet wide and be covered once in spring with three-inch semidouble pink flowers in clusters. It is completely hardy in Zone 6B. It provides spectacular autumn color of plum purple with traces of orange, pink, and yellow. It needs protection from blackspot.

'Drummond's Thornless' is a "lost rose." It has disappeared from most catalogs and nurseries, but can be found in many backyards in the Milwaukee area. It is especially attractive in autumn.

We cut canes twelve to eighteen inches from the ground, depending on their use in the landscape. We remove about one-third of the oldest canes.
DARYL JOHNSON
PORTLAND, OREGON

In the fall, after the first freeze, we prune to thirty inches; in spring, we prune to twelve to fifteen inches.
JIM BROWNE
MEMPHIS BOTANIC GARDEN

We cut canes to three feet in the fall, and to five to seven buds in the spring–wherever those buds are, and they aren't always close to the ground.
MICHAEL RUGGIERO
THE NEW YORK BOTANICAL GARDEN

In our climate, canes should be pruned to no larger than ten inches at the beginning of the growing season.
WILLIAM RADLER
BOERNER BOTANICAL GARDENS

We prune to five to six inches from the ground at the beginning of the growing season. We have to be careful not to cut back too early, as cold damage sometimes takes a while to show up.
NANCY ROSE
MINNESOTA LANDSCAPE ARBORETUM

We prune much less severely than in northern gardens, with excellent results.
CLAIR MARTIN
THE HUNTINGTON BOTANICAL GARDEN

For most of our hybrid teas, we prune to the desired height, usually not pruning lower than eighteen inches feet from the ground, sometimes up to three feet.
NELSON STERNER
OLD WESTBURY GARDENS

Opposite: 'Elina'.

MODERN ROSES

HYBRID TEA ROSES

The activities of the nineteenth-century rose breeders culminated in the creation of the first modern rose, the Hybrid Tea. Although opinions differ on which rose was the original Hybrid Tea, the American Rose Society has recognized 'La France' (created by Jean-Baptiste Guillot in Lyons, France) as the first Hybrid Tea and has designated the date of its introduction, 1867, as the dividing line between old garden roses and modern roses. The original Hybrid Teas were a cross between Tea roses and Hybrid Perpetuals, which yielded plants with the large globular flowers of the short-stemmed Hybrid Perpetuals borne on the long, elegant stems of the teas. Hybrid teas bloomed sooner and more often than the Hybrid Perpetuals, with a more compact growth habit, and their long stems suited them ideally for use as cut flowers and exhibition blooms. Hybrid Teas soon became very popular, and the Hybrid Perpetuals began to vanish from gardens.

Another French rose breeder of Lyons, Joseph Pernet-Ducher, experimented with *R. foetida persiana,* Persian Yellow, to produce hybrids whose yellow coloring would survive crossbreeding. He introduced a Hybrid Foetida named 'Soleil d'Or' in 1900 and then, from it, Hybrid Teas, of which 'Rayon d'Or' was the first in 1910. This opened a whole new palette of colors to rose breeders, including apricot, copper, and salmon. Strangely, many modern yellow roses prove to be less hardy than other roses in their classes, even though Persian Yellow is hardy through Zone 4.

Today's Hybrid Teas are the world's most popular roses. They come in a wide variety of colors, with elegant high-centered blooms opening from long, pointed buds, borne all season, on plants with an upright, rather formal growth habit. Fragrance varies from slight to intense. Flowers are mostly double or semidouble, although a few single varieties do exist. Many Hybrid Teas are hardier and stronger than their tender tea forebears and breeders continue their attempts to create a Hybrid Tea that will be reliably hardy in regions with extremely cold winters.

Hybrid Teas require attentive pruning. The desired large blooms on long stems are produced on vigorous new growth, which in turn is produced from severely pruned-back older canes. In colder climates, canes should be cut to clear wood and/or desired height at the beginning of the growing season—about ten inches from the ground in cold areas, slightly less in warmer regions. After removing dead and crowded wood, open up the center of the bush and cut out all but three to four strong canes, and prune these back to an outward-facing bud. To promote good rebloom, deadhead spent flowers until one month before first frost, cutting back along the stem down to the first set of five leaflets facing away from the bush's center.

'Azure Sea' (Christensen, 1983) This slightly fragrant rose has silvery lavender flowers with thirty ruby-blushed petals on an upright bush. Fairly winter hardy.

'Blue Moon' (Tantau, 1965) Called 'Mainzer Fastnacht' in Germany. The double, three-and-one-half- to four-and-one-half-inch lavender flowers are the closest to blue of all roses. The strongly scented blooms have about forty petals and are borne all season; they hold color well and are fine for cutting. Plants are upright and moderately vigorous with large, semiglossy leaves. Disease resistant and fairly winter hardy.

'Brandy' (Swim & Christensen, 1981) Long, tight, burnt orange buds open to beautiful, broad-petaled loose-form flowers of rich gold apricot with a moderate, fruity tea scent. Blooms are four to six inches across, with about thirty petals, produced abundantly throughout the season and set off well by large, dark green, glossy foliage. Vigorous, bushy plants grow four to five feet tall, with good disease resistance. This cultivar has trouble in winter even with protection at The New York Botanical Garden and has been reported tender in Portland, Oregon, as well. AARS 1982.

'Canadian White Star' (Mander, 1980) The point on each curled-back petal makes the large, pure white flowers resemble stars. The full blossoms are borne best in cooler weather. Plants are tall and upright with leathery leaves.

'Cherry Brandy' (Tantau, 1965) Orange blend, coral to salmon, flowers open from small, exhibition-type buds on long stems. Blooms are five inches across, fragrant, full, cupped to flat, with about thirty petals, borne best in cooler weather. Moderately tall plants have dark, glossy foliage; disease resistant.

'Chicago Peace' (Johnson, 1962) This sport of 'Peace' was discovered by a Chicago gardener in her backyard. Colors are more intense than on the parent, a bright blend of apricot, yellow, and shades of pink. Finely formed, full flowers are five to six inches across, with fifty to sixty slightly fragrant petals, borne well all season and excellent for cutting. Upright, vigorous, bushy

'Chicago Peace' (below) displays a typical growth habit for a Hybrid Tea, upright bushes about four feet high.

'AZURE SEA' Hybrid Tea. Upright bush, three to four feet tall.
Ruby-blushed, silvery lavender flowers. Slightly fragrant.
Moderately hardy.

'BLUE MOON' ('Mainzer Fastnacht') Hybrid Tea. Upright, moderately vigorous bush, four to five feet tall. Double, three-
and-one-half- to four-and-one-half-inch lavender flowers
borne all season. Strongly scented. Large, semiglossy leaves.
Fairly winter hardy.

'BRANDY' Hybrid Tea. Vigorous, bushy plants grow four to
five feet tall. Broad-petaled loose-form flowers, four to six
inches across, of rich gold apricot. Blooms produced abundantly throughout the season. Moderate, fruity tea scent.
Large, dark green foliage.

'BRIGADOON' Hybrid Tea. Tall, upright, spreading bush. Very
double high-centered, coral pink, rose pink, and white flowers, with colors blending on reverse. Spicy fragrance. Medium
dark green semiglossy fragrance.

'CANADIAN WHITE STAR' ('Dr. Wolfgang Poschi') Hybrid Tea. Tall upright plants, three to five feet tall. Large, pure white flowers, which grow singly on long stems, resemble stars. Moderately fragrant. Leathery, glossy dark green leaves.

'CHERRY BRANDY' Hybrid Tea. Moderately tall plants. Full, cupped orange blend flowers, five inches across. Fragrant. Dark, glossy foliage. Disease resistant.

'CHICAGO PEACE' Hybrid Tea. Upright, vigorous, bushy plants, four-and-one-half to five-and-one-half feet tall. Full flowers, five to six inches across, in a blend of apricot, yellow, and shades of pink, borne all season. Slightly fragrant. Leathery, glossy, dark green leaves. Moderately thorny.

'CHRYSLER IMPERIAL' Hybrid Tea. Upright, bushy plants grow four to five feet tall. Classic, high-centered blooms, deep crimson, four-and-one-half to five inches across. Rich fragrance. Dark green, dull foliage. Moderately thorny. Good disease resistance, but subject to mildew.

plants grow four-and-one-half to five-and-one-half feet tall, with leathery, glossy, dark green leaves. Disease resistant and winter hardy with protection in colder climates.

'Chrysler Imperial' (Lammerts, 1952) In return for this rose's name, the breeder received a free car. Large, full deep crimson flowers with rich old-rose fragrance open from shapely buds. Classic, high-centered blooms are four-and-one-half to five inches across, with forty to fifty petals; color turns toward magenta with age, and flowers tend to ball in cool weather. Upright, bushy plants grow four to five feet tall, with dark green, dull foliage. Subject to mildew in cool and wet weather, as well as other diseases. Not winter hardy in Zone 5. Climbing form available. AARS 1953.

'Dainty Bess' (Archer, 1925) The best and most popular of the single Hybrid Teas. The five petals are large, ruffled, and a beautiful deep pink, contrasting effectively with distinctive wine-colored stamens. Blooms are four to five inches across, somewhat fragrant, borne all season, singly and in clusters. Moderately vigorous, well-branched plants grow three to four feet tall, with dark green, leathery foliage, few thorns. Susceptible to several diseases and not winter hardy in Zone 5. Climbing form available.

'Dolly Parton' (Winchel, 1984) Like its namesake, this rose commands attention. Long, pointed buds open to brilliant orange-red blooms six inches or more across, intensely fragrant and exceptionally long-lasting, both on the bush and cut. Classic, high-centered flowers are fully double, with thirty to thirty-five

ALL-AMERICA ROSE SELECTIONS (AARS)

Established in 1938, the AARS is an organization of commericial rose growers that sponsors two-year tests of new rose varieties. The roses are grown and evaluated at twenty-five official AARS test gardens in varied climates and soils around the United States.

The roses under trial are evaluated four times a year in fourteen different categories, including bud form, flower form, disease resistance, vigor, growth habit, stem strength, foliage, opening and finishing color, novelty, hardiness, flower production, and fragrance. Scores are totaled at the end of the two-year trial, and AARS members vote on which new roses are to receive the prestigious and commercially very valuable AARS award.

The Hybrid Tea 'Charlotte Armstrong' was the first recipient of the AARS award, in 1941.

The American Rose Society sponsors a separate award just for miniature roses—the American Rose Society Award of Excellence for Miniature Roses (ARSAE).

Not all Hybrid Teas are double; some are single, such as 'Kathleen' (left) and 'Ellen Wilmot' (far left).

AMERICAN ROSE SOCIETY (ARS)

The ARS was founded in 1899 by commercial florists and nursery operators in response to the growing interest in roses in the United States. It remained small and semiprofessional until the printer, horticulturist, and photographer J. Horace McFarland became editor of its publications. Under McFarland, the ARS published the first edition of its yearbook, *American Rose Annual,* in 1916, and turned into a dynamic organization devoted to dissemination of knowledge about roses and rose-growing among amateurs and nonprofessionals.

Today, the ARS–whose motto is "A rose for every home, a bush for every garden"–has over thirty thousand members and scores of chapters throughout the United States and even abroad. It records and regulates rose names, sets standards for judging at rose shows, and sponsors meetings, seminars, and various standing committees.

ARS publications for members include the yearly *American Rose Annual,* which describes all new roses of the past year; *The American Rose,* a monthly rose-information magazine; and *Handbook for Selecting Roses,* a buyer's guide rating roses currently available. Members also have access to the ARS lending library of books, videos, films, and slides. The ARS also provides Consulting Rosarians, available to share their knowledge with individual rose growers.

petals, borne well all season. Vigorous, upright, well-branched plants grow three to four feet tall, with large, dark green leaves that are susceptible to mildew.

'Double Delight' (Swim & Ellis, 1977) The large flowers of this popular rose are distinctive: the ruffled outer petals are creamy white with ruby edges, and the inner petals are buttery yellow tipped with raspberry red. Blooms become increasingly red as they age. Double five-and-one-half-inch flowers have thirty-five to forty-five petals, with a delightful spicy fragrance, borne well right into autumn. Spreading, very bushy plants grow three to four feet tall, with medium green foliage. Not very winter hardy or disease resistant; susceptible to mildew in cool, wet weather. Climbing form available. AARS 1977.

'Duet' (Swim, 1960) Ruffled petals of this bicolor are light dusty pink above and darker reddish pink on the reverse. Fragrant, double four-inch blooms have twenty-five to thirty-five petals, borne abundantly in clusters all season. Flowers are very long-lasting, both on the bush and in the vase. Tall, vigorous, bushy plants grow four-and-one-half to five-and-one-half feet tall, with large, leathery, medium green leaves. Disease resistant and winter hardy to 10° F. AARS 1961.

'Electron' (McGredy, 1970) Called 'Mullard Jubilee' in Europe. Exhibition-quality glowing deep pink flowers open from plump, deep rose buds. Five-inch blooms have thirty petals, with classic Hybrid Tea form, and repeat freely all season, even in summer heat, holding their shape well. Compact, vigorous, bushy plants grow two-and-one-half to three-and-one-half feet tall, with dark green foliage. Not winter hardy in Zone 5; not particularly disease resistant. AARS 1973.

'Elina' (Dickson, 1984) Dark green foliage contrasts beautifully with pale yellow to ivory double flowers, four to five inches across with light fragrance. A vigorous upright grower. Most Hybrid Teas could use this cultivar as a model for hardiness, vigor, and beautiful form.

'First Prize' (Boerner, 1970) As suggested by its name, this is a top-rated exhibition and Hybrid Tea rose; flowers are very long-lasting in the vase if cut when in tight bud. Exceptionally long deep pink buds open to five- to six-inch double blooms, deep rose pink with ivory at the center and thirty to thirty-five fragrant petals; repeats well. Vigorous, spreading plants grow four to five feet tall, with dark green, leathery leaves that are susceptible to both blackspot and mildew. Very tender. Climbing form available. Excellent as a tree rose; its stocky canes easily support its large flowers. AARS 1970.

'Folklore' (Kordes, 1977) Good exhibition rose, with classic Hybrid Tea form. Richly fragrant flowers are four- to four-and-one-half inches across, with forty-five petals, soft pink or orange above with yellow-orange reverse. Very winter hardy (with protection) plants grow five to eight feet tall, with long, leathery, disease-resistant foliage.

'Fragrant Cloud' (Tantau, 1963) Long, scarlet-orange buds open to five-inch coral red flowers with twenty-five to thirty petals and intense old-rose fragrance. Blooms are initially high-centered, then spread to an even fullness, and are

'DAINTY BESS' Hybrid Tea. Moderately vigorous, well-branched plants, three to four feet tall. Single four- to fiveinchflowers with five large ruffled silvery rose pink petals, distinctive wine-colored stamens, borne all season, singly and in clusters. Somewhat fragrant. Large, dark green foliage.

'DOLLY PARTON' Hybrid Tea.Vigorous, upright, well-branched plants, three to four feet tall. Brilliant orange-red blooms six inches or more across. Classic, high-centered fully double flowers, borne well all season. Large, dark green leaves. Susceptible to mildew.

'DOUBLE DELIGHT' Hybrid Tea. Spreading, very bushy plants, three to four feet tall. Large, double five-and-one-half-inch flowers; ruffled outer petals creamy white with ruby edges; inner petals buttery yellow tipped with raspberry red. Spicy fragrance. Medium green foliage. Susceptible to mildew in cool, wet weather.

'DUET' Hybrid Tea. Tall, vigorous, bushy plants, four-and-one-half to five-and-one-half feet tall. Double four-inch bicolor blooms with ruffled petals light dusty pink above and darker reddish pink on reverse. Fragrant flowers borne abundantly in clusters all season. Large, leathery, medium green leaves.

borne both singly and in clusters. Sturdy, freely branching plants grow three to five feet tall, with large, dark green leaves. Good resistance to rose rust and powdery mildew; winter hardy. Easy to grow.

'Fragrant Memory' ('Jadis') (Warriner, 1974) When first marketed as 'Jadis' (French for "formerly," or "days of yore"), this rose sold poorly in spite of its rich, sweet fragrance; removed from commerce in 1979, it was reintroduced successfully in 1989 under the more descriptive name of 'Fragrant Memory'. Elegant, urn-shaped buds open to bright pink five-inch flowers with a slight shading of lavender. Blooms have classic Hybrid Tea form, with twenty-five petals, borne prolifically through the season on stems suitable for cutting. Vigorous, upright, bushy plants grow three to five feet tall, with large, light green leaves. Hardy with protection.

'Headliner' (Warriner, 1985) Creamy white petals are lightly edged with red at the center and become increasingly washed with pink and then red toward the outside of the four-inch forty- to sixty-petaled blooms. Five-foot plants are abundantly covered with medium green foliage. Needs winter protection above Zone 6 and is very susceptible to mildew.

'La France' (Guillet Fils, 1867) The officially recognized first Hybrid Tea rose. Long, pointed buds open to large, globe-shaped silvery pink flowers with brighter pink reverse. Blooms are three-and-one-half to four-and-one-half

Roses are doubly effective when they are reflected in water. Roses with a cascading habit are often used near ponds and pools, manmade or natural. *Below:* 'Curley Pink', a Hybrid Tea, growing near Brooklyn Botanic Garden's Cranford Rose Garden.

'ELECTRON' Hybrid Tea. Compact, vigorous, bushy plants, two-and-one-half to three-and-one-half feet tall. Deep pink, five-inch flowers with classic Hybrid Tea form repeat freely all season. Dark green foliage.

'ELINA' Hybrid Tea. A vigorous upright grower, to four feet tall. Pale yellow to ivory double flowers, four to five inches across. Very fragrant. Dark green foliage.

'ELIZABETH TAYLOR' Hybrid Tea. Bushy, upright shrub. Deep pink medium-sized high-centered blooms, usually appear singly on long stems. Fragrant. Dark green semiglossy foliage.

'FIRST PRIZE' Hybrid Tea. Vigorous, spreading plants, four to five feet tall. Long-lasting five- to six-inch double blooms, deep rose pink with ivory at the center; repeats well. Fragrant. Dark green, leathery leaves. Very tender.

'FOLKLORE' Hybrid Tea. Plants five to eight feet tall. Four- to four-and-one-half-inch flowers, with thirty-five petals, soft pink or orange above with yellow-orange reverse. Richly fragrant. Long, leathery, disease-resistant foliage. Very winter hardy (with protection).

'FRAGRANT CLOUD' Hybrid Tea. Sturdy, freely branching plants, three to five feet tall. Five-inch coral red flowers, initially high-centered then evenly full, borne both singly and in clusters. Intense old-rose fragrance. Large, dark green leaves. Winter hardy.

'FRAGRANT MEMORY' ('Jadis') Hybrid Tea. Vigorous, upright, bushy plants grow three to five feet tall. Elegant, urn-shaped buds open to bright pink five-inch flowers with a slight shading of lavender, borne prolifically through the season. Rich, sweet fragrance. Large, light green leaves.

'HEADLINER' Hybrid Tea. Five-foot plants. Four-inch blooms with creamy white petals lightly edged with red at the center become washed with pink and then red. Abundant medium green foliage. Needs winter protection above Zone 6 and is very susceptible to mildew.

inches across, with sixty very fragrant petals, reflexed at the edges. Upright, branching plants grow three to four feet tall, with medium green semiglossy foliage. Fairly vigorous and winter hardy. Mildew susceptible. Flower production slows in hot weather, as does the size of the bloom. Flowers fail to open in hot weather. Climbing form available. Though it is often grown because of its historical significance, it is not the showiest of Hybrid Teas.

'Lady Ursula' (Dickson, 1908) Strongly tea-scented dusty pink flowers with light pink reverse have high, pointed centers with curled and pointed petals; good for cutting. Plants are very vigorous.

'Lemon Sherbet' (Kern Rose Nursery, 1973) Spicily scented white flowers with creamy centers open from long, pointed buds on long stems; bloom all summer and are good for cutting. Vigorous bushes grow six feet tall with dark, delicate foliage.

'Maid of Honour' (Weddle, 1984) Fragrant amber-yellow flowers are double (forty-five petals); large, dark foliage. A prolific bloomer with long stems. A vigorous plant, it grows to six feet. Fairly disease resistant and hardy, but is somewhat susceptible to mildew.

'Madame Violet' (Teranishi, 1981) High-centered, spiraled flowers are pink-tinted lilac, three to four inches across, with forty-five petals, borne most often in clusters. Vigorous plants grow four to five feet tall, with semiglossy grayish green leaves. Fairly good disease resistance and winter hardiness. No fragrance.

'Miss All-American Beauty' (Meilland, 1967) Called 'Maria Callas' in Europe. Full, cupped, peonylike deep pink flowers are very fragrant, five inches across, with fifty-five large, rounded petals, good for cutting and exhibition, produced prolifically all season. Vigorous, bushy, disease-resistant plants grow three to four feet tall, with leathery, medium green foliage. Not dependably hardy over winter in Zone 5, even with protection. AARS 1968.

'Mister Lincoln' (Swim & Weeks, 1964) One of the most popular red roses. Long, lovely buds open to rich, dark red flowers, four-and-one-half to six inches across, with thirty to forty petals. Blooms are very fragrant and fully double, initially high centered and then evenly full, borne freely all season on long stems, excellent for cutting and exhibition. Velvety red petals do not lose color. Vigorous, well-branched plants grow to six feet tall, with glossy dark foliage. Especially recommended for gardens in the South. AARS 1965.

'Night 'n' Day' (Swim & Weeks, 1968) One of the so-called black roses. Fragrant, dark red flowers have up to forty petals, with lighter shades of scarlet, and good rebloom. Moderately growing plants have disease-resistant leaves.

'Olympiad' (McGredy, 1984) One of the best red roses. Lightly fragrant, exhibition-type flowers are brilliant red, cupped and slightly reflexed, borne on long stems. Blooms are four to five inches across, with good all-season repeat and color fastness. Classic Hybrid Tea form and long, strong stems make this an excellent and long-lasting cut flower. Vigorous, compact plants grow four to five feet tall, with medium green disease-resistant foliage. Good winter hardiness. An earlier rose with the same name was introduced in 1931 and is now

THE GAMBLE FRAGRANCE AWARD

English rosarian James Alexander Gamble wanted hybridizers to work at developing rose scents as well as colors and forms. So he gave $25,000 to the American Rose Society to support research on rose fragrance and to reward new roses that were also fragrant.

The James Alexander Gamble Award for Fragrant Roses is only given periodically. To date, these are the intensely fragrant roses that have won the award (all are hybrid teas, except as otherwise noted):

'Crimson Glory' (1961)
'Tiffany' (1962)
'Chrysler Imperial' (1965)
'Sutter's Gold' (1966)
'Granada' (1968)
'Fragrant Cloud' (1970)
'Papa Meilland' (1974)
'Sunsprite' (Floribunda, 1979)
'Double Delight' (1986)

'LA FRANCE' Hybrid Tea. Upright, branching plants grow three to four feet tall. Long, pointed buds open to large, globe-shaped silvery pink flowers, three-and-one-half to four-and-one-half inches across, with brighter pink reverse. Very fragrant. Medium green semiglossy foliage.

'LADY URSULA' Hybrid Tea. Vigorous plants. Dusty pink flowers with light pink reverse; high, pointed centers with curled and pointed petals. Strong Tea scent.

'LEMON SHERBET' Hybrid Tea. Vigorous bushes grow six feet tall. White flowers with creamy centers bloom all summer. Spicy scent. Dark, delicate foliage.

'MAID OF HONOUR' Hybrid Tea. Vigorous plant grows to six feet. Double amber-yellow flowers bloom prolifically on long stems. Fragrant. Large, dark foliage. Fairly disease resistant and hardy.

considered extinct. AARS 1984.

'Peace' (Meilland, 1945) Called 'Gioia,' 'Gloria Dei,' and 'Mme. A. Meilland' in Europe, this is often referred to as the "Rose of the Century," the most popular rose in the world. Primrose buds open to yellow petals edged in rosy pink and orange blends that spread as the flowers unfold. Beautiful, fully double blooms are five to six inches across, with forty to forty-five petals, borne on long, sturdy stems, with light fragrance and high-centered form. Long-lasting flowers are excellent cut and for exhibition. Very vigorous, bushy plants grow five to six feet tall, with large, leathery, dark green, glossy foliage. Winter hardy with protection. Fine climbing form available. AARS 1946.

'Polar Star' ('Polarstern') (Tantau, 1982) White flowers with thirty-five petals, mostly in long-stemmed clusters on bushy plant. No fragrance. Although most white Hybrid Teas are winter tender, this one is hardy with protection in Zone 5.

'Princess de Monaco' (Meilland, 1981) Sometimes called 'Princess Grace', for whom it is named. Rouge and cream buds open to high-centered four- to six-inch flowers with thirty-five to forty creamy ivory petals edged in deep pink blush. High-centered, tea-scented blooms are exhibition quality and fine for cutting, produced throughout the season. Vigorous, bushy plants grow three to four feet tall, with dark, glossy foliage.

'Pristine' (Warriner, 1978) Long, pink-tinged ivory buds open to classic hybrid-tea-form flowers, nearly white with blush pink edges. Lightly fragrant blooms are five to six inches across, with thirty petals, borne singly on long stems throughout the season, excellent for exhibition. Moderately vigorous, upright bushes grow four to five feet tall, with very large, deep green, handsome leaves and nearly thornless canes. Disease resistant and tender. New growth is red, which contrasts with the pale flowers. 'Pristine' is a parent of 'Secret', 1994's AARS rose.

'Radiance' (Cook, 1908) Also known as 'Pink Radiance', this is one of the best pink roses ever, and one of the most popular Hybrid Teas (although its flowers are not classicly shaped). Globe-shaped buds open to large, deep rose-pink, very fragrant cupped flowers with twenty-five petals and long stems. Everblooming, winter hardy, and disease resistant.

'Senior Prom' (Brownell, 1964) Double pink flowers, up to five inches across; upright plant.

'Sheer Elegance' (Twomey, 1989) Exhibition-type three- to four-inch flowers have thirty-five to forty soft pink to pale salmon petals edged with a deeper salmon borne on long stems. Plants grow four to five feet tall, with dark green foliage. Disease resistant, susceptible to mildew. Nice fragrance. Reported tender in New York area, hardy in Portland, Oregon, fairly dependable with protection in Milwaukee. Winner of the Portland Gold Medal Award in 1994.

'Sunbright' (Warriner, 1984) Flat, bright yellow, double flowers open from long, urn-shaped buds. Lightly fragrant four-inch blooms have twenty-four to thirty petals and are borne constantly, singly and in clusters. Very vigorous plants

Hybrid Teas have been bred for excellence as cut flowers, and many of the best cut roses are of this class, such as 'Night 'n' Day', above.

'MADAME VIOLET' Hybrid Tea. Vigorous plants grow four to five feet tall. High-centered, spiraled flowers three to four inches across, pink-tinted lilac; borne most often in clusters. No fragrance. Semiglossy grayish green leaves.

'MISS ALL-AMERICAN BEAUTY' Hybrid Tea. Vigorous, bushy plants grow three to four feet tall. Full, cupped, peonylike deep pink flowers, five inches across, produced prolifically all season. Very fragrant. Leathery, medium green foliage.

'MISS AMERICA' Hybrid Tea. Vigorous, upright bush to five feet tall. Six-inch pink blend blooms are very double. Fragrant. Dark leathery foliage.

'MISTER LINCOLN' Hybrid Tea. Vigorous, well-branched plants grow to six feet tall. Long buds open to fully double dark red flowers, four-and-one-half to six inches across. Very fragrant. Glossy dark foliage.

'NIGHT 'N' DAY' Hybrid Tea. Moderately vigorous. Dark red flowers with lighter shades of scarlet, and good rebloom. Fragrant.

'OLYMPIAD' Hybrid Tea. Vigorous, compact plants grow four to five feet tall. Brilliant red, cupped and slightly reflexed flowers, four to five inches across, borne on long stems; good all-season repeat and color fastness. Lightly fragrant. Medium green disease-resistant foliage.

'PEACE' Hybrid Tea. Very vigorous, bushy plants grow five to six feet tall. Primrose buds open to yellow petals edged in rosy pink and orange blends that spread as the flowers unfold. Fully double blooms, five to six inches across, borne on long, sturdy stems, Light fragrance. Large, leathery, dark green, glossy foliage. Winter hardy with protection.

'PERFECT MOMENT' Hybrid Tea. Upright bushy shrub, to five feet tall. Pointed buds open to double, cupped flowers, that are red on outer half of petals and yellow on inner half, with reverse yellow blushed with red. Slight fragrance. Medium green semiglossy foliage.

'Polar Star', growing at Boerner Botanical Gardens.

grow three to five feet tall, with dark green leaves that are more disease resistant than on most yellow roses. Long-lasting, fade-resistant flowers are good for cutting. Was severely damaged in winter at The New York Botanical Garden, even with protection; middle hardiness reported at Boerner Botanical Gardens.

'Swarthmore' (Meilland, 1963) Elegant buds open to high-centered four-inch flowers in shades of rose-pink and red, darker at the edges than the centers. Lightly tea-scented blooms are four to five inches across, with forty-five to fifty-five petals, borne prolifically on long, straight stems; excellent exhibition rose and for cutting. Vigorous, bushy plants grow four to seven feet tall, with dark green, leathery foliage. Good winter hardiness.

'Tiffany' (Lindquist, 1954) An extremely popular Hybrid Tea with intense old-rose fragrance. Beautifully formed buds open into classic high-centered flowers, medium to light pink shaded yellow at the base. Blooms are four to five inches across, with twenty-five to thirty silky petals, produced abundantly all summer, usually singly; long-lasting and long-stemmed flowers are good for cutting and exhibition. Sturdy, upright, vigorous bushes grow four to five feet tall, with moderately thorny canes and full, light green foliage. Disease resistant (but susceptible to powdery mildew) and winter hardy. Climbing form available. AARS, 1955; also winner of fragrance award.

'Touch of Class' (Le Clerc, 1984) A top-rated exhibition rose. Tapered salmon pink buds open to spiraled, high-centered flowers, warm pink shading into coral and fading with age to a soft salmon. Blooms are four-and-one-half to five-and-one-half inches across, with thirty to thirty-five slightly ruffled and slightly fragrant petals. Upright bushes grow four to seven feet tall, with reddish young and dark green older foliage. Though unscented and highly susceptible to powdery mildew, this rose displays many other good qualities, including winter hardiness and disease resistance. AARS 1968.

'Tropicana' (Tantau, 1962) The first orange-red Hybrid Tea, called 'Super Star' in Europe, and the third biggest-selling rose in the twentieth century. Sweetly scented fluorescent orange flowers hold their intense color well. Cup-shaped four- to six-inch blooms are initially high-centered, with thirty to thirty-five petals; long-lasting, prolifically produced all season, and good for cutting. Vigorous, thorny bushes grow four to six feet tall, with leathery, dark green foliage. Disease-resistant, but may be troubled by mildew; good winter hardiness. Climbing form available. AARS 1963.

'World Peace' (Perry, 1987) Pink-blend double flowers suffused with cream at the tips of petals; fruity fragrance. Average green leaves on six-foot-tall bushes. Good disease resistance.

'Yves Piaget' (Meilland, 1985) Named for the Geneva jeweler who designed the gold rose presented to the winner of the Geneva rose competition. Peonylike five- to six-inch pink flowers are strongly fragrant, with eighty petals, borne prolifically and constantly on disease-resistant four- to five-foot-tall plants. Good winter hardiness, excellent fragrance.

'POLAR STAR' ('Polarstern') Hybrid Tea. (Tantau, 1982) Bushy plant grows three feet tall by two feet wide. White flowers mostly in long-stemmed clusters. Light green foliage. Winter hardy with protection.

'PRINCESS DE MONACO' Hybrid Tea. Vigorous, bushy plants grow three to four feet tall. Rouge and cream buds open to high-centered four- to six-inch ivory flowers edged in deep pink blush, produced throughout the season. Tea scented. Dark, glossy foliage.

'PRISTINE' Hybrid Tea. Moderately vigorous, upright bushes grow four to five feet tall. Classic Hybrid-Tea-form flowers, nearly white with blush pink edges, five to six inches across, borne singly on long stems throughout the season. Lightly fragrant. Very large, deep green, handsome leaves.

'RADIANCE' Hybrid Tea. Globe-shaped buds open to large, deep rose-pink, very fragrant cupped flowers on long stems. Everblooming, winter hardy, and disease resistant.

'SECRET' Hybrid Tea. A descendant of 'Pristine', with similar growth habit and shape but deeper shading of pink at the edges of the petals.

'SHEER ELEGANCE' Hybrid Tea. Plants grow four to five feet tall. Three- to four-inch soft pink to pale salmon flowers edged with a deeper salmon, borne on long stems. Dark green foliage. Nice fragrance.

'SUNBRIGHT' Hybrid Tea. Very vigorous plants grow three to five feet tall. Flat, bright yellow, double, four-inch flowers, borne constantly, singly and in clusters. Lightly fragrant. Dark green leaves.

'TIFFANY' Hybrid Tea. Sturdy, upright, vigorous bushes grow four to five feet tall. Classic high-centered flowers, medium to light pink shaded yellow at the base, four to five inches across, produced abundantly all summer, usually singly. Intense old-rose fragrance. Moderately thorny canes and full, light green foliage.

'TOUCH OF CLASS' Hybrid Tea. Upright bushes grow four to seven feet tall. High-centered flowers, warm pink shading into coral. Blooms are four-and-one-half to five-and-one-half inches across, with slightly ruffled petals. Slightly fragrant. Reddish young and dark green older foliage.

'VOL DE NUIT' Hybrid Tea. Upright and bushy to five feet tall. Large, deep lilac, double blossoms. Very fragrant. Medium to light green matt foliage.

'WORLD PEACE' Hybrid Tea. Six-foot-tall bushes. Pink-blend double flowers suffused with cream at the tips of petals. Fruity fragrance. Average green leaves. Good disease resistance.

'YVES PIAGET' Hybrid Tea. Four- to five-foot-tall plants. Peonylike five- to six-inch pink flowers are borne prolifically and constantly. Strongly fragrant. Disease-resistant, good winter hardiness.

EXHIBITING ROSES

The American Rose Society sponsors many local, regional, and national shows; local garden clubs do, too. Roses are judged by variety within each class (Floribunda, Polyantha, Hybrid Tea, etc.) by ARS-accredited judges. The grand-prize-winning Queen of the Show is then chosen from among the single-bloomed (one on one stem; achieved by disbudding) Hybrid Teas and Grandifloras.

Single blooms are judged on the following criteria:

Form: 25 points
Color: 20 points
Stem and Foliage: 20 points
Substance: 15 points
Balance and Proportion: 10 points
Size: 10 points

For detailed instructions on exhibiting roses, contact the American Rose Society, Box 30,000, Shreveport, LA 71130 (318-938-5402)

FLORIBUNDAS

Floribunda, or "abundantly flowering" roses originally resulted from crosses between Polyanthas and Hybrid Teas. A pioneer in the development of Floribundas was the Danish breeder D. T. Poulsen, who sought the larger flowers of the Hybrid Teas on hardier plants, plus the all-season bloom of both parents. Poulsen introduced his first Floribunda, 'Rödhätte' ('Red Riding Hood') in 1912. These new roses were at first known as Hybrid Polyanthas. A new name was needed and the term *Floribunda* was adopted in a successful marketing plan by Gene Boerner of the Jackson and Perkins rose firm. The class was officially recognized around 1940. Hybridization continues, with flowers increasingly resembling Hybrid Teas and clusters becoming smaller. New classes are likely to emerge.

Today's Floribundas can be large and shrubby with clusters of blooms all season long in a range of colors. Plants have the same disease susceptibility as Hybrid Teas, often requiring treatment from June through September. They are fine bedding plants and also combine well with other roses; they make an attractive hedge and an excellent border. To prune Floribundas, clean out centers, remove dead wood, and cut back remaining canes by one-third to outward-facing buds at the beginning of the growing season. In the North, prune to ten inches if any wood survives above ground level. For bedding plants, trim bushes to even heights. Deadhead through the growing season, up to one month before first frost.

'Angel Face' (Swim & Weeks, 1968) Short pointed buds open to ruffled, deep lavender flowers with ruby red edges, initially high-centered and then cupped. The very spicily fragrant blooms are three-and-one-half to four inches across, with thirty-five to forty petals, usually borne in clusters; excellent for cutting and exhibition. Unfortunately, the low height makes it difficult for the wonderful fragrance to reach passersby. Bushy, spreading plants grow two-and-one-half to three feet tall, with dark green, glossy, leathery foliage. Not winter hardy in the Milwaukee or Portland areas; subject to blackspot and mildew.

'Betty Prior' (Prior, 1935) One of the all-time most popular Floribundas. Single, five-petaled medium to dark carmine-pink flowers (color is richer when the weather is cool), two to three inches across, mildly fragrant, and resembling dogwood, are produced prolifically and constantly in large clusters. Vigorous, bushy plants are the tallest of the Floribundas, growing four to five feet tall or more, with medium green, semiglossy leaves. Especially resistant to blackspot (but susceptible to powdery mildew) and winter hardy (with protection), this makes an excellent border, edging, or hedge.

'Frensham' (Norman, 1946) Semidouble, nonfading, deep scarlet flowers are exceptionally long-lasting. Blooms are two to three inches across, with fifteen petals and slight fragrance, borne freely in clusters from midseason on. Vigorous, spreading, bushy plants grow three feet tall and more, with dark green, semiglossy foliage. Thorny plants make a fine hedge and are hardy with protection and disease resistant.

'Gene Boerner' (Boerner, 1968) Named for the outstanding Floribunda hybrid-

'ANGEL FACE' Floribunda. Bushy, spreading plants grow two-and-one-half to three feet tall. Ruffled, deep lavender flowers with ruby red edges, three-and-one-half to four inches across, usually borne in clusters. Very spicily fragrant. Dark green, glossy, leathery foliage.

'BETTY PRIOR' Floribunda. Vigorous, bushy plants to five feet tall or more. Single, five-petaled medium to dark carmine-pink flowers, two to three inches across are produced prolifically and constantly in large clusters. Mildly fragrant. Medium green, semiglossy leaves. Disease resistant and winter hardy.

'EUROPEANA' Floribunda. Vigorous upright bush, two and one half to three feet tall. Clusters of deep crimson, semidouble flowers with fifteen to twenty petals; midseason with autumn repeat bloom. Fragrant. Leaves reddish when young, age to dark, leathery green.

'FRENCH LACE' Floribunda. Well-branched upright plant, three to four feet tall. Double white blooms, three-and-one-half to four inches across in midseason with good repeat. Semiglossy medium green leaves.

'FRENSHAM' Floribunda. Vigorous, spreading, bushy plants grow three feet tall and more. Semidouble, nonfading, deep scarlet flowers are two to three inches across, borne freely in clusters from midseason on. Dark green, semiglossy foliage.

'GENE BOERNER' Floribunda. Vigorous plants to five feet high. Double vibrant medium pink flowers, three to three-and-one-half inches across, with exposed yellow stamens, blooming profusely all season, usually in clusters. Lightly Tea-scented. Medium green, semiglossy foliage.

'GOLDEN SLIPPERS' Floribunda. Compact, low-growing bush, two feet tall and wide. Pointed buds open quickly to loose, semidouble orange flowers with yellow centers and reverse. Lightly fragrant. Glossy, leathery foliage.

'ICEBERG' Floribunda. Bushy plants grow four to five feet tall. Double, cupped, three- to four-inch pure white flowers with a touch of pink in the center, almost always borne in clusters. Sweetly fragrant. Light green foliage.

er. Hybrid Tea-type flowers are vibrant medium pink with exposed yellow stamens, blooming profusely all season, usually in clusters. Double, lightly Tea-scented blooms are three to three-and-one-half inches across, with thirty-five petals; long-lasting flowers are good for cutting and exhibition. Vigorous plants are tall for Floribundas, growing up to five feet high, with medium green, semiglossy foliage. Disease resistant; hardy with protection at The New York Botanical Garden. AARS 1969.

'Golden Slippers' (Abrams, 1961) Pointed buds open quickly to beautifully shaded orange flowers with yellow centers and reverse, lightly fragrant, with twenty petals. Plants are compact and low growing, excellent for bedding. AARS 1962.

'Gene Boerner' can be a good low hedge if pruned severely at the beginning of its growing season.

'IVORY FASHION' Floribunda. Vigorous, well-branched bush, three-and-one-half to four feet tall. Clusters of semidouble, ivory white blooms, three-and-one-half inches across, with good repeat bloom. Fragrant. Medium green foliage.

'KIRSTEN POULSEN' Floribunda. Vigorous, bushy plants. Single, cupped, five-petaled bright scarlet flowers borne in long sprays. Slightly fragrant.

'REDGOLD' Floribunda. Vigorous, bushy plants three to five feet tall. Double, chrome yellow flowers, edged in red, two to three inches across are borne singly and in clusters throughout the season. Slightly fruit-scented. Glossy green leaves.

'SIMPLICITY' Floribunda. Vigorous, bushy plants are dense and fully branched. Semidouble cupped medium pink flowers borne abundantly in clusters on freely flowering plants. Slightly fragrant Medium green, semiglossy foliage.

'Iceberg' (Kordes, 1958) Called 'Fée des Neiges' in France and 'Schneewittchen' in Germany. Sweetly fragrant, pure white flowers with a touch of pink in the center. Double, cupped blooms are three to four inches across, with thirty-five to forty petals, almost always borne in clusters. Profusely blooming, bushy plants, grow four to five feet tall, forming an excellent hedge. Light green foliage is very disease resistant (but needs some protection from blackspot and sometimes has mildew on bud stems), and plants are extremely winter hardy. There is a climbing sport available as well.

'Kirsten Poulsen' (Poulsen, 1924) An early Floribunda, important in establishing the class. Single, five-petaled deep pink flowers borne in long sprays are cupped and slightly fragrant. Plants are vigorous and bushy and bloom constantly.

'Redgold' (Dickson, 1971) Double, chrome yellow flowers are edged in red, two to three inches across, with twenty-five to thirty large petals. Slightly fruit-scented blooms are borne singly and in clusters throughout the season; long-lasting flowers are good for cutting. Vigorous, bushy plants grow three to five feet tall, with glossy green leaves and very thorny canes. Hardy with protection. AARS 1971.

'Simplicity' (Warriner, 1979) Classed as a Floribunda, but often sold as a Shrub Rose or "living fence." Semidouble medium pink flowers are slightly fragrant, with eighteen to twenty petals. Cupped blooms are borne abundantly in clusters on freely flowering plants. Vigorous, bushy plants are dense and fully branched, forming a fine hedge, with medium green, semiglossy foliage. Fairly hardy in Connecticut with protection.

'Sun Flare' (Warriner, 1983) Semidouble, bright lemon yellow flowers have a mild licorice scent. Nicely shaped three-inch blooms are initially high-centered and then cupped, with twenty-seven to thirty petals, borne abundantly singly or in clusters, holding their color well. Vigorous, spreading, plants grow two to three feet tall, with light green, glossy foliage. Susceptible to blackspot; winter tender. AARS 1983.

'Sunsprite' (Kordes, 1977) Very bright and fragrant, nonfading yellow flowers are three to four inches across, with twenty-eight petals, but are not long lasting. Compact plants grow two to five feet tall and are very disease resistant (but not in the North), especially for a yellow rose, and winter hardy, though they need some protection in Portland and Milwaukee. It is the most fragrant modern yellow rose at The New York Botanical Garden.

'Trumpeter' (McGredy, 1977) Brilliant orange-red blooms are double, two-and-one-half to three-and-one-half inches across, with thirty-five to forty ruffled petals, lightly fragrant, borne singly or in clusters. Spreading, vigorous plants grow to three feet, with glossy green foliage, and bloom constantly and prolifically. A fine choice for colorful mass plantings.

'Vogue' (Boerner, 1951) Long, elegant buds open to high-centered, deep coral flowers, two to four inches across, with twenty-five slightly fragrant petals, loosely arranged. Long-lasting blooms are borne in large clusters, but plants may be slow to bloom in heat. Vigorous, bushy plants grow three feet tall and

'Simplicity' and 'Iceberg', both Floribundas, are often grown together.

more, with medium green, semiglossy leaves. Good resistance to mildew but not to blackspot. AARS, 1952.

GRANDIFLORAS

Yet another step in the line of Hybrid Tea cross-breeding, the Grandifloras were created by crossing a Hybrid Tea with a Floribunda. The class was created to encompass 'Queen Elizabeth', an outstanding cross created by American breeder Dr. Walter E. Lammerts and introduced in 1954. Grandiflora flowers are clustered and produced in quantities like the Floribundas, but are larger, with the shape and longer stems of the Hybrid Teas; they are excellent for cutting. As implied by their name, Grandifloras grow very tall, often over six feet (they are usually much smaller in the North). They bloom more often than Hybrid Teas and more vigorously later in the season. Contrary to popular opinion, they are not more hardy than Hybrid Teas; all Grandifloras are protected in winter at Minnesota Landscape Arboretum. Because of their

Floribundas and Grandifloras at The New York Botanical Garden.

'SUN FLARE' Floribunda. Vigorous, spreading, plants grow two to three feet tall. Semidouble, three-inch bright lemon yellow flowers are initially high-centered and then cupped, borne abundantly singly or in clusters. Mild licorice scent. Light green, glossy foliage.

'SUNSPRITE' Floribunda. Compact plants grow two to five feet tall. Nonfading yellow flowers are three to four inches across, not long lasting. Very fragrant and disease resistant, especially for a yellow rose.

'TRUMPETER' Floribunda. Spreading, vigorous plants grow to three feet. Brilliant, double orange-red blooms are two-and-one-half to three-and-one-half inches across, borne singly or in clusters. Lightly fragrant. Glossy green foliage. Very disease resistant.

'VOGUE' Floribunda. Vigorous, bushy plants, three feet tall or more. Loose, high-centered, deep coral flowers, two to four inches across, borne in large clusters. Medium green, semi-glossy leaves.

'Queen Elizabeth', the first Grandiflora.

height, Grandifloras are often grown as background plants or as a screen; in this case, prune back only to the desired height. If the aim is to produce the largest flowers, however, prune severely as with the Hybrid Teas.

'Arizona' (Weeks, 1975) Urn-shaped buds open into high-centered, long-stemmed blooms with colors reminiscent of a desert sunset: coppery orange with tints of gold. Flowers are three to four inches across, double and intensely fragrant, with twenty-five to forty petals, borne singly and set off attractively against semiglossy, coppery green, leathery foliage. Tall, upright plants grow five to six feet (to three feet in the North) and make fine specimens or hedges. They are somewhat tender and highly susceptible to mildew and to winter canker, which kills plants. AARS, 1975.

'Gold Medal' (Christensen, 1982) Long-lasting classically shaped yellow blooms, tipped in pink and orange, lightening as they age. Double flowers are four to five inches across, with thirty-five to forty petals and a light Tea fragrance, borne singly and in clusters all season. Vigorous plants can grow over six feet and are generally disease resistant but with some susceptibility to blackspot. In the North, they are generally under four feet tall; they need protection under 15° F. and clusters of blooms are light unless much wood survived the winter and the plant was trimmed lightly. It is one of the best of its class at the Memphis Botanic Garden.

'Hotel Hershey' (J. B. Williams, 1977) An offspring of 'Queen Elizabeth', the original Grandiflora. Pointed, urn-shaped buds open to high-centered, deep coral-orange flowers with thirty-five to forty ruffled petals and a light Tea fragrance. Dark-leaved plants have a moderate growth habit.

'June Bride' (Shepherd, 1957) Clusters of creamy, red-tinged buds open to fragrant, soft white flowers, high-centered at first but later cupped, with about thirty petals. Upright, vigorous bush has fierce prickles and crinkled, leathery foliage. Now rare.

'Lagerfeld' (Christensen, 1985) Pale lavender blossoms come from elegant long pointed buds; an excellent cut flower. Intensely fragrant flowers are borne profusely from long stems on upright, vigorous plants, to six feet tall, hardier than most. Mildew can be a problem; this cultivar does not grow well at the Memphis Botanic Garden.

'Love' (Warriner, 1980) Short, pointed buds open to classic, high-centered bright red flowers with white reverse, slightly fragrant. Double three- to four-inch blooms have thirty-five to fifty petals and are freely borne singly or, later in the season, in clusters. Upright plants are short for a Grandiflora, reaching only four feet in height; new foliage is red, and turns dark green. Disease resistant and fairly winter hardy, dependable in Zone 5 with protection.

'Mount Shasta' (Swim and Weeks, 1963) Large, double, pure white flowers are four-and-one-half to five inches across, with twenty to thirty moderately fragrant petals. Upright, vigorous plants have soft green, leathery foliage with good disease resistance and good growth in cool regions. AARS, 1980.

'Prima Donna' (Shirakawa, 1984) Very slender, long buds open to high-centered rich pink flowers, three to four inches across and slightly fragrant, with twen-

'GOLD MEDAL' Grandiflora. Vigorous plants can grow over six feet. Double yellow blooms, tipped in pink and orange, four to five inches across, borne singly and in clusters all season. Light Tea fragrance.

'HOTEL HERSHEY' Grandiflora. Moderately vigorous. Pointed, urn-shaped buds open to high-centered, deep coral-orange flowers. Light Tea fragrance. Dark leaves.

'LAGERFELD' Grandiflora. Upright, vigorous plants, to six feet tall. Pale lavender blossoms come from elegant, long pointed buds; profuse bloom. Intensely fragrant.

'LOVE' Grandiflora. Upright plants to four feet in height. Short, pointed buds open to classic, high-centered bright red flowers with white reverse, slightly fragrant; double three- to four-inch blooms freely borne singly or, later in the season, in clusters. New foliage is red and turns dark green.

'Lagerfeld', like many other modern flowers, makes an excellent, long-lasting cut flower.

'Queen Elizabeth' (Lammerts, 1954) The first Grandiflora, named by its American hybridizer in commemoration of the new queen's accession to the English throne in 1952, this became the twentieth century's second most popular rose after 'Peace' and a prolific award-winner. Salmon-pink buds open to clear pink, high-centered and cupped blossoms, three to four inches across and lightly fragrant, borne singly or in small sprays. Abundant, long-lasting flowers are excellent for cutting and bloom all season. Very vigorous, bushy plants grow five to seven feet, with nearly thornless canes and glossy, dark green, leathery foliage. This rose is usually considered disease resistant and very hardy, though it is found to be susceptible to disease at Boerner Botanical Garden. It mkaes an excellent hedge or screen. Mike Ruggiero of The New York Botanical Garden considers it to be the best modern rose for the beginning grower. A climbing sport is also available. AARS, 1955.

'Scarlet Knight' (Meilland, 1966) Rich, black-red buds open to velvety, cupped, fire-red flowers, four to five inches across, with thirty-five to forty petals and a light Tea fragrance. Blooms are borne singly or in clusters, holding their color well and lasting a long time both on the plant and as a cut flower. Hardy with protection, very vigorous plants grow to medium height; they are thorny and have large, leathery foliage. AARS, 1968.

'Sundowner' (McGredy, 1978) Pointed buds open to double, very fragrant golden orange flowers with tints of apricot and salmon. Double, informally styled blooms are four inches across, with thirty-five to forty petals, borne singly on long stems early in the season and in small clusters later. Vigorous, upright, bushy plants are four-and-one-half to five-and-one-half feet tall (up to twelve feet in California). The large, coppery green leaves are somewhat susceptible to mildew and blackspot. AARS, 1979.

'Tournament of Roses' (Warriner, 1988) Oval buds open to small clusters of high-centered, four-inch, warm pink flowers with a darker coral reverse and twenty-five to thirty mildly fragrant petals. Blooms are borne profusely on disease-resistant, winter-hardy plants that grow four to five feet high (to two-and-one-half feet in the North), with glossy dark green leaves.

'White Lightnin'' (Swim & Christensen, 1980) Long, pointed buds open to double, cupped, clear white flowers, three-and-one-half to four inches across, with twenty-five to thirty-six ruffled petals. The strongly lemon-rose-scented blooms are borne prolifically all season, usually in small clusters. Upright, bushy, vigorous plants grow three to five feet tall, with leathery dark green foliage, and are winter tender and mildly disease resistant. At Boerner Botanical Gardens, this rose did not survive its first winter; it is still grown there, but is replaced periodically. AARS, 1981.

'MOUNT SHASTA' Grandiflora. Upright plant grows four to five feet high. Large, double clear white blossoms borne singly on long stems. Glossy dark green leaves.

'PINK PARFAIT' Grandiflora. Upright, vigorous plant grows four to five feet tall. Double three-and-one-half- to four-inch flowers borne singly and in clusters in midseason; good repeat. Mild fragrance. Medium green semiglossy leaves.

'TOURNAMENT OF ROSES' Grandiflora. Four to five feet high, shorter in the North. Oval buds open to small clusters of high-centered, four-inch, warm pink flowers with a darker coral reverse. Mildly fragrant. Glossy dark green leaves.

'WHITE LIGHTNIN' ' Grandiflora. Upright, bushy, vigorous plants grow three to five feet tall. Long, pointed buds open to double, cupped, clear white flowers, three-and-one-half to four inches across. Strongly lemon-rose-scent. Glossy dark green foliage.

POLYANTHAS

The name *Polyantha* means "many-flowered," an apt description of these low-growing roses covered with extensive clusters of small blooms, which are attractive but not very fragrant. This class—the first repeat-blooming low-growing rose—was created by the originator of the Hybrid Tea, the French breeder Jean-Baptiste Guillot, in the 1870s and 1880s. They were a cross between *R. multiflora* and a dwarf China rose. Polyanthas bloom continuously all season long and are often quite hardy; a few are crown-hardy in Zone 5. Their low and bushy growth habit makes them well adapted for borders, edgings, and low hedges; they fill in nicely around the feet of the taller-growing Floribundas and Grandifloras.

Polyanthas are generally pruned like Old Garden Roses: Trim them out at the beginning of the growing season, removing old, dead, and diseased wood. If bushes have become too large, cut them back, either lightly or up to one half. Deadhead throughout the season to maintain profuse repeat bloom.

'The Fairy' is popular for its constant bloom. It is shown here in Old Westbury Garden's Cottage Garden among annuals and perennials.

'BABY FARAUX' Polyantha. Bushy plant grows to one foot tall, one foot wide. Double violet flowers in large clusters. Fragrant. Medium green foliage.

'CAMEO' Polyantha. Stocky, bushy shrubs, two feet tall and wide. Small, semidouble cupped flowers, soft salmon darkening to darker pink with age; flowers continuously through the summer. Abundant gray-green foliage.

'CLOTILDE SOUPERT' Polyantha. Bushy one-and-one-half by one-and-one-half-foot shrubs. Clusters of round, red-tinted buds open to very double white flowers with blush to deep pink centers. Very fragrant. Rich green foliage.

'DICK KOSTER' Polyantha. Low-growing, compact shrub, to one foot tall. Light bright red, cupped, one-and-one-half-inch flowers borne in clusters. No fragrance. Nearly thornless plants. Good medium green foliage.

'GABRIELLE PRIVAT' Polyantha. Compact plants grow two to three feet high. Large clusters of double medium pink flowers, one-and-one-half to two inches across appear in midsummer; good repeat. Glossy, medium green foliage.

'LA MARNE' Polyantha. Bushy, compact plants grow about two feet high. Everblooming, cupped, two-inch pink flowers have blush white centers and are borne freely in large, loose clusters. Light fragrance. Glossy, medium green foliage.

'MARGO KOSTER' Polyantha. Sport of 'Dick Koster', with similar habit but salmon flowers.

'MARIE PAVIÉ' Polyantha. Low-growing, thornless shrubs, under two feet in height. Pale white flowers with deep pink centers and golden stamens borne in clusters throughout the season. Long, pointed leaves.

'Cecile Brunner' ('The Sweetheart Rose', 'Mignon', 'Maltese Rose') (Pernet-Ducher, 1881) Although grown on a fairly short, spindly bush with sparse foliage, 'Cecile Brunner' is loved for its exquisite cream/blush pink blossoms, just one-and-one-half inches across, that bloom profusely in midsummer and again in early fall. Often used as a buttonhole rose, it has a faint but distinctive perfume. Not very hardy. A climbing sport is also popular.

'Clotilde Soupert' (Soupert & Notting, 1890) One of the first Polyanthas on the market, this was a valued member of the White House Rose Garden by 1894. Clusters of round, red-tinted buds open to very double and fragrant white flowers with blush to deep pink centers, resembling Old Garden Roses. This fine bedding plant has large, hooked prickles. In cool or damp weather, buds do not open fully. Plants tend to produce some red blossoms.

'Dick Koster' (Koster, 1929) Light bright red, cupped, one-and-one-half-inch flowers are borne in clusters, with twenty to twenty-five petals and no fragrance. Nearly thornless plants are well suited for forcing to produce gift plants.

'Jean Mermoz' (Chenault, 1937) This cross between *R. wichuraiana* and a Hybrid Tea has quartered, full, one-inch pink flowers with light pink edges and dark pink centers, opening from clusters of tight, round buds. The scentless flowers are constantly in bloom on low-growing, disease-resistant plants.

'La Marne' (Barbier, 1915) Cupped, two-inch pink flowers have blush white centers and fifteen petals; they are borne freely in large, loose, lightly fragrant clusters. Color darkens in cooler weather. Bushy, compact plants grow about two feet high, with glossy, medium green foliage. Disease resistant, winter hardy, everblooming plants are excellent for the border and bedding.

'Marie Pavié' (Alégatière, 1888) An old Polyantha, once very popular as a boutonniere or "sweetheart" rose. Pale white flowers with deep pink centers and golden stamens are borne in clusters throughout the season, set off against long, pointed leaves. Low-growing, thornless, very hardy shrubs make an excellent everblooming hedge.

'Nathalie Nypels' ('Mevrouw Nathalie Nypels') (Leenders, 1919) Popular in Great Britain and throughout Europe, 'Nathalie Nypels' produces silky-textured deep-pink to salmon flowers that appear in clusters throughout the season, borne on strong stems on a two-and-one-half-foot shrub amid dark green foliage.

'Orange Triumph' (Kordes, 1937) In spite of its name, the two-inch, semidouble flowers are medium red, blooming in large clusters with long stems starting late in the season. Cupped blooms have little fragrance but last well when cut. Vigorous, compact, three-foot plants (will grow taller in warm climates) are moderately thorny, with glossy dark green foliage. Winter hardy (crown-hardy in Zone 5); moderately susceptible to powdery mildew and blackspot.

'Perle d'Or' (Dubreuil, 1884) Also known as 'Yellow Cécile Brunner', another old Polyantha that it resembles; both were very popular as "sweetheart" or

VIEWPOINT
CUT FLOWERS

Cut flowers early in the day and condition them in deep, warm water. Recut stems under water and use a floral preservative. If a floral preservative is not available, add flat lemon-lime soda; the sugar will feed the flowers and the acid will control the bacteria. Diet soda won't work, though.
CLAIR MARTIN
THE HUNTINGTON BOTANICAL GARDEN

Always cut (or recut) stems underwater; this prevents air bubbles in the xylem which can cause bent necks.
NANCY ROSE
MINNESOTA LANDSCAPE ARBORETUM

I try to cut roses as early in the morning as possible, before they have been exposed to higher temperatures. I carry around a container of water and place the cut flowers in the water immediately. I cut them again about an inch or two above the last cut before placing them in their final receptacle; I make this cut to them while it is under water. A few ounces of any lemon-lime soda helps eliminate bacteria.
MIKE RUGGIERO
THE NEW YORK BOTANICAL GARDEN

Use only clean warm water (105-110 F) to hydrate roses; recut prior to using. Use a preservative in the water such as Flora Life. Remove lower foliage and thorns.
NELSON STERNER
OLD WESTBURY GARDENS

Cut stem one-quarter inch each day and add fresh water.
DAVID SATTIZAHN
HERSHEY GARDENS

'Nathalie Nypels' growing with *Verbena bonariensis*.

buttonhole roses. While 'Cécile Brunner' is blush pink on a yellowy/creamy buff ground, 'Perle d'Or' replaces the pink with apricot. Small, starburst-form flowers have button eyes and are very fragrant, borne in clusters throughout the season. Dwarf, branching plants are somewhat tender, with glossy, dark green foliage.

'The Fairy' (Bentall, 1932) A very popular, easy-to-grow rose. Buttonlike medium pink one-inch flowers fade to blush. Although blooms have no fragrance and are tiny, they are borne nonstop in enormous domed clusters from late in the season until after frost. The shiny, pointed, medium green leaves are tiny, abundant, and disease resistant. Hardy plants do well in spite of neglect and less-than-ideal growing conditions; cutting them back heavily in the spring keeps them young and vigorous at The New York Botanical Garden. Bushes grow two to three feet tall and spread up to four feet wide; they make a fine groundcover, container plant, hedge, or border.

'Tip-Top' (Lambert, 1909) Long buds and small flowers are excellent "sweetheart" or boutonniere roses. White flowers are edged with rose and slightly yellow at the base, with sixteen petals, borne singly or in clusters, with little fragrance. Small, compact bush has long, pointed leaves. Rare; not to be confused with the Floribunda 'Tip-top'.

'NATHALIE NYPELS' Polyantha. Dwarf, spreading shrub. Semidouble rose-pink flowers, two to three inches across. Very fragrant. Dull green foliage.

'MRS. R.M. FINCH' Polyantha. Spreading shrub two to three feet tall. Semidouble cupped medium pink flowers, two to two-and-one-half inches across. Abundant medium green foliage.

'THE FAIRY' Polyantha. Bushes grow two to three feet tall and spread up to four feet wide. Buttonlike medium pink one-inch flowers fade to blush; borne nonstop in enormous domed clusters from late in the season until after frost. No fragrance. Shiny, tiny, pointed, medium green leaves.

'YESTERDAY' Polyantha. Low bushy growth. Semidouble one-and-one-half-inch lilac-pink flowers in trusses. Slight fragrance. Small glossy leaves.

MINIATURE ROSES

Miniature Roses range in size from just one-half inch to over one inch. In many cultivars, everything about them is miniaturized, from bushes, to leaves, to classically formed blossoms.

The Miniature Rose class originated with 'Roulettii', a dwarf rose found growing in pots on window ledges in a Swiss village in 1916. Most cultivated Miniature roses can trace their lineage back to this found rose, but scholars are unsure of where it came from. It is assumed that 'Roulettii' was left over from the by-then passed Victorian craze fro "fairy" or "Lawrenceana" roses. It all started in the early 1800s, when the China Rose (*R. chinensis*) was first brought to Europe. A miniuature form of the China Rose was also shipped, but received less attention. Nevertheless, from this miniature rose, many varieties were developed and then lost when the craze ended. One of these, 'Roulettii' apparently survived to be found on the Swiss window ledge.

Rose breeders saw the potential of the new Miniature Rose, and many hybrids were soon created. The Dutch nurseryman Jan de Vink introduced the crimson 'Peon' in 1935, which became 'Tom Thumb' when U.S. breeder Thomas Pyle brought it home in 1936 and made it the first Miniature Rose patented in the United States. Ralph Moore of California then moved to the forefront of Miniature Rose hybridization, creating a wide array of cultivars, including spreading groundcover minis and mini Moss Roses. Many of Moore's original creations were based on 'Oakington Ruby', a Miniature bred in Oakington, Cambridge, England. Another very old Miniature Rose used by early hybridizers was 'Pompon de Paris', grown since about 1839. Today, rose breeders are extremely active in producing new varieties of Miniatures, which are rapidly moving to the forefront of popularity among rose classes.

Miniature roses range in height from three inches to over two feet. Although Miniatures closely resemble the classes they have been crossed with–Hybrid Teas and Floribundas, for example–all parts of a Miniature– flowers, leaves, stems–are reduced in relation to plant size. The great current popularity of Miniature Roses lies in their versatility. While they do require abundant sunshine like other roses, they are quite hardy, very free-flowering, and can be grown almost anywhere. They are easy to propagate by rooting cuttings because most Miniatures are grown on their own rootstock. They are ideal container and window box plants, making them the choice of city and apartment dwellers, and can make fine borders for larger roses or other shrubs (though some are too small for this purpose). They do well in the rock garden and provide an appropriate scale for the small yard or planting area. They can even be grown indoors, on a sunny south-facing windowsill or under artificial lights. In addition to mini shrub types, there are climbing, cascading, and trailing Miniatures, plus micro-Miniatures and even Miniature tree roses. All of these are available in a wide range of colors.

Since Miniature Roses are grown on their own roots, they have no bud union; locate plant lower than the level they grew in the nursery or in their pots. To prune Miniature Roses, cut back to the height you want; if you want them small, prune them hard. Keep dead wood and twiggy growth cleared out. Tie climbing Miniatures in place as you would for full-size climbers. All

'CHILD'S PLAY' Miniature. Prolific plant. Masses of picotee blooms of white edged in red with semidouble petals, borne singly or in sprays of three; reblooms constantly. Dark green foliage.

'CINDERELLA' Miniature. Bushy plant grows eight to ten inches tall; nearly thornless. Very small micro-mini has long-stemmed, perfectly formed blooms one-half to three-quarter inch wide, opening light blush pink and fading to white; very double; fine repeat bloom. Spicy scent.

'DEBUT' Miniature. Bushy growth, to twelve inches high. Single (sometimes double) blooms are scarlet blending to cream and yellow at base, fading to cherry red with white at the base. Medium dark green semiglossy foliage.

'HOLY TOLEDO' Miniature. Vigorous well-branched bush, fifteen to eighteen inches tall. High-centered double orange blossoms, yellow at base, one-and-one-half to two inches across. Bloom midseason, and repeat well. Slight fragrance. Dark green glossy foliage.

'KO'S YELLOW' Miniature. Bushy growth, to eighteen inches tall. Double flowers with classic form are yellow with red markings, fading to cream. Dark, glossy foliage.

'MAGIC CAROUSEL' Miniature. Very vigorous spreading shrub, usually under one foot tall, but sometimes growing to thirty inches. Fully double cupped or flat white blossoms with red edges, one-and-one-half to two inches across. Medium green semiglossy foliage.

'MOSSY GEM' Miniature. Flat, bright magenta flowers, one inch across, borne on single stems early in season. Mossy calyxes. Lightly scented.

'ORIENTAL SIMPLEX' Miniature. Bushes grow just four inches tall. Simple, five-petaled, fire-orange flowers on long stems with massed yellow stamens. Good repeat flowering.

varieties listed here by name are hardy and disease resistant except as otherwise noted.

'Apricot Mist' (Saville, 1987) Produces double, exhibition-form flowers on long
stems, in varying shades of apricot, one inch across and fragrant. Has fine
repeat bloom. This is a fine Miniature for containers and mass plantings.

'Arizona Sunset' (Jolly, 1985) One-inch cupped flowers have up to twenty yellow
petals edged with orange and red. Fragrance is slight. The plant's low, spreading growth habit makes it good for bedding. Bushes may be slow to flower in
hot weather.

'Beauty Secret' (Moore, 1965) Very fragrant, medium red, double blooms are
one-and-one-half inch wide, with twenty-four to forty petals and excellent
repeat bloom throughout the season. High-centered flowers resemble Hybrid
Teas. Vigorous, bushy, upright plants grow ten to eighteen inches high. Leaves
are medium green and semiglossy. Plants overwinter well indoors and are
winter hardy outdoors as well.

'Child's Play' (Harmon, 1991) This 1993 AARS winner is a prolific plant, covered in picotee blooms of white edged in red with semidouble petals. Flowers
are borne singly or in sprays of three; reblooms constantly. Foliage is dark
green. Disease resistant and hardy.

'Cinderella' (de Vink, 1953) Popular for years, this very small micro-mini
(directly descended from 'Tom Thumb') has long-stemmed, perfectly formed
blooms one-half to three-quarter inch wide. Blooms open light blush pink
and fade to white; they are very double, with forty-five to fifty-five spicy-
scented petals and fine repeat bloom. The bushy, disease-resistant plant grows
eight to ten inches tall and is nearly thornless; it is, however, susceptible to
mildew. Excellent for Miniature Rose beds and hedges.

'Jean Kenneally' (Bennett, 1984) Appropriately named for a California rosarian
and judge, this Miniature produces apricot blooms with perfect Hybrid Tea
form on individual stems and in clusters. The slightly scented flowers are one-
and-one-half inches wide, with twenty-two petals; repeat bloom is excellent.
Bushy plants grow ten to sixteen inches high, with semiglossy foliage.
Susceptible to mildew.

'Lavender Jewel' (Moore, 1978) Lavender-mauve semidouble blooms are high-
centered and one inch across, with up to thirty-eight lightly fragrant petals.
Compact plants with dense, bushy growth and dark green, semiglossy foliage
are ten to fifteen inches high. This is a fine ever-blooming mini for edging or
pot (especially hanging) culture.

'Mossy Gem' (Kelly, 1984) This is a modern Moss Rose in Miniature. Its flat,
bright magenta flowers, one inch across and lightly scented, are one of the
earliest-blooming roses, borne on single stems. The plant's ancestry is evident
from its mossy calyxes.

'New Beginning' (Saville, 1988) The very double, vivid orange blooms have a
yellow reverse. Flowers are one-and-one-half inches across, with forty-five to
fifty petals. Plants grow fourteen to twenty inches tall, with dark green
foliage. AARS, 1989.

To be sure, an ordinary passer-
by would think that my rose
just looked just like you. . . But
in herself alone she is more
important than all the hundreds
of you other roses; because it is
she that I have watered;
because it is she that I have put
under the glass globe; because
it is she that I have sheltered
behind the screen; because it is
for her that I have killed the
caterpillars; because it is she
that I have listened to when she
grumbled, or boasted, or even
sometimes when she said nothing. Because she is my rose.
ANTOINE DE SAINT EXUPERY,
THE LITTLE PRINCE

'PRIDE 'N' JOY' Miniature. Spreading bushy plant. Double medium orange blossoms, with orange and cream on reverse. Moderate fruity fragrance. Medium dark green semiglossy foliage.

'PUPPY LOVE' Miniature. Compact bushy plant, twelve to fifteen inches tall. High-centered, double flowers, orange blended with pink and yellow, one-and-one-half inches across, bloom midseason with good repeat bloom. Medium green semiglossy leaves.

'STARINA' Miniature. Vigorous, bushy plants grow twelve to sixteen inches tall. Classic, high-centered Hybrid Tea-form blooms are vivid orange-red with a touch of yellow at the base, one-and-one-half inches across, produced abundantly throughout the season. Little fragrance. Leaves are dark green and glossy.

'Sweet Chariot' Miniature. Upright plants grow two to-and-one-half feet tall. Deep magenta, double clustered flowers with a quartered shape. Very fragrant. Light green leaves.

'Oriental Simplex' (Williams, 1987) As its name indicates, this rose produces simple, five-petaled flowers, whose fire-orange petals are strikingly set off by massed yellow stamens. Blooms are borne on fairly long stems. Bushes grow four inches tall, with good repeat flowering. A good bedding plant.

'Red Cascade' (Moore, 1976) This is a climbing Miniature that grows fifteen to twenty feet in warm climates; in cooler areas, it grows three to four feet and looks good as a groundcover, in a hanging basket, or cascading down a wall. The double, deep red flowers are slightly fragrant and long-stemmed, one-and-one-half inches across, with thirty-five to forty petals, produced in clusters. A good repeat bloomer, but susceptible to mildew. Slightly fragrant.

'Rise 'n' Shine' (Moore, 1977) An outstanding yellow Miniature, with pure yellow double blooms, borne singly and in clusters, one-and-one-half inches wide, with thirty to thirty-five petals and slight fragrance. Abundantly produced flowers have excellent, high-centered Hybrid Tea form and are popular for exhibition. Bushy, compact plants grow vigorously to ten to fourteen inches and have dark green, glossy leaves.

'Starina' (Meilland, 1965) The world's favorite Miniature Rose, with the classic, high-centered Hybrid Tea bloom form. The long-lasting double flowers are vivid orange-red with a touch of yellow at the base, one-and-one-half inches across, with thirty-five petals. Blooms have little fragrance but are produced abundantly throughout the season. Vigorous, bushy plants grow twelve to sixteen inches tall; leaves are dark green and glossy.

'Sweet Chariot' (Moore, 1984) One of the most fragrant Miniature Roses; produces deep magenta, double, clustered flowers with a quartered shape. Each bloom of forty petals has a subtle stripe down the center of each petal. Upright plants grow two to two-and-one-half feet tall, with light green leaves. A fine container plant that does best in cool rather than hot, dry weather.

'Sweet Fairy' A light pink micro mini with Tea fragrance.

'Beauty Secret'.

CLIMBING ROSES

Climbing Roses are roses with exceptionally long canes that are suitable for growing on or around a support. Climbing Roses don't climb on their own, with tendrils or self-twining canes; the canes have to be trained and secured into place. Climbers have a varied ancestry. Many were developed from *R. wichuraiana* and *R. multiflora,* both hardy species from the Far East, and *R. setigera,* a species native to North America. Some modern Climbers have some tall Bourbon and Noisette ancestry. Many are sports of bush roses, including Hybrid Teas and Floribundas; the flowers of these are similar to the parent but tend to be much larger. Many of these sports share their parent's name–for example, 'Climbing Peace' and 'Climbing Chrysler Imperial'. *R. kordesii* also has contributed its genes to produce Kordesii Climbers, the hardiest Climbing Roses.

Because of the varied backgrounds of Climbers, their growth and flowering characteristics vary as well. They produce relatively stiff canes from the base of the plant and from other, older canes. Most also produce laterals, or side shoots, off the canes, which in turn bear flowers. Some Climbers also produce blooms at the ends of new canes. Most Climbers bear flowers in clusters, sometimes only once at the beginning of the season, sometimes throughout the season. Sports of Hybrid Teas, Grandifloras, and Floribundas are less hardy than other Climbers. Size varies widely, from small eight- to twelve-foot types (well-suited for use as pillar roses) to those that grow twenty feet or more.

Climbers can be trained along fences and across and up walls; they can be wrapped spirally around posts and archways. Training the canes parallel to the

Above and right: 'New Dawn'.

'AMERICA' Large-flowered Climber. Plants grow slowly, to about six to eight feet high. Pointed coral buds open to full, salmon-pink flowers, three to four inches across. Strong spicy scent. Bloom is recurrent.

'BLAZE' Large-flowered Climber. Grows ten to fifteen feet. Bright red, semidouble, cupped flowers, two to three inches across, borne in clusters; covered in bloom all season. Slightly fragrant. Dark green, leathery leaves.

'CHARLOTTE ARMSTRONG' Large-flowered Climber. Vigorous, fast-growing climber, to fifteen feet. Large, cerise red flowers, three inches across. Abundant medium green foliage.

'NEW DAWN' Large-flowered Climber. Vigorous, upright plants grow ten feet and more in a season. Blush-colored flowers, three to three-and-one-half inches across, borne singly or in clusters from midseason up until frost. Tea-scented. Glossy foliage turns yellow in fall.

'RED FOUNTAIN' Large-flowered Climber. Vigorous plant, grows eight to ten feet. Clusters of blood red flowers. Thick, dark green leaves.

'ROYAL SUNSET' Large-flowered Climber. Vigorous plant, grows ten to fifteen feet. Apricot blend flowers, pink at base, bloom singly all season. Slight fragrance. Abundant dark green foliage.

'DEBUTANTE' Rambler. Vigorous habit, spreading to twelve feet by ten feet. Clusters of small, fully double rose-pink flowers. Fragrant. Dark green glossy foliage.

'TAUSENDSCHOEN' Multiflora Rambler. Strong, fast-growing plant to ten feet. Clusters of large double flowers, pink with white at center. Abundant medium green foliage.

ground encourages the production of laterals and, thus, more profuse bloom. Don't start pruning Climbers until after their second or third year of growth in the garden. Prune single bloomers after flowering has finished; prune everbloomers during winter dormancy. Cut canes back by one-third, and trim flowering laterals by two-thirds (see page 90 for alternate views on pruning).

'Altissimo' (Delbard-Chabert, 1966) Velvety blood red four- to five-inch flowers are single, with seven petals, golden stamens, and a slight clove fragrance, borne in small clusters intermittently throughout the season, even in partial shade. Vigorous plants have glossy dark green, disease-resistant foliage. As a Climber, 'Altissimo' can grow ten to twelve feet in a season when mature, or it can be pruned as a tall shrub. Its large flowers, which are good for cutting, are borne only on the ends of canes unless the canes are trained horizontally. Blooms on old wood.

'America' (Warriner, 1976) Pointed coral buds open to full, salmon-pink flowers, three to four inches across, with thirty-five to forty-five petals, fine Hybrid Tea form, and strong spicy scent. Bloom is recurrent. Plants grow slowly, to about six to eight feet high; they are not winter hardy in Zone 5 and need protection in Zone 6. Susceptible to blackspot. One of the few AARS Climbers, this is a good pillar rose. AARS, 1976.

'Blaze' (Kallay, 1932) Bright red, semidouble, cupped flowers are two to three inches across, with twenty to twenty-five petals, slightly fragrant, borne in clusters. This is one of the most popular Climbers, as it is covered in bloom all season and plants are hardy, vigorous, fast-growing, easy to train, and winter hardy in Zone 6. Grows ten to fifteen feet, with dark green, leathery leaves.

'Golden Arctic' (Brownell, 1954) Very double, starlike, deep yellow flowers, three to four inches across with over forty petals, are extremely fragrant. Blooms are borne in clusters on single long stems. Vigorous plants have light green foliage and strong red prickles; they bloom constantly.

'Joseph's Coat' (Armstrong and Swimm, 1964) As its name implies, this is a multicolored large-flowering Climber. Yellow and red buds open to yellow blooms that gradually turn orange and then red as they mature. The clusters of three- to four-inch, double, twenty-five-petaled flowers are produced prolifically all season long, so plants are always covered with blooms of many shades. Plants grow eight to ten feet, with glossy dark green foliage; they can be trained as Climbers or around pillars, or they can be pruned as free-standing shrubs. Susceptible to blackspot, but tender in cold climates.

'Lawrence Johnston' (Ducher, 1923) Also called 'Hidcote Yellow', after Hidcote, the influential garden established by Mr. Johnston, son of an expatriate American family, in Gloustershire, England. This is a hybrid of *R. foetida persiana*. Large, semidouble, bright yellow flowers are up to five inches across and fragrant. Blooms appear very early in the season, continuing through the spring, and may repeat. Very vigorous plants can grow twenty to thirty feet; they are hardy, but canes may die back in very cold climates. Very susceptible to blackspot, especially in the South.

'New Dawn' (Dreer, 1930) An everblooming sport of 'Dr. W. Van Fleet' and the

Many Climbing Roses are sports of Hybrid Teas, Polyanthas, and other classes. *Above:* 'Climbing Cecile Brunner', a sport of the popular Polyantha.

THE LANUAGE OF ROSES

The colors, shapes, and classes of roses have become symbols of virtues, emotions, and ideas, forming a language of their own.

Burgundy Rose: unconscious beauty

Cabbage Rose: ambassador of love

Carolina Rose: love is dangerous

Centifolia Rose: pride

China Rose: beauty always new

Damask Rose: brilliant complexion

Dog Rose: Pleasure and pain

Moss Rose: Superior merit

Moss Rosebud: Confession of love

Multiflora Rose: Grace

Musk Rose: Capricious beauty

Musk Rose Cluster: Charming

Red-leaved Cluster: Beauty and prosperity

Red Rose: Love

Red Rose, deep: Bashful shame

Red Rose, full: Beauty

Red Rosebud: Purity & loveliness

Single Rose: Simplicity

Thornless Rose: Early attachment

White Rose:I am worthy of you

White Rose, withered: Transient impression

White Rosebud: Secrecy; youthful innocence & purity

White and Red Rose together: Unity

Yellow Rose: Jealousy or infidelity

---

first plant to be patented, 'New Dawn' is the parent of many other roses. Like its parent, 'New Dawn' has blush-colored, Tea-scented flowers, three to three-and-one-half inches across, that are borne singly or in clusters from midseason up until frost and are good for cutting. Vigorous, upright plants grow ten feet and more in a season, with strong prickles and glossy, disease-resistant foliage that turns yellow in the fall. Winter hardy to Zone 6, plants can be grown as climbers or shrubs.

'Piñata' (Suzuki, 1978) Clusters of egg-shaped yellow and red buds open to three- to four-inch multicolored blooms, yellow washed with orange-red, with twenty-eight petals. Plants are slow-growing, reaching only a medium height, with glossy green leaves and good repeat bloom; they train well on a pillar, or can stand alone as a shrub. Best bloom is in cool weather. Plants prefer partial shade and are susceptible to frost dieback.

'White Cap' (Brownell, 1954) Nearly pure white, cupped and quartered flowers have fifty to sixty petals, borne singly or in clusters, with old garden rose fragrance. Carefree, hardy plants grow ten feet tall, with dark green foliage and many hooked prickles. Blooms nonstop all season.

RAMBLERS

Ramblers are similar to Climbers in that they produce long, pliable canes suitable for growing on supports. They were developed mostly from *R. wichuraiana* and *R. multiflora.* They bloom only once, at the season's beginning or midpoint, producing clusters of flowers in bright shades of pink, red, and yellow, as well as white. Their foliage and flowers are smaller than those of the Climbers, and their canes are more flexible, growing from ten to twenty feet in a year. Laterals that grow from these canes produce flowers the following season.

The pliability of Rambler canes makes them easy to wrap around pillars and archways, and along fences. In an informal setting with plenty of room, they can also be left to sprawl, as a groundcover. As with the Climbers, Ramblers whose canes are trained parallel to the ground will produce the most flowers. Because Ramblers are quite susceptible to diseases, especially mildew, they are not good choices for training along a wall, where air circulation will be impaired. Because Ramblers bloom on second-year wood, cut most old canes back to the ground right after flowering to encourage production of new growth for next year's blooms and to allow for good air circulation. While most Ramblers produce canes from the base of the plant, some grow new canes from old wood; for these types, prune back only a moderate amount of the old growth.

'Chevy Chase' (Hansen, 1939) Massive erect clusters of one- to two-inch deep red fragrant flowers are produced once per season in clusters of ten to twenty blooms. Foliage is grayish green. Plants are extremely vigorous, hardy to -5° F., with many strong, straight prickles. Grows up to fifteen feet in a season. Unlike other Ramblers, not susceptible to mildew.

'Dorothy Perkins' (Jackson & Perkins, 1901) A very popular *Wichuraiana* hybrid

Rambler named for the granddaughter of Jackson & Perkins' founder. Fragrant, double, rose-pink flowers are one to two inches across, almost always borne only once per season. Vigorous plants grow ten to twenty feet high, with dark, glossy foliage and many prickles. Highly susceptible to mildew and insects. Has produced many important sports.

'Excelsa' (Walsh, 1909) Also called the 'Red Dorothy Perkins'. Large, hanging clusters of deep pink (fading lighter), double, cupped two-inch blooms with little fragrance are produced once later in the season. Plants are very vigorous and hardy to -5° F., growing twelve to eighteen feet tall, with glossy green foliage and many thorns. Susceptible to disease, especially mildew, and mites. Often confused with the 'Seven Sisters Rose'.

'Ivy Alice' (Letts, 1927) Soft pink and salmon flowers become tinged with carmine as they fade. Grows like 'Excelsa', with light green foliage.

Below: 'Chevy Chase' and 'New Dawn'.

plant selector

HYBRID MUSK ROSES

Hybrid Musk Roses were developed in England early in the twentieth century by the Reverend Joseph Pemberton, who retired from his priesthood in the Church of England to devote the rest of his life to breeding roses. In spite of their name, Hybrid Musks are not closely related to *R. moschata*, the Musk Rose; instead, they were a mix of Teas, Hybrid Teas, and Chinas, plus the early Ramblers 'Trier' and 'Aglaia'. Hybrid Musks are Shrub Roses that resemble large-growing Floribundas; they can be grown as freestanding bushes or hedges, or trained as Climbers. Plants are tender as Tea roses. They are reported to be hardy at The New York Botanical Garden without protection; at Minnesota Landscape Arboretum, they usually die back to the snowline or the ground, but they put out vigorous new growth and bloom on new wood. They are disease resistant and can tolerate some shade and poor soil. Blooms are generally fragrant and single, and they repeat well, in large clusters, when plants are grown in full sun. Some Hybrid Musks set good hips after blooms are spent. Pruning consists simply of removing old wood; for climbing Hybrid Musks, prune back laterals also after the first burst of growth. Deadheading promotes good production of new flowers.

'Ballerina' (Bentall, 1937) This Hybrid Musk derives its name from the dense, arching and then draping clusters of bloom, which resemble a ballerina's skirt. White-centered single pink flowers are two inches across, with a slightly musky sweet-pea fragrance, appearing midseason with good repeat. Arching plants grow three to four feet high and wide, with few thorns and light green, semiglossy foliage. Disease resistant and winter hardy.

'Belinda' (Bentall, 1936) Large clusters of small, semidouble, medium pink flowers, two inches across, with twelve to fifteen petals, appear in midseason with good repeat. Upright, vigorous plants grow four to six feet high and wide, with glossy disease-resistant foliage and few thorns. Dense, bushy plants do well in partial shade and make a good hedge.

'Bloomfield Dainty' (Thomas, 1924) Clear yellow single flowers, two to three inches across, open from orange-coral buds and fade to creamy pink-tinged white. Both fragrance and repeat bloom are light. Plants grow five to seven feet, with scattered and large hooked prickles; foliage is not very disease resistant. This is a good Climber or pillar rose, but canes stiffen as they age, so they need to be trained while young and still flexible.

'Clytemnestra' (Pemberton, 1915) One of the Reverend Pemberton's early Hybrid Musk creations. Small, fragrant apricot-blend flowers have eighteen to twenty ruffled petals and are borne in clusters of ten to twelve at the ends of canes. Disease-resistant plants produce masses of bloom early in the season, with intermittent repeat bloom until frost. Procumbent long-caned plants can be trained on pillars.

'Daybreak' (Pemberton, 1918) Single lemon yellow flowers are produced amid foliage that is copper when young and turns dark green later. Blooms recur on the four-foot bush.

'Felicia' (Pemberton, 1928) A later creation of the Reverend Pemberton.

'BALLERINA' Hybrid Musk. Arching plants three to four feet high and wide. Dense, arching and then draping clusters of white-centered single pink flowers, two inches across, appear midseason with good repeat. Slightly musky sweet-pea fragrance. Few thorns. Light green, semiglossy foliage.

'BELINDA' Hybrid Musk. Upright, vigorous plants grow four to six feet high and wide. Large clusters of small, semidouble, medium pink flowers, two inches across, appear in midseason with good repeat. Glossy foliage, few thorns.

'BLOOMFIELD DAINTY' Hybrid Musk. Plants five to seven feet tall. Clear yellow single flowers, two to three inches across, open from orange-coral buds and fade to creamy pink-tinged white. Light fragrance.

'DAYBREAK' Hybrid Musk. Four-foot bush. Recurrent, single, lemon yellow flowers. Foliage is copper, turning dark green with age.

Above: 'Bonica'. *Below:* 'Carefree Wonder'.

Semidouble, cupped and ruffled flowers are fragrant and have blush pink outer petals, with deeper pink inner petals and a touch of yellow at the base of petals. Vigorous plants have dark foliage and few prickles and are good for training around a pillar.

'Prosperity' (Pemberton, 1919) A wonderfully vigorous Shrub-Floribunda, probably hardy to -5° F., which is unusual for a white.

SHRUB ROSES

This is a catch-all category of roses, encompassing shrub-type roses that don't fit neatly into any other class. Because Shrub Roses vary in parentage, generalizations about them do not apply to all members, but many of them are robust, spreading plants that require little maintenance and fit easily into the landscape like other ornamental shrubs. Some are constantly in bloom. Flowers range from single to semidouble to fully double, Hybrid Tea-type blooms and are often followed by hips. Some Shrub Roses are low-growing and can be used as groundcovers; others can be trained as short climbers; others are bushy mounds, widespreading or upright. Shrub Roses can be planted as single specimens or in groups to form borders, hedges, and screens. Pruning is minimal, consisting simply of removing dead and crowded wood; light thinning out and cutting back of older wood will keep hedges and specimen plants in shape and within bounds.

Hybrid Species Roses–including hybrid Eglantines, Spinosissimas, and

'BELINDA'S DREAM' Shrub Rose. Vigorous, compact shrub. High-centered, shell pink flowers, four inches across, borne on short stems throughout the season. Very fragrant.

'BONICA' Shrub Rose. Dense, arching three foot by four foot plants. Full, one- to two-inch, soft pink flowers with lighter pink outside petals are borne in large clusters; the shrub blooms freely from early in the season until after frost. Very small, dark green foliage.

'GOLDEN WINGS' Shrub Rose. Vigorous shrub to five feet tall and four feet wide. Clear yellow, single flowers with visible dark stamens, to three inches across, borne singly and in clusters from midseason through fall. Slightly fragrant. Pointed medium green leaves.

'SEA FOAM' Shrub Rose. Vigorous, trailing plants with three- to six-foot canes. Pink buds open to two-inch double, light pink flowers that fade to creamy white, borne abundantly all season in clusters. Lightly fragrant. Small, glossy, leathery leaves.

'SPARRIESHOOP' Shrub Rose. Vigorous, upright plants grow five to ten feet tall. Single, four-inch flowers have five wavy petals, light pink fading to a white or light pink center with golden stamens. Fragrant. Medium green, leathery leaves.

'WILD AT HEART' Shrub Rose. Vigorous, upright plants grow five to ten feet tall. Semidouble four-inch flowers have dark pink, wavy petals with golden stamens. Fragrant. Light green semiglossy leathery leaves.

'ILLUSION' Shrub Rose. Vigorous upright shrub to five feet tall. Double medium red flowers, to two-and-one-half inches across, are borne singly and in clusters throughout the season. Slightly fragrant. Small light green leaves.

'WHITE MEIDILAND' Shrub Rose. Bushy, spreading plant, to two feet tall and four feet wide. Clusters of pure white semidouble flowers. Slightly fragrant. Abundant small semiglossy foliage.

Rugosas—can also be considered Shrub Roses; they are described in the earlier section on Species Roses.

'All That Jazz' (Devor, 1991) A new variety that has gained a lot of attention, this vigorous shrub produces sprays of three to five coral-salmon blend cupped blossoms with a Damask fragrance.

'Autumn Bouquet' (Jacobus, 1948) An older variety, now rare. Very tight buds open to wonderfully fragrant three-inch carmine pink flowers with tight, pointed centers; blooms recur. Upright, vigorous bushes have tough, leathery leaves and fierce prickles.

'Belinda's Dream' (Basye, 1988) Very fragrant, high-centered, exhibition-type shell pink flowers, four inches across, are borne on short stems throughout the season. Vigorous, compact, disease-resistant shrub closely resembles a Hybrid Perpetual.

'Bonica' (Meilland, 1981) Also known as 'Bonica '82' and 'Meidomonac' (its official name), this was the first Shrub Rose awarded an AARS (in 1987). The shrub blooms freely from early in the season until after frost. Full, one- to two-inch, soft pink flowers with lighter pink outside petals are borne in large clusters on dense, arching three foot by four foot plants with very small, dark green foliage. Bears attractive red hips, but is often defoliated by blackspot by mid September at Boerner Botanical Gardens. At Minnesota Landscape Arboretum, it is fairly disease-free but lacks vigor and has much winter dieback.

'Carefree Wonder' (Meilland, 1989) True to its name, this rose is disease resistant, very winter hardy (to -15° F.), and grows vigorously but compactly. Semidouble four-inch blooms are borne prolifically in clusters throughout the summer. Flowers are vivid pink with a creamy white reverse, borne against glossy medium green foliage. Orange hips follow in fall and winter. An exceptional plant, singled out for praise by many consultants on this volume for its beauty and easy maintenance. AARS, 1981.

'Henry Kelsey' (Department of Agriculture, Canada, 1984) Three-inch red blooms with sweet fragrance repeat all season, especially if spent blooms are removed. This is the only red everblooming climbing rose that is hardy to -20° F.

'Sea Foam' (Schwartz, 1964) Pink buds open to two-inch double, lightly fragrant light pink flowers that fade to creamy white, borne abundantly all season in clusters that cover the bush like sea foam. Carefree, vigorous plants are trailing, with large, hooked prickles and small, glossy, leathery leaves. The three- to six-foot canes make an excellent groundcover and can also be trained to climb. Extremely hardy, to -5° F.

'Sparrieshoop' (Kordes, 1953) Single, fragrant four-inch flowers have five wavy petals, light pink fading to a white or light pink center with golden stamens. Clusters rebloom after a long delay. Vigorous, upright plants grow five to ten feet tall, with medium green, leathery leaves, and are winter hardy to 0° F.

'White Meidiland' (Meilland, 1986) One of a series of Shrub Roses introduced by France's famed Meilland Nursery; others in the series include red and white

Many roses that were formerly thought of as Species Roses have now been reclassified as Shrub Roses, like 'Micrugosa' (above).

'CAREFREE BEAUTY' Shrub Rose. Plants grow four to six feet tall. Long buds open to semidouble, rich light pink blooms, four-and-one-half inches across, borne in small clusters all season.

'COUNTRY DANCER' Shrub Rose. Spreading plants, two-and-one-half to three feet tall. Well-formed, cup-shaped pink flowers.

'HAWKEYE BELLE' Shrub Rose. Well-formed pale pink buds open to small white blooms, four to four-and-one-half inches across. Very fragrant. Leathery dark foliage.

'PRAIRIE PRINCESS' Shrub Rose. Vigorous, tall bushes. Ruffled clear pink flowers open from long, pointed buds.

varieties. The plants are spreading and require little maintenance and are often used in large plantings, such as city parks.

KORDESII ROSES Kordesii Shrubs are exceptionally hardy and easy-to-grow varieties developed from the new Species Rose introduced by the German hybridizer Kordes, *R. kordesii* in 1952. Cultivars include **'Champlain',** which looks like a red Floribunda and is hardy to -5° F., but susceptible to blackspot and mildew, and **'Illusion',** a medium red upright grower that can be used as a tree rose in Zone 6 and above. **'William Baffin'** (Svedja, Canada, 1983) Deep pink blooms in clusters repeatedly all season. The only repeat-blooming disease-resistant climbing rose hardy to -20° F.

DR. BUCK ROSES

Professor Griffith Buck of Iowa State University has hybridized a series of Shrub Roses that are extremely hardy and carefree, including those listed below.

'Carefree Beauty' (Buck, 1977) Long buds open to semidouble, rich light pink blooms, four-and-one-half inches across, with fifteen to twenty lightly fragrant petals. Small clusters of blooms are borne all season. Disease-resistant plants (blackspot reported at The New York Botanical Garden) grow four to six feet and make an excellent hedge. Orange hips appear in the fall and last over the winter, but for effective repeat bloom it is best to remove spent bloom.

'Country Dancer' (Buck, 1975) Well-formed, cup-shaped pink flowers are borne on medium-sized disease-resistant spreading plants, two-and-one-half to three feet tall.

'Hawkeye Belle' (Buck, 1975) Well-formed pale pink buds open to small white blooms, four to four-and-one-half inches across. Very fragrant. Disease resistant, leathery dark foliage. Hardy.

'Carefree Beauty'.

plant selector

'Prairie Flower' (Buck, 1975) Single, cardinal red flowers are lightly fragrant, two to three inches across, with seven petals and white centers. Blooms are borne singly or in clusters all season on four-foot plants with leathery, dark green foliage.

'Prairie Princess' (Buck, 1972) Ruffled clear pink flowers open from long, pointed buds, borne on vigorous, tall bushes. Somewhat susceptible to blackspot. Hardy to -20° F. Stops blooming in late summer.

'Summer Wind' (Buck, 1975) Large, salmon pink flowers have eight to ten petals, with a slight white stripe down interior petals, and exposed yellow stamens. Sweetly scented blooms are borne all season on vigorous, disease-resistant four-foot by five-foot plants.

ENGLISH ROSES

English breeder David Austin created this type of rose, often by crossing spring-flowering Old Garden Roses with modern types such as the Floribundas and Hybrid Teas. His object has been to create repeat-flowering disease-resistant shrubs, with old-time rose fragrance and double bloom plus the modern range of colors. English Roses are crown hardy to Zone 5, and may survive to Zone 4 with extra protection; some, like 'Symphony', are winter tender and subject to blackspot. All are given winter protection at Minnesota Landscape Arboretum.

'Abraham Darby' (Austin, 1990; introduced into commerce in 1985) Named for a prominent figure in the Industrial Revolution. Large, cupped pale apricot-yellow flowers bloom singly or in clusters from early spring on through the

Among the charms of David Austin's English Roses are abundant bloom and very double flowers. *Above:* 'Graham Thomas'. *Right:* 'Abraham Darby'.

'ABRAHAM DARBY' Shrub Rose. Vigorous, bushy shrubs grow five feet tall. Large, cupped pale apricot-yellow flowers bloom singly or in clusters from early spring on through the season. Spicy fragrance. Large, glossy foliage.

'EVELYN' Shrub Rose. Compact shrubby plant to four feet tall. Rich yellow cupped double flowers, three to four inches across, borne in clusters. Strong fragrance.

'GERTRUDE JEKYLL' Shrub Rose. Vigorous, upright plants grow four to five feet tall. Tightly rolled buds open to large, rich pink flowers, four inches across, with petals spiraling from the center; dependably repeats bloom if spent blooms are removed. Strongly scented.

'GRAHAM THOMAS' Shrub Rose. Vigorous, bushy plants grow four to eight feet tall. Apricot buds open to pure yellow flowers, medium-sized double blooms borne in sprays; good repeat. Strong Tea fragrance. Shiny light green foliage.

'HERITAGE' Shrub Rose. Robust plants, four feet wide and tall. Clear shell pink double flowers are cupped, three to four inches across and borne profusely in sprays, repeating regularly through the season. Strong spicy, lemony fragrance. Dark green leathery foliage.

'MARY ROSE' Shrub Rose. Compact, vigorous shrubs grow four feet tall and wide. Rich rose-pink, double flowers, three or more inches across, bloom in small clusters all season. Strong Damask fragrance. Foliage is dull green.

'OTHELLO' Shrub Rose. Vigorous, thorny plants grow five to six feet tall and wide. Cupped, dark crimson, full-petaled, four-inch flowers produced freely through the season. Strong fragrance. Dusky dark green foliage.

'SIR WALTER RALEIGH' Shrub Rose. Bushy plant, to four feet tall and four feet wide. Large, peonylike flowers, in clear rich pink with golden stamens. Very fragrant. Large, medium green foliage.

season, with a spicy fragrance. Vigorous, bushy shrubs grow five feet tall and wide, with large, glossy, and disease-resistant foliage.

'Constance Spry' (Austin, 1961) The first English Rose introduced to the market. Double, myrrh-scented, light pink flowers are four to five inches across, borne in clusters on often droopy stems. Once-blooming. Arching, disease-resistant plants grow six to eight feet tall and are best grown as climbers to fifteen feet. Not hardy in Zone 6.

'Evelyn' (Austin, 1993) 'Evelyn' is one of Austin's most recent introductions, a cross between 'Graham Thomas' and 'Tamora', it also has the Hybrid Rugosa 'Conrad Ferdinand Meyer', the Floribunda 'Iceberg', and the Noisette 'Gloire de Dijon' in its ancestry. The compact shrubby plant has cupped flowers in an unusually deep and rich yellow and strong fragrance.

'Gertrude Jekyll' (Austin, 1986) Named after the renowned English horticulturist. Tightly rolled buds open to large, strongly scented, rich pink flowers, four inches across, with petals spiraling from the center; dependably repeats bloom if spent blooms are removed. Vigorous, upright plants grow four to five feet tall. Hardy to Zone 6.

'Graham Thomas' (Austin, 1983) Named after a famous English rosarian who played an important role in reestablishing interest in old Shrub Roses. Apricot buds open to rich, pure yellow flowers with a strong Tea rose fragrance. Medium-sized double blooms are borne in sprays and repeat well. Vigorous, bushy plants grow four to eight feet tall, with shiny light green foliage, and are best treated as pillar roses because of the long canes produced after the first bloom. Disease resistant and hardy to -5° F.

'Heritage' (Austin, 1984) David Austin considers this the best English Rose to date. Clear shell pink double flowers are cupped, three to four inches across, and have a strong spicy fragrance with overtones of lemon. Flowers are borne profusely in sprays, repeating regularly through the season, on robust plants that grow four feet wide and tall. Dark green leathery disease-resistant foliage, hardy to -10° F., but leaves tend to burn in southern California heat and sun.

'Mary Rose' (Austin, 1983) Named after Henry VIII's flagship. Rich rose-pink, many-petaled, double flowers are three or more inches across, with the Damask Rose's strong fragrance and appearance. Blooms in small clusters from very early to very late in the season. Compact, vigorous shrubs grow four feet tall and wide and can be pruned hard. Foliage is dull green. Disease resistant and hardy to -10° F.

'Othello' (Austin, 1990) Cupped, full-petaled, four-inch flowers are rich, dark crimson, aging to soft shades of purple and mauve. The strongly scented blooms are produced freely through the season on vigorous, thorny plants that grow five to six feet tall and wide. Foliage is dusky dark green; plants are very disease resistant.

'Sir Walter Raleigh' (Austin, introduced to commerce in 1985) Large, peonylike flowers, in clear rich pink with golden stamens. Very fragrant. Large, medium green foliage.

TREE ROSES

Tree roses are not a class or variety created by hybridizers. Instead, they are plants created by grafting together several different roses, usually three. The rose variety desired for flowers and foliage is grafted onto a straight stem, which in turn is grafted onto a sturdy rootstock, producing a rose "tree." Tree roses can be very upright and formal-appearing; others are somewhat more spreading and rounded; yet others, with pliable canes as the top flowering portion, produce weeping "trees." Tree roses are not very hardy, even if the various individual parts are, because the upper bud union is easily damaged by cold temperatures. Trunks should be supported by stakes; stakes should be as inobtrusive as possible, since they can detract from the beauty of the plant. Tree roses can be treated like Climbers by digging and laying them down in late fall and by covering them with soil. At The New York Botanical Garden, tree roses are dug and potted in the fall and stored in a cool storage area (about 37° F.) until spring. *Above:* 'First Prize' as a tree rose.

Once you've decided to incorporate some roses into your landscape, what's your next step? It is *not* rushing off to your local nursery, buying the specimens that appeal to you visually, and then planting them willy-nilly where you think they might look good. You'll be preparing the soil thoroughly for your roses, so you're not going to be happy moving them if you carelessly put them in an inappropriate spot. And you definitely aren't going to want to try to move the large, sprawling Species Roses, or Climbers and Ramblers. Before choosing and planting roses, you need to work out a plan, a garden design that will provide optimal growing conditions for your roses and optimal enjoyment for you and your family. Many factors come into play: amount of sunlight, type of garden, space available, type of rose, color, the mix of plants, structural elements, edgings, and shapes, sizes, and textures, plus personal preference. You also want to consider the amount of time you are willing to spend maintaining your rose garden. Most modern roses require much more work, in the form of winter protection, pruning, and disease and pest control, than most of the Old Garden and Species Roses or Dr. Buck and David Austin Shrub Roses.

Choosing the Site Survey possible sites for growing roses in your outdoor areas. Of primary importance is sunlight—most roses require at least six hours of sun a day. Remember that as nearby trees grow, their shade will encroach on areas that are sunny today. Also, you must keep roses away from trees and large

Roses planted outside a window can be enjoyed from inside as well as out.

shrubs that would compete with the rose roots for water and soil nutrients.

Be sure to consider access to water when siting your garden; roses need ample water for maximum growth and flower production. If you are choosing a very sloping site, you'll have to level it out, terrace it, or break it up into smaller individual areas so the abundant water your roses will require and the enriched soil you've created won't wash away with every rainstorm.

While your roses need good air circulation, they don't want to be in an exposed, windy site, which would both buffet them and dry them out; nor do they want to be in a low area that will collect cold air and become a frost pocket. Finally, you'll greatly increase the enjoyment you derive from your rose garden if you can see it when you look out the windows of your home.

Planning on Paper Now you're ready to draw up a garden plan on paper. First, figure the exact dimensions of your site (or sites) with a tape measure, and draw these to scale on graph paper; a scale of one-quarter inch to one foot is useful. Next, fill in the existing structures–a large tree, a pool, building, or deck, a fence along which to train Climbers, a bench that will serve as a focal point, walkways, paths. If it's a large garden, allow for working and access paths–four feet for the former, two feet for the latter. Or design beds (garden

Above: Sunlight is an important factor in choosing a site for your roses. Observe possible sites throughout the day to make sure that they are not shaded by nearby trees.

islands) and borders (gardens alongside a wall, fence, walkway) that you can work without having to walk into them: six feet wide for a free-standing bed that you can reach from either side, three feet wide for a border you can approach from only one side.

Consider structural edgings for your garden beds, especially formal beds. They give a clean, more defined look and keep some invasive plants out but your improved garden soil in. For wood edgings, use treated lumber or naturally rot-resistant wood like cedar or redwood; bricks or attractively arranged rocks are other possibilities. Once you know how much space will be taken up by pathways, edgings, and structures, you can figure out just how much space you have for your roses and other plants, if any.

Garden Types The next step, before choosing which roses to grow, is to consider what kind of garden you want to create. Roses are often grown in formal beds and borders, which have a linear or geometrical layout–rectangular, circular, square, or curved–and commonly include structured walkways and architectural elements as well. Formal gardens complement houses with a formal, classical architectural style especially well. Modern roses are best for formal gardens, as they have a tidy, upright growth habit, and similar varieties will grow to similar heights in uniform rows, which is the effect you want for a formal bed. Cutting gardens, devoted to providing cut flowers, are usually

Below: **The Peggy Rockefeller Rose Garden at The New York Botanical Garden is a formal garden with carefully laid out, symmetrical beds.**

formal beds filled with rows of Hybrid Teas and Grandifloras; Floribundas are a possibility for this purpose, too.

Perhaps the structured look and meticulous grooming required of a formal rose garden don't appeal to you. In this case, you might prefer a cottage, or informal, garden—still carefully planned, but with a free-flowing, relaxed look, especially well suited for the country farmhouse or cottage-style home. Informal beds and borders will have curved shapes. The carefree growth habits and interesting foliage of Old Garden and Species Roses are perfect for cottage gardens. In northern areas, the pre-China Old Garden Roses, Species Roses, and English Roses are especially good, while in the South, Teas and Chinas work well. Climbers and Ramblers or, in mild climates, Noisettes and Hybrid Musks can form a background. If you have an older home, you might want to plant the roses that were popular in the era when your house was built—Hybrid Perpetuals, the so-called Victorian rose, for example, for a Victorian-style house that dates from 1870. David Austin's Shrub Roses also have an old-world look that evokes the Victorian era.

If you're especially fond of fragrance in the garden, and the heavenly scent of roses in particular, you might want to design a garden full of the most fragrant roses, or plant these types of roses where their scent will waft into open windows or suffuse your patio, deck, or poolside area. In general, the Old

Below: This informal garden mixes roses with annuals and perennials.

Above: 'Old Red Moss' hips. In late summer and autumn, foliage and hips provide interest in the rose garden.
Right: Deep pink, striped 'Rosa Mundi' contrasts with lighter pink 'Albertine', a Rambler.

Garden (especially the Damasks), Species, and English Roses are the most fragrant, although some specific varieties of modern roses, especially the dark red ones, are noted for their scent. *R. eglanteria,* the sweetbrier rose, has fragrant, apple-scented leaves.

You can enhance your rock garden with low-growing summer-blooming roses such as Miniatures and small Polyanthas. Roses create a lovely background in an herb garden, too, where they traditionally belong. A terrace garden—in your backyard or on your apartment or condo balcony—of container-grown roses is also possible; best for this purpose are the low-growing

Floribundas, Polyanthas, and Miniatures, perhaps with a tree rose or two thrown in. (See Chapter 5 for information on growing roses in containers.)

Wild gardens, too, can have their roses, along the edges of fields and woodlands, or along otherwise empty hillsides; Species, Climbers, Ramblers, and Shrub Roses are best for this, and many Species and Shrub Roses add autumn and winter interest with their colorful foliage and hips. If you're looking for a groundcover, low-growing Floribundas, Miniatures, and Ramblers left supine serve well for this purpose. Some Climbers, too, can be turned into groundcovers by pegging (attaching their canes to the ground). Rugosas are perfect for seaside gardens; many Old Garden Roses do well in salty air also.

Color In the rose world, every color is represented except blue and black (green is provided by the foliage, and by the startling 'Green Rose', also known as *R. chinensis viridiflora*). So placement and distribution of color is an important consideration in the design of your rose garden. Warm colors—reds, yellows, oranges, and golds—create a cheerful, vibrant, and, logically, warm atmosphere. They also catch the eye, so they make the far end of the garden seem nearer. These same qualities make warm colors not the best choice for small or hot-climate gardens. Cool colors—blues, purples, violets, mauves—along with whites and pastels have a calming, refreshing feel. They can cool off an overly sun-drenched area, create an aura of peace, and make a small garden seem to expand. Light colors—pastels and whites—stand out at twilight and night.

Above: The vivid colors of modern roses can be difficult to incorporate into a garden. *Below:* A mass planting of 'Cerise Bouquet', with lavender.

Above: A symmetrical conifer contrasts with Species Roses in shape and color. *Right:* Tall Hybrid Tea growing with dahlias.

garden design

You can also choose monochromatic or mixed color schemes. In a monochromatic design, all flowers are of a single hue—as in a mass planting of the Hybrid Tea 'Apricot Nectar' or a hedge of white Floribundas—or of tones and shades of a single hue, as in a blend of pinks. This creates a unified effect. Bold, bright colors can be placed next to each other, but an entire garden of this tends to be tiring. White roses are always an effective contrast or buffer for these vivid colors. Softer colors and blends may also pick up the stronger tones of adjacent flowers. Give some thought, too, to the color of any background: a brick or mahogany-colored wall may not blend well with the red or mauve Climber you'd like to plant. If you're just starting off with roses, it's best to start cautiously, with only a few colors in any one area, adding more as the garden becomes established.

Note that rose color is affected by climate, culture, and stage of growth. Heat can cause deep pink and red roses to darken and yellow and peach-col-

ored roses to fade. The low light of spring favors pale bloom, while intense summer light heightens color–except for the yellows, which develop their best color in less intense light. Water and nutrient levels also affect flower color, and many roses change hues as they develop from bud to full to spent bloom.

Remember that color in your rose garden is not restricted to blooming season. A number of roses–especially the Species, Old Garden Roses, and Shrub Roses–have colorful autumn foliage and ornamental hips in a variety of colors, sizes, and shapes, some of which remain on the plant into the winter. Notable among these are *R. rugosa,* with its hips resembling cherry tomatoes, used for tea and jelly; *R. moyesii,* with bright orange-red bottle-shaped hips; and *R. virginiana,* whose small red hips are enhanced by vari-colored autumn foliage.

Mixing Plants Although roses are often, and appropriately, grown alone, they also mix readily with other landscape plants. Annuals and perennials are wonderful companions for roses. Low-growing and shallow-rooted annuals like alyssum and lobelia serve as groundcovers, filling in attractively at the feet of

VIEWPOINT
MIXED PLANTINGS

I like mixing Shrub and Old Garden Roses into perennial borders and mixed flowering shrub plantings. Choose plants that continue to bloom when the roses have petered out. I also like a pink rose (like 'Carefree Beauty') edged with catmint for nice contrast with blue-lavender flowers.
NANCY ROSE, MINNESOTA LANDSCAPE ARBORETUM

I use roses in a mixed landscape, planting perennials, annuals, and herbs along with the roses; this provides color throughout the season and separates the roses, minimizing disease spread. Plants that host spider mites, like violets and strawberries, should not be planted if mites are a problem.
CLAIR MARTIN, THE HUNTINGTON BOTANICAL GARDEN

Many shallow-rooted perennials, annuals, and biennials that don't compete with roses.can be used with good effect. Pansies make good groundcover for early spring or fall, while sweet alyssum and portulaca (individual colors) can be used in the summer months. Perennial catmint makes a great twelve- to fifteen-inch border of gray foliage that is an excellent foil to the green foliage of Shrub Roses; the masses of tiny blue flowers give the garden a uniform appearance when all of the various colored shrubs are in bloom.
MIKE RUGGIERO, THE NEW YORK BOTANICAL GARDEN

A formal edging like boxwood or holly is nice, as are violas or alyssum, planted six to twelve inches away from the roses. We have used roses in perennial plantings, but find the perennials outgrow the roses and cause poor air circulation.
NELSON STERNER,
OLD WESTBURY GARDENS

Left: 'Bantry Bay' combines beautifully with *Clematis* 'Perle d'azur'.

Hybrid Teas and Grandifloras and helping to keep the roses' roots cool; perennial groundcovers such as periwinkle do the same. Perennials and herbs that bloom all season are perfect partners for the Species and Old Garden Roses that bloom only once; in fact, Old Garden Roses look better combined with perennials than in exclusive groups by themselves. Early spring-flowering perennials and bulbs start off the season in rose gardens before the main event.

Blue-flowered plants supply a color missing from the rose palette; possibilities include lavender, delphinium, campanula, and cornflower. Plants with silver-gray foliage–the artemisias, santolina, lamb's ears, dusty miller–provide a lovely contrast to the darker green foliage and bright blooms of roses. Miniature Roses and Polyanthas can be used in perennial or annual flower beds or borders as edgings, while Shrub Roses and Floribundas make fine border backdrops. Keep annuals and perennials six inches or more away from the base or main cane of each rose, and don't plant heavy-feeding or deep-rooted companions with your roses.

Roses also combine well with other landscape shrubs, to extend or complement the season of bloom. Roses and evergreen shrubs are wonderful companions, the roses providing a beautiful splash of color against the green, and the evergreens supplying color and texture when the roses are dormant. While roses should mostly be kept away from trees, whose roots can compete for water and nutrients, you can plant Miniature Roses near small ornamental trees, and in the South, Climbing Roses enjoy scrambling up through the

Below: 'Fantin-Latour', a Centifolia, combined with geraniums.

branches of larger trees, so long as their base is planted several feet from the trunk of the tree. The spacing varies with the type of tree, and whether it's evergreen or deciduous. Keep climbers away from river birches or willow to avoid competition for root moisture and nutrients.

Shape, Size, and Texture A cutting garden filled with uniform rows of Hybrid Teas may provide a feast of color, but it lacks other interest. Most garden designs strive for a mix of shapes, sizes, and textures that complement one another, adding visual interest and a sense of harmony. When choosing roses, select different types to provide variation in height, texture, width, and color patterns. Hybrid Teas and Grandifloras, in particular, need companions to fill in their sparse foliage and soften their stiff growth habit. Edging these roses with lower-growing Floribundas, Polyanthas, and Miniatures achieves that purpose, as does backing them with Climbers, Ramblers, and tall Shrub Roses.

In a formal rose garden, Climbing Roses (suitably trained on pillars or festooned on ropes) or tree roses add height, and clipped shrubs such as boxwood and yew provide a contrasting border or background texture. In an informal garden, Old Garden Roses combine beautifully with the modern roses like Hybrid Teas and Floribundas, as the older roses have interesting foliage throughout the season even though they bloom only once. Other contrasts are provided by interplanting roses with perennials and annuals, as noted above–for example, spiky foxglove, tall and bold yellow daylilies, soft and low-growing petunias, and fuzzy and gray lamb's ears.

Spacing The amount of space each rose needs in your garden depends on the type of rose, type of garden, and your climate. Rose bushes in colder climates do not grow as large as the same variety in warmer climates with a longer growing season, so roses are planted closer together in northern areas than in southern regions. Wherever you plant, be sure not to crowd your roses, remembering that they grow rapidly. Poor air circulation encourages disease.

In regions with cold winters, where temperatures regularly drop below 20° F., space Hybrid Teas and Grandifloras about two feet apart; wider spacing will allow easier access for maintenance and winter covering. In areas with mild winters, where temperatures drop to between 20° F. and 30° F., those same roses need spacing two-and-one-half to three feet. In warm-winter sections with temperatures seldom below freezing, allow three-and-one-half feet between these roses.

Floribundas and Polyanthas are lower-growing than Hybrid Teas and Grandifloras, but they are also spreading. Space these roses two feet apart in cold climates and two to two-and-one-half feet apart in warmer areas. In all climates, space Miniature roses at least that far apart; their tight, compact growth habit makes them prone to spider mites, mildew, and other problems that are aggravated by crowding. Give Climbers six or more feet. Spacing for Shrub and Old Garden Roses depends on the class and/or variety. Many will need four to six feet. Reduce spacing by about six inches for roses planted as hedges and edgings.

Keep roses two to three feet away from any wall you're planting them along so they have room to fill out evenly and enjoy free air movement.

Stone benches complement shrub roses at Boerner Botanical Gardens.

Climbers, however, should only be about one to one-and-one-quarter feet away from a wall they'll be trained up; they can be planted even closer to a fence. Be sure roses planted near a building are not in a position to be pelted by rain runoff or ice or snow falling or melting from overhead eaves.

Planning Around Structures Structures of all kinds are ideally suited for the rose garden. Roses call to mind images of trellises and arbors engulfed with hundred of blooms, of flowering walls and fences, of rose-covered cottages. And what better setting for a garden bench than surrounded by fragrant roses?

Climbers, with relatively stiff canes, and the more pliable Ramblers can both be trained on fences, walls (with hooks, clips, or a trellis), pillars, and pergolas, and festooned on chains or ropes. Add interest to the exterior of your house, and fragrance within, by training Climbers and Ramblers to twine around doorways and windows, or over and around a porch. Let pink or red Ramblers spill over a weathered gray split-rail fence or stone wall. Leave Climbers free to cover old and unsightly tree stumps or garden sheds, fill an empty bank, clamber up among tree branches. Once established, Climbers can easily support weaker-stemmed vines; an arbor of pink and white roses combined with purple clematis is breathtaking. (See Chapter 4 for training methods.)

Other roses besides the Large-flowered Climbers and Ramblers can be trained to climb up and along garden structures, notably the Noisettes and

Above: Yellow 'Lady Hillingdon' a Tea rose, and 'Allister Stella Gray', a Noisette, contrast with pink Species Roses and gray stone.

Hybrid Musks, and individual varieties of many classes, such as the Tea rose 'Sombreuil', the Damask 'Mme. Hardy', the Bourbon 'Zépherine Drouhin', and the Hybrid Perpetual 'Frau Karl Druschki'. (The Plant Selector, Chapter 2, will guide you to others.)

Edgings and Hedges As noted above, structural edgings such as wood, brick, or stone will give your garden a crisper, more defined look. You can also create edgings from plants, with or without the structural elements. Common edging plants include low-growing annuals such as sweet alyssum and lobelia. Or you can create a low front border with roses themselves, using Miniatures, Polyanthas, and low-growing Floribundas such as 'Showbiz'. Be careful not to overshade these low growers.

Roses also make attractive and interesting hedges and screens. Albas, Damasks, Rugosas, many Shrub Roses, and most Species Roses will grow large enough to create a living background fence that can also screen out unpleasant sights and sounds. The thornier, denser varieties such as the Species and Hybrid Eglantines will also become an impenetrable barrier, should you wish to deter uninvited human or animal visitors. Floribundas are a good choice for low- and mid-growing, low-maintenance hedges, especially the white 'Iceberg'; so are the pink 'Carefree Wonder' or yellow 'Sun Flair'. When planting roses for edgings or hedges, reduce the recommended space between them so they will grow together, with no gaps in between foliage.

Visiting Rose Gardens and Nurseries Once you've worked out your garden design and have an idea of which roses you want to grow where, visit if at all possible rose gardens and nurseries in your area. In the gardens, you will be able to see what the different kinds of roses actually look like growing, as individual plants and as part of a larger landscape. From both gardens and nurseries you can find out which classes and varieties are best suited for your region, and

Below: A brick path and a stone fountain provide focus and definition to an informal garden at The New York Botanical Garden.

Above: Large rocks provide an easy border for this mixed garden. *Left:* A row of Hybrid Teas is more interesting when laid out along a curve.

which are likely to disappoint you. For more advice specific to your particular area, seek out a local rose society, whose members will be delighted to share their knowledge with you. Or, call the American Rose Society in Shreveport, Louisiana (see page 217), and request a visit from a local consulting rosarian.

Key:
A: 'Frau Dagmar Hastrup'
B: Ligularia
C: 'Rosa Mundi'
D: 'Wedding Day'
E: Catmint
F: 'Madame Isaac Pereire'
G: 'Constance Spry'

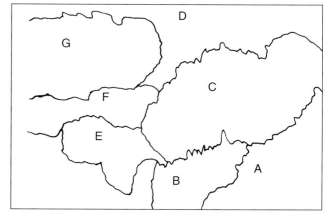

This garden combines a group of old roses with perennials; the yellow of the ligularia and purple of the catmint are good counterpoints for the different shades of pink.

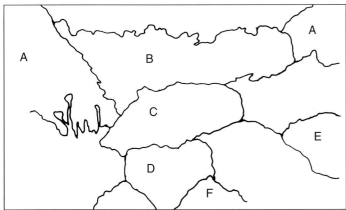

Key:
A: Boxwood
B: 'Seafoam'
C: Catmint
D: Geranium
E: Artemesia
F: Dusty miller

In Old Westbury Garden's Gray Garden, a shrub rose forms a backdrop for a group of foliage plants.

TECHNIQUES 4

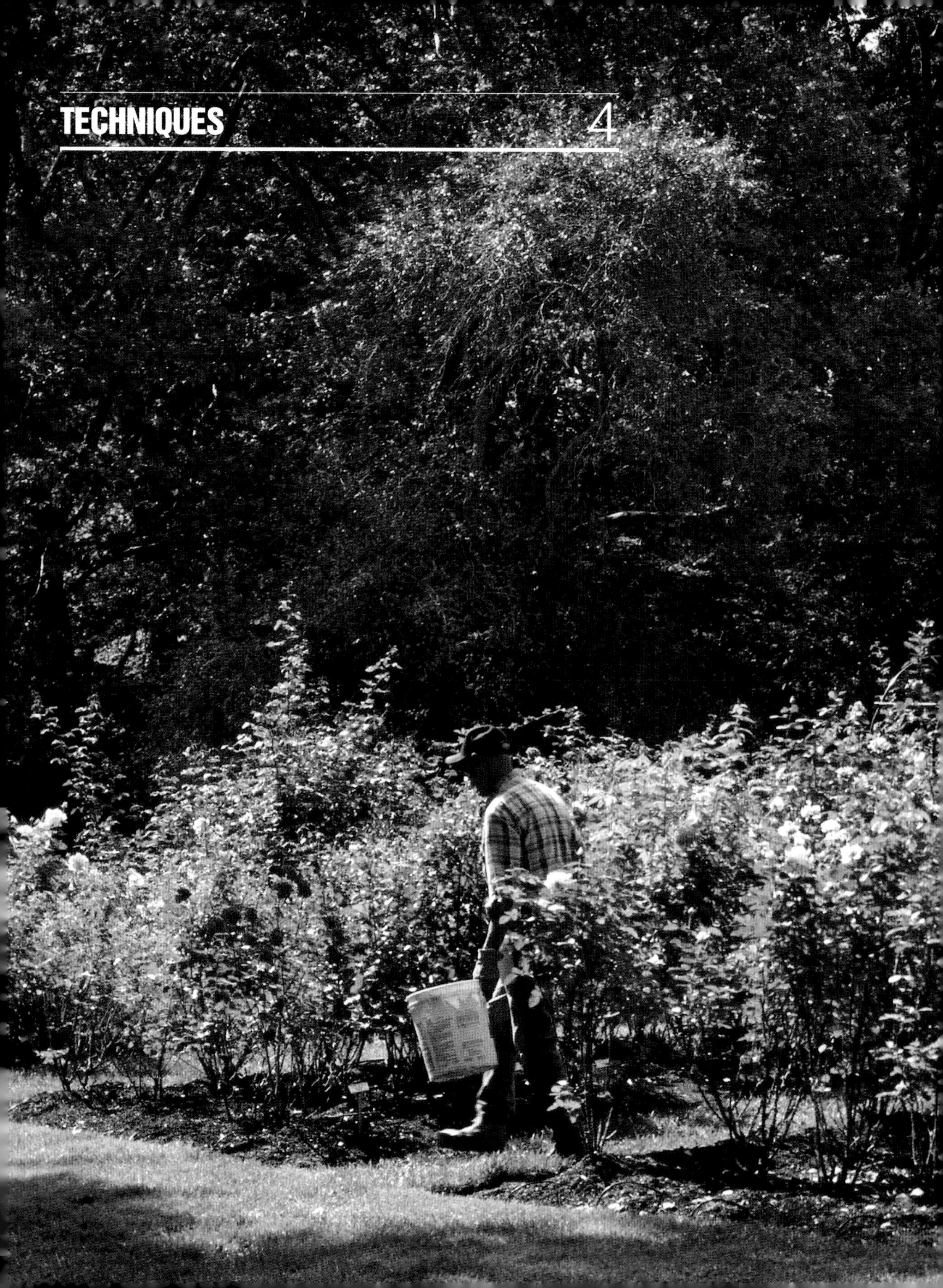

Growing roses need not be as difficult and time-consuming as many people imagine it. Although they would never be considered anything but high-maintenance plants, roses are actually quite tenacious shrubs. Many are more care-free than the most difficult types and demand a concentrated period of attention only at planting time. Others, such as the Hybrid Teas, do require your time and frequent attention, but in return they reward you fully with the exquisite colors and form of their blooms. The basic rose-growing techniques described in this chapter will guide you to success in rose culture. As you gain experience in growing roses, you'll discover methods—perhaps unique to your gardening conditions—that work best for you.

CHOOSING AND IMPROVING THE SITE Chapter 3 (Garden Design) discusses several important site selection factors for roses (except for the Species Roses, which, being wild in origin, will grow almost anywhere): at least six hours of sun per day, access to plenty of water, and sufficient distance from competing trees and large shrubs. Only the right site will supply these requirements. Other important needs of roses include good air circulation, so foliar moisture dries out during the day or after a rainstorm, and fertile, well-drained, workable soil. If the site does not meet the last two requirements, you can make improvements so it does. Providing good air circulation is a relatively simple matter of cutting back competing vegetation and keeping the rose itself adequately pruned or cut back. Improving the soil and ensuring adequate drainage require more work, but are the essential first steps for success with roses.

Site Improvement The first step in preparing a site in which your roses will flourish is a general cleanup, the removal of rocks, sticks, stumps, or other debris. Once the area is relatively clean, lay out the boundaries of your site using string, garden hose, or spray paint. If the site is a grassy area, skin the turf off using a shovel or spade. Take the top two inches off—grass and roots—and knock the soil loose from the roots. Don't throw away the turf—use it to start a compost pile. Or, use a product like Roundup to remove grass instead of skinning off the turf; this will preserve the top two inches of soil, and all the nutrients in them. If the area is covered with brush or weeds, mow first and then skin off the vegetation. Once you have bare ground, you're ready to begin improving the soil for a productive garden.

Drainage Since roses require abundant water but dislike wet feet, good drainage is vital for your rose garden. In well-drained soil, water moves through at a moderate rate so roots can absorb the moisture but don't get waterlogged, and nutrients also percolate through so roots can absorb them. If you're not sure about your soil's drainage capacity, test it: dig a hole the size of a one-gallon pot, fill it with water, and see how long it takes to drain. If it drains in less than two hours, your soil is sandy and needs organic matter added to boost moisture retention. If it drains in two to four hours, your soil is loamy and will provide fine drainage for your roses. If the drainage time is over four hours, you have clayey soil that needs both sand and organic matter to make it more friable and permeable to water and nutrients; recheck drainage after amend-

To determine whether your drainage is adequate, dig a hole large enough to hold a gallon pot. Fill the hole with water, and see how long it takes to drain.

ing the soil. Several years ago, the roses in the Wilson Rose Garden at the Minneapolis Landscape Arboretum were doing poorly. A drainage test was done—and the water dropped only one-quarter inch in two hours! The beds were renovated, old soil was excavated to two feet deep, drain tiling was installed, and new soil (sand:peat:loam) was added. The roses have been thriving ever since. There are several other ways to provide good drainage:

1. Use raised beds, which always provide better drainage, allow you to mix better soil from elsewhere into your rose-growing site, and are also essential if your soil is not workable down to three feet.

2. Install a drainage pipe. These pipes, usually plastic, are sold at most garden supply or hardware stores; laid in a foot-deep trench below the planting areas, they move water away from your rose garden. This works only if you can provide a place for the water to drain to.

3. Grade a severely sloped area with terraces or retaining walls.

4. If your problem is serious, or if you think it is worth the investment, talk to a professional landscaper about inserting a drainage system, such as tile, gravel beds, or a more elaborate piping system.

According to William Radler of Boerner Botanical Gardens, the only practical solutions for poor drainage are drainage tile and raised beds; you cannot add enough sand to make a difference. Also, he notes that sandy soil will drain in about five minutes, and soil that does not drain in two to four hours might have drainage problems.

ANALYZING AND IMPROVING SOIL Soil is the backbone of your garden, the medium that shelters your plants' roots and provides the nutrients needed for health, growth, and bloom. There are three basic types of soil: clay, sand, and loam. Clay soil has very little space between its particles; this type of soil is often very rich in nutrients, but water and nutrients have trouble traveling through clay soil to the roots of the plant. Clay soil is often very sticky when wet. Sandy soil transports material easily, but it can't hold nutrients and water for very long; this type of soil does not stick together. The best is a mix of the two: loam, which is light but rich. This type of soil is often called "friable," which means it is easily pulverized.

To identify the level of nutrients in your soil, and what additions are needed, a soil test is required. A small but representative amount of garden soil is analyzed for nutrient deficiencies and excesses. To get an accurate reading for your entire garden area, take small amounts from several different spots in your garden, mixing them to make a total of about one-half cup of soil. Very different garden areas within your property will require separate soil tests. A full analysis of the soil mix can be done by a county extension service, an agricultural university, or perhaps even a local garden center. The analysis will generally be accompanied by recommendations for needed nutrients and their application rates. Note that it can take three weeks (more, in the busy spring) to get the report.

Most soil-test analyses will also report on the pH level of your soil—its acidity or alkalinity. You can also test pH levels yourself with a simple home kit.

VIEWPOINT

IMPROVING THE SOIL BEFORE PLANTING

We add Mill's Magic Rose Mix before planting. This material is 100% natural organics. Mill's Rose Mix is manufactured by a contributor to the Garden. To treat weeds, we use a granular herbicide known as Snapshot 2.5 TG, a mixture of Gallery and Treflan only for pre-emergent purposes.
DAVID SATTIZAHN, HERSHEY GARDENS

We add lots of organic matter—composed horse manure or leaf mold, up to a 50% mixture. We cultivate to remove weeds. and mulch with shredded leaf mulch to prevent weeds.
NELSON STERNER, OLD WESTBURY

We do use some chemical herbicide to remove weeds. We also remove the old rose bushes, removing all roots and then amend soil with our own compost, at a 50-50 mixture.
CLAIR MARTIN, THE HUNTINGTON BOTANICAL GARDENS

We take the opportunity before planting to add organic material to our soil, which is for the most part already organic. Leaf compost or well-rotted cow manure and some peat moss is mixed thoroughly with the soil that is taken from the hole before the rose is planted. In addition, we thoroughly mix super-phosphate into all of the soil (phosphate does not move well in the soil) which will aid in root development. We sometimes use pre-emergents in the spring to reduce weeds.
MICHAEL RUGGIERO, THE NEW YORK BOTANICAL GARDEN

We add oodles of organic matter (leaf and garden compost, aged manure, sphagnum peat moss, etc.). If adding just one or a few bushes to existing beds, we just add as much organic matter as possible without disturbing roots. We recommend hand weeding because roses are very sensitive to herbicides.
NANCY ROSE, MINNESOTA LANDSCAPE ARBORETUM

COMPOST

In forests and prairies, swamps and backyards, an amazing process is continuously taking place. Plant parts and animal leavings rot or decompose with the help of fungi, bacteria, and other microorganisms. Earthworms and an assortment of insects do their part digesting and mixing the plant and animal matter together. The result is a marvelous, rich, and crumbly layer of organic matter we call compost.

BENEFITS OF COMPOST Compost encourages the growth of earthworms and other beneficial organisms whose activities help plants grow strong and healthy. It provides nutrients and improves the soil. Wet clay soils drain better and sandy soils hold more moisture if amended with compost.

HOW TO MAKE COMPOST A compost pile keeps organic matter handy for garden use and, as an added advantage, keeps the material from filling up overburdened landfills. To make your own compost, start with a layer of chopped leaves, grass clippings, and kitchen waste like banana peels, eggshells, old lettuce leaves, apple cores, coffee grounds, and whatever else is available. Keep adding materials until you have a six-inch layer, then cover it with a three- to six-inch layer of soil, manure, or finished compost.

Alternate six-inch layers of organic matter and two- to three-inch layers of soil or manure until the pile is about three feet tall. A pile that is three feet tall by three feet square will generate enough heat during decomposition to sterilize the compost. This makes it useful as potting soil, topdressing for lawns, or soil-improving additives.

COMPOST CARE Keep your compost pile in a semishaded area to keep it from drying out too much. But if your compost pile is near a tree, turn it frequently to make sure tree roots don't grow into it. Make an indentation in the top of the pile to hold water and sprinkle the pile with a garden hose when it looks dry. Keep the compost moist, but not wet. Beneficial organisms cannot survive in soggy conditions.

USING COMPOST When your compost is ready, it can be mixed into the soil before planting, or applied to the surface of the soil as a soil-enriching mulch.

QUICK COMPOST If you need compost in a hurry, speed up the process by turning the pile with a pitchfork once a week for a month. Mixing the compost allows oxygen into the center of the pile, where it encourages the growth of bacteria and fungi. A pile that is turned regularly will become finished compost in four to eight months.

MAKING A COMPOST BIN As illustrated below, many elaborate compost bins are sold. Some of these have devices for turning the compost and for removing it from the bin. Although these store-bought bins don't do the compost pile any harm, they are really not necessary. An enclosure made from chicken wire or from five wood pallets (one on the bottom, and four wired together for the sides) does the job just as well.

WHAT TO COMPOST
- kitchen waste
- lawn clippings (in thin layers so they do not mat down)
- chopped leaves (large leaves take a long time to break down)
- shredded branches
- garden plants
- shredded paper
- weeds (but be sure to use before they go to seed or weeds may sprout in the garden)
- straw or hay

WHAT NOT TO COMPOST
- orange and other citrus peels
- meat scraps, fatty trash (to avoid rodents and animals)
- excessive wood ashes

The pH level is measured on a scale of 1 to 14; 7.0 is neutral, with readings below that indicating an acid soil and above that indicating alkaline soil. For best growth, roses prefer a slightly acid soil with a pH of about 6.0 to 6.6, with a slight tolerance in either direction. If the soil is too acidic (common in the eastern United States), add limestone, worked well into the soil several months before planting. If the soil is too alkaline (common in the western United States), add agricultural grade sulfur, compost, sphagnum peat moss, or ground oak leaves (or aluminum sulfate if the pH is very high). Soil needing pH change will need to be adjusted on a yearly basis; soil pH is a critical factor.

To meet the nutrient needs indicated by your soil test, add organic materials, such as compost and well-rotted manure for nitrogen, bonemeal or powdered rock phosphate for phosphorus, and wood ashes or New Jersey Greensand for potassium. Organic soil amendments will create the well-balanced, friable, well-drained soil in which roses thrive, and unlike the "quick fixes" of chemical fertilizers, will not harm your roses or the environment and will build the soil for long-term fertility. Since organic materials are slower to break down, however, they must be added in advance of planting in order for their nutrients to be available to your plants.

All weeds must be removed from the soil; these weeds will compete with the roses. William Radler of Boerner Botanical Garden states that without chemical treatment, such deep-rooted weeds as Canadian thistle, quackgrass, and bindweed will resprout from root pieces left in the ground; he suggests treating a new flowerbed with Roundup (glyphosate) because when used properly it is efficient and saves much work. (A note of caution: Roundup is applied to the weeds, not the soil; it kills anything green that it touches.)

PREPARING THE SOIL FOR PLANTING When your rose garden site has been graded and drained properly and is free of turf, weeds, and other debris, you can begin preparing the soil. If you are preparing your soil in the spring, be sure

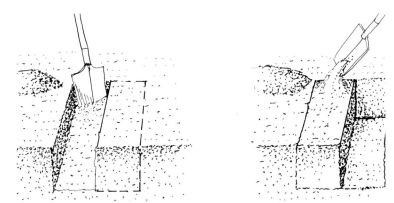

Double digging is a method of creating a loose, well-tilled bed; it requires digging two shovels deep, breaking up clods as you dig. Soil from the first digging is used to fill the adjacent rows. It is hard work, and some of our experts think it is unnecessary.

the soil has dried out enough. Squeeze a handful of soil in your hand; if it forms a lump that breaks apart easily in your palm when you open your fist, the soil is ready for tilling. If it stays in a sticky ball, it's too wet, and if it won't form a ball at all, it's too dry. In either of these cases, tilling will destroy the soil's structure.

To till, loosen and turn the soil over to a depth of four to six inches. If tender vegetation is growing on the site, turn it into the top part of the soil. Pull out any woody stems. Wait at least two weeks after this initial tilling to allow the tilled plants to decompose; then turn the soil under again to a depth of four to six inches to ensure the breaking up of dead plants and to loosen the soil further.

After the second tilling, apply soil amendments such as lime, compost, sand, manure, or bonemeal. Till once again, this time to a depth of at least eighteen inches with a tiller or by hand with a spading fork. Several of our

When buying rose bushes, look for strong canes and laterals.

experts suggested tilling even deeper, because the deeper the ground is broken up and organic matter is worked, the deeper the roots will travel to pick up nutrients and moisture. On the other hand, Nancy Rose of the Minnesota Landscape Arboretum finds that digging twelve to eighteen inches is far enough, because the soil is loosened further during the planting process.

Double digging is a process by which two spadesful of dirt are lifted and loosened to create a deep, loose, well-tilled bed. It is time-consuming and back-breaking, but it is greatly beneficial to the future health of your roses. Although it seems complicated, the procedure simply requires digging down an extra shovel-depth. As you dig, place the soil you've removed alongside the trench; fill each trench with the soil from the trench before it. Break up all clods in the soil and add soil amendments as necessary. If your site is very large, consider hiring or renting a tractor-tiller to do the double digging for you.

You may not be able to provide deeply prepared, well-drained soil at your chosen site because of hardpan (an impermeable layer below the surface), bedrock, or severely compacted clay soil (as at a recent construction site). In this case, create raised beds in which your roses can thrive, or install drainage pipes. Enclose the garden area with lumber or brick and fill with two feet of soil mixed generously with organic materials. Let the bed settle for several weeks before planting, and add more soil if necessary.

BUYING ROSES The basic rule for buying roses is to get strong, healthy plants from reputable sources. Local nurseries with good reputations can help you select varieties that are reliable in your area. Mail-order nurseries are also good sources of roses and may offer a wider variety than is available locally. It doesn't matter whether the nursery is located in your part of the country or climate zone; if the rose is suitable for your climate, it will adjust after you plant it.

Mail-order roses are shipped dormant and with bare roots wrapped in a moisture-retaining material (except for Miniatures, which are potted). As soon as you receive the roses, open the package to be sure the roots are moist; if they aren't, water them immediately. Local nurseries start with bare-root roses also; they then plant them in containers and sell them after they develop some leaves and even flowers. Bare-root plants establish themselves more quickly than container plants, whose roots take time to spread out. If you can't plant bare-root roses immediately, keep the bush moist in its plastic protective covering and store it in a cool, dark place. If you cannot plant these roses within two weeks after receiving them, heel them into the garden (dig a trench, lay the rose in it, and cover the plant up to the canes). If you can't plant container-grown roses right away, keep them in a warm, sunny spot sheltered from the wind, and be diligent about keeping their soil moist. Above all, do not let the roots of either a bare-root or container rose dry out at any time before planting.

Roses are sold by grade: 1, 1 1/2, and 2. All of these must have a well-developed root system and a balanced growth pattern; the grades also specify number, diameter, and length of canes for each class of rose. Grades 1 1/2 and

VIEWPOINT

STORING UNPLANTED ROSE BUSHES

We either heel in roses until we can plant them or pot them up in five-gallon containers. Depending on the weather, bare root rose bushes can be stored up to two weeks in water.
CLAIR MARTIN
THE HUNTINGTON BOTANICAL GARDENS

All roses are shipped to us out of cold storage and are planted immediately.
DAVID SATTIZAHN
HERSHEY GARDENS

We like to plant roses as soon as we receive them, but this is not always possible. Roses that cannot be planted immediately are stored in our root cellar, where the temperature remains cool and the air is slightly moist. Before we plant these stored bare root roses, we will soak the root system in water for a few hours. If for any reason we can't plant them for a week or two, we pot them.
MIKE RUGGIERO, THE NEW YORK BOTANICAL GARDEN

We keep them in a flower cooler at 40 F. If kept moist, they will survive for two to three weeks. We always soak roots for twenty-four hours prior to planting.
NELSON STERNER
OLD WESTBURY GARDENS

We store them wrapped in plastic in a cool, dark box, up to three or four weeks.
DARYL JOHNSON

WHEN TO PLANT
Pacific Northwest: January to April
Pacific Seaboard: January to
February
Southwest: December to January
South Central: December to
February
Mid South: November, February
to March
Subtropical: December to January
North Central: April to May,
October to November
Eastern Seaboard: March to May,
October to November
Northeast: March to May, October
to Novembe.

2 will have fewer, thinner, and/or shorter canes, so they are cheaper to buy but require more time and care to develop into thriving rose bushes (even with the extra attention, the Grade 2 roses are usually unsatisfactory). In addition to grade, look for green bark (a few roses, like 'Love', don't have green bark) and healthy, moist canes (three or more for most rose classes of Grade 1) with no shriveling. Roots should be vigorous and undamaged. If you are buying potted roses, select only those in containers of at least two gallons. The boxed roses you frequently encounter at supermarkets and nurseries are a risk–in some cases, plants have dried out and have damaged roots, which you won't discover until you get them home–in other cases, they are just fine. Also, avoid waxed roses; this material helps them retain moisture in the stores, but must be removed before planting (in the North, the wax is beneficial and need not be removed).

WHEN TO PLANT Bare-root plants need to be planted while they are still dormant. This means early in the spring in colder climates and in late winter in climates with above-freezing winters. Bare-root roses can also be planted in the late fall in regions with cold winters if soil temperatures remain above 40° F. into early winter, allowing the plant roots to grow and become established (Nelson Sterner at Old Westbury Gardens recommends against this). Container roses can be planted anytime during the growing season, from early spring to midfall–again, allowing roots time to become established before the ground freezes.

There is a common theory that roses should not be grown in a spot where they have been grown before; this is because chemicals left by the old plant may exist in the soil. Most of our experts agree that if a site has been home to successful roses, there is no reason not to plant them there again; most botanic gardens plant roses in the same site over and over. If debris is cleaned each time, no problems have been reported. If there has been disease in a particular spot, soil should be replaced before replanting. However, micronutrients that the first plant pulled out of the ground won't be available to the next one.

HOW TO PLANT The best day to plant a rose is still and overcast, with no sun or wind to dry canes and roots. If you must plant on a sunny day, plant late in the afternoon so the rose isn't shocked by the full force of the burning sun. Soak the roots or the entire plant for twenty-four hours (some consultants suggest up to forty-eight hours, some as little as an hour or two) in a bucket of water before planting

Spacing of roses, as discussed in Chapter 3, depends on several factors: type of rose, your climate, and garden design. See Chapter 3 for specific requirements.

The most important rule in planting rose bushes is to dig a very large hole, much larger than you might think necessary. This provides an environment in which the plant can establish a strong, healthy root system, the foundation for years of vigorous growth. For most roses, other than minis, this means a hole eighteen to twenty-four inches wide and twenty-four inches deep, or at least one-and-one-half times the diameter or the root system–measuring the exact

PLANTING

1. Dig hole twice the length and width of the rosebush's roots.

2. Incorporate amendments such as peat moss, compost, leaf mold, or fertilizer.

3. Clean debris and clumps of soil off roots.

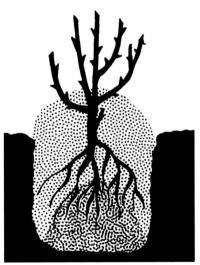

4. Build a mound of earth in the hole, and position the rose bush.

5. Position rootball in desired location; see text on page 180. for further information.

6. Water well. Some gardeners like to build a well around the hole to hold water.

Preparing a bed for roses is a little like getting the house ready for the arrival of a difficult old lady, some biddy with aristocratic pretensions and persnickety tastes. Her stay is bound to be an ordeal, and you want to give her as little cause for complaint as possible. All of a sudden, the soil that's served you well for years seems lacking, its drainage dubious, its pH off. So I've been double-digging, hauling bales of peat moss, and blowing all at once and in one place the precious cache of compost it's taken me years to accumulate.

MICHAEL POLLAN, *SECOND NATURE*, 1991

size of the hole is not as important as making sure it is is large enough to accommodate the rose's roots comfortably. Mix the soil you remove from the hole with one-third its volume of organic matter–compost, well-rotted manure, leaf mold, and/or peat moss. Remove the rose bush from the water it has been soaking in, and cut off any broken canes. Prune each cane back to about ten inches, just above an outward-facing and swelling bud, cutting at a 45° angle (some of our experts say this is unnecessary; others say it looks nicer that way). Now make a mound (cone) of the soil-organics mixture in the hole. The purpose of the mound is to prevent air pockets. Place the rose bush on this mound, spreading its roots evenly down around the mound.

To position the rose correctly in the planting hole, find its bud union. Most roses consist of a hardy rootstalk to which the desired variety has been grafted. The swollen place where the two roses join at the base of the stem is called the bud union. In northern areas with below-zero winter temperatures, position the bud union one to two inches inches below the soil surface. At Old Westbury Gardens, bud unions are positioned one inch above soil; at The Huntington Botanical Gardens, just at soil level. Daryl Johnson of Portland recommends against positioning the bud union above soil level because he finds that positioning below bud union discourages basal growth. William Radler of Boerner Botanical Garden near Milwaukee states that it is very important to position the bud union two inches below soil level in the North, as roses planted with bud union above soil level are more likely to winter kill. In regions where winter temperatures do not drop below 20° F., position the bud union just above the soil level. In frost-free regions, position the bud union one to two inches above soil level. Note that Species and Old Garden Roses, plus most Miniatures, are grown on their own rootstock, so they have no bud union; plant these with the crown at or one inch below soil surface.

With the bud union or crown at the correct level, fill the planting hole half to two-thirds full with the soil mixture (some experts suggest adding several tablespoons of Epsom salts after planting for sturdy stems), anchoring the plant securely and firming down to remove air pockets. Fill the hole with water. When the water is completely absorbed, fill the planting hole to the top with more of the soil mixture and again tamp down gently. Make a shallow trench around the hole and water thoroughly again. Mound up an additional six to ten inches of soil around the plant and leave this in place for several weeks to shelter the plant and keep it moist while it establishes itself in its new surroundings (this is not done at Boerner Botanical Garden). Jim Browne covers newly planted roses with large brown paper sacks, inverted over the top with the bottoms opened a bit to let off any heat buildup; the sack holds sufficient moisture to keep the canes from drying out. Once the plant has sent out an inch or two of new growth, you can remove the protective soil mound by spraying gently with the garden hose. If you are planting in the fall, add winter protection as detailed later in this chapter.

Container-grown roses, as noted, can be planted any time the ground is not frozen (but make sure they'll have time to establish themselves before frost).

Dig a hole at least one-and-one-half times the size of the rootball; combine the removed soil with manure and compost. (At Memphis Botanic Garden, where the soil is heavy clay, holes are dug wider and deeper to allow for better drainage.) Being sure the rose and its soil are thoroughly damp, tap the rose out of its container, gently loosen the roots (without letting the soil fall off), and place the plant in the hole, positioning the bud union as described above. If you cannot tap the rose loose, cut away the bottom of the container, slit the sides, and slide the plant out of the pot or pull the pieces of the container up and away. Fill and water as above, and adjust the bud union or crown level if needed once the soil has settled.

Help your newly planted roses along by giving them plenty of water, especially in the first few weeks. Miniatures have shallower root systems, so be diligent about keeping them moist during this settling-in period. Deep, slow watering is better than frequent sprinklings, which encourage surface roots, though frequent light sprinklings are of benefit in hot or windy weather.

TRAINING CLIMBERS AND RAMBLERS Neither Climbers nor Ramblers can naturally attach themselves to supports, so you must tie them loosely to the structures you want to train them to. Most Climbers have very stiff canes, Ramblers more pliable ones, which makes Ramblers easier to train than Climbers,

'Ivy Alice' trained on an arch.

TRAINING

Above: When training climbers, tie loosely with twine. Do not wrap the twine tightly around the cane. *Above right:* Plants with very pliable canes (usually Ramblers instead of Large-flowered Climbers) can be trained on low fences. Tie them in a slight curve. *Right:* Some gardeners advocate training more than one cane, wrapping them in a spiral fashion. The advantage is a fuller effect; the disadvantage is that the plant is almost impossible to remove for winter protection or for maintaining the support. If you live in a area where winter protection is not necessary and if the material in your support will not require painting or other maintenance, consider this method.

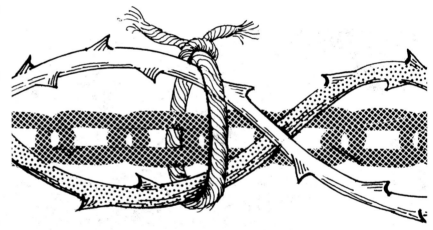

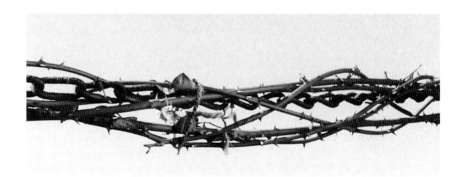

TRAINING

1. Choose a strong, vigorous cane, at least as thick as a pencil and preferably as thick as your middle finger. Discard woody canes if you have newer, healthier canes available.

2. Begin by training the canes vertically up the trellis; by doing this, you are encouraging the plant to grow taller.

3. As the plant grows up the trellis, continue tying it, securing it to the trellis. It may take two to three years before it reaches the top of a six-foot trellis.

4. Secure to the plant to diagonal as well as vertical and horizontal surfaces; this provides a fuller effect.

5. Tie the plant at intervals of three to five inches. Some gardeners advocate wrapping or spiralling the cane around the support; this gives a very full effect, but makes it difficult to remove the plant.

6. Once the plant reaches the top of the trellis, train it horizontally. Continue tying as it grows.

although the stiff canes of Climbers are excellent for upright posts or trellises. To train Climbers and Ramblers over fences, on arches, and up walls, spread the canes out fanlike, spacing them evenly and horizontally, and tie in place with a soft material like twine. The more horizontal and spread apart they are, the more flowers and blooming laterals they will produce.

Climbers and Ramblers can be trained to grow up poles and around chains. Wrap two or three canes around a pole in a spiral; when the canes produce laterals, wrap them horizontally around and along a chain or rope leading to a second pole (this step is done more easily with the more pliable Rambler canes). Do this while the plant is dormant, just after flowering. Wrapping spirally, as with the canes, encourages the production of laterals and, therefore, blooms, but makes it hard to remove them for winter. Tie loosely. Roses trained up a pillar or post are often called "pillar roses," which describes the way they are being grown, not the class or variety.

Use the same methods to train Ramblers and Climbers on arches, which may be slender for Ramblers but must be heavier for Climbers. To keep roses from cluttering up an arch, start with only about four to six canes. Carefully wrap each cane around the arch, tying at intervals with soft twine. Wrapping encourages the production of laterals that produce next season's bloom and also improves the appearance of both rose and arch. Try to keep the canes separate from each other.

Ramblers and the more pliable of the Climbers are best for training on low fences. Remove older, crowded wood immediately after flowering. Then train the newer growth in slightly curving arches over the fence. Tie loosely in place. If you will need to remove them for winter, do not allow canes to weave themselves through the supports.

Note, too, that many modern bush roses, including the Hybrid Teas, have climbing sports with large flowers that can be trained on supports. Hybrid Musks, some Chinas, vigorous Noisettes, taller Albas and Centifolias, and some Shrub Roses (like 'William Baffin') can also be trained as climbers.

Pegging is an alternate form of training for Climbers. The long canes are bent down and pegged horizontally along the ground (Ramblers will spread supinely on their own). The horizontal positioning stimulates more profuse bloom. Other long-caned roses that can be pegged include Damasks, Bourbons, Hybrid Perpetuals, and many Albas.

PRUNING All roses need some amount of pruning, which strengthens the plant and makes it more productive by stimulating new growth. In the case of Species, Shrub, and many Old Garden Roses, pruning consists simply of cutting out diseased, dead, and unproductive wood and perhaps shaping the plant. Modern roses like the Hybrid Teas and Grandifloras require more elaborate pruning. The most severe pruning is done early in the season, just before the rose plants begin to grow but while buds are beginning to swell so you can easily identify healthy growth. In the North, this would be in very early spring; in areas with mild winters, January is the month to prune. One rule of thumb is to prune roses when forsythia starts to bloom.

PRUNING

1. Begin by removing any suckers beneath soil grade. Removal of suckers should be done throughout the season.

2. Choose three or four vigorous canes, and remove the rest. The goal is create an open framework that provides good air circulation. Buds should face outwards.

3. Remove any canes or stems that overlap or cross with others.

4. Reduce height of canes. This is done for two reasons: to achieve the right height and to remove parts of the cane injured during winter. At Old Westbury Gardens, plant is pruned to white pith; see text for more information on pruning in different parts of the country.

5. Cut away any dead branches or stubs as close to the stem as possible.

6. The finished product: this bush, at Old Westbury Gardens is pruned properly for its situation. Pruning in spring might be more severe in colder climates, and less drastic in warmer ones.

Arm yourself with sharp pruning shears, long-handled lopping shears, and a small pruning saw. Disinfect tools after use with rubbing alcohol or bleach, and be sure to clear up and discard all pruning debris. These are vital steps in disease and pest control. (Some gardeners disagree.)

Here are some general guidelines for pruning roses; specifics for the different classes of roses follow. The first step is to remove all dead and diseased wood, which will be blackened, shriveled, split, or unusually or unevenly colored. You'll know if you've gotten to healthy, live wood when you reach white pith. If winter kill has been severe, you may need to prune the rose bush to the ground. Also remove any portions of canes infested by borers. Then thin out the bush from the center so the canes are not crowded together, removing crossed canes and older growth rather than the newer canes, which have an even green or reddish color and many swelling buds. To promote growth away from the center of the bush, prune the remaining canes one-quarter inch above a healthy, swelling bud that points outward, making the cut at a 45° angle that slants downward away from the bud, toward the center of the bush. This stimulates all the remaining buds on that cane to grow; they will become new flowering canes. Some gardeners add Epsom salts to promote strong stems and production of shoots from the bud union (these are called basal breaks). Remove faded flowers (deadhead) continually to promote repeat bloom; this too is a form of pruning. Keep on deadheading as needed. You may choose to seal cuts of canes thicker than a pencil with white glue, clear nail polish, or a similar sealing compound to prevent borers. Pruning paint works too, but it's messier.

Species Roses are the simplest to maintain; they need pruning only when they become too large, invasive, or overcrowded. Thin out old wood with sharp shears, preferably but not necessarily while the plant is dormant. Removing up to one-third of the wood on some varieties such as Rugosas and Eglantines promotes better bloom and discourages rose stem girdler.

Pruning for the Gallicas, Damasks and Damask Perpetuals, Albas, Centifolias, and Moss Roses consists only of thinning out old wood to keep the plants from becoming too dense. Prune after blooming to encourage new wood, which will produce next year's flowers, but wait until new plants have been growing for two or three years, because the blooms are on second-year wood. An occasional hard pruning for these types of roses will cause better flower production. After pruning the canes of Damasks and Damask Perpetuals, you can cut the laterals, which are the flowering branches, by one-third. Let the taller Albas and Centifolias reach their full height, and then prune and thin only laterally.

China and Tea roses will do well with no pruning at all in areas where they flower continually on both old and new growth. You can, however, prune to shape the plant and remove old and dead wood. During dormancy or periods between bloom, you can cut back Chinas by one-third to stimulate productive new growth.

As with the Chinas, some pruning of the everblooming Bourbons and

Hybrid Perpetuals stimulates new growth with many flowers. Prune early in the season while the plant is still dormant, after two or three years' initial growth. Cut main shoots of Bourbons by one-third and others by two-thirds; after blooming, cut laterals back again by one-third. For Hybrid Perpetuals, cut back all canes by two-thirds during dormancy, and repeat after the first bloom.

Most Noisettes need very little pruning; simply remove old flowers and dead wood. Prune vigorous, climbing Noisettes as you do Climbers.

When pruning modern roses, such as the Hybrid Teas, Floribundas, and Grandifloras, choose a height that fits your garden and then cut all canes to an even level, for uniform growth, at the beginning of the growing season. Daryl Johnson prunes to slightly different heights for a less topped-off effect. Remove old, dead, and crowded canes and clear out the centers. In general, the more severe the pruning for these types of roses, the stronger the new growth will be, which will produce large flowers on long stems and good rebloom. Hybrid Teas, in particular, should be cut back by at least two-thirds of their height. In areas with very cold winters, cut Hybrid Teas down to live wood and the desired height at the beginning (not the end) of the growing season (see page 90 for further information on pruning Hybrid Teas). In cold climates, the pith is often injured or discolored to ground level or below, but if it is alive below ground, it will resprout on its own no matter how it's pruned. Prune so the center of the bush is open. Failure to prune Hybrid Teas will severely weaken and eventually kill the plant. Removal of spent blooms is also

Cutting at a 45 degree angle when deadheading or pruning exposes more of the cane to the air. Some gardeners think this is beneficial because it deflects water from the bud, promotes healing, and looks neater; others think it is unnecessary. What is more important is making the cut about one-quarter inch from the nearest bud, and angling it away from the bud. Prune to outward facing buds whenever possible.

important for rebloom; cut flower stems along with the blooms. To stop production of tender new growth that could be damaged by harsh weather, stop deadheading one month before the first frost.

Polyanthas need thinning and clearing out of dead wood at the beginning of the growing season, plus a light cutting back. If a larger bush is getting out of hand, you can cut it back by two-thirds. Prune Floribundas grown as hedges only gently during the growing season, to encourage quick production of their abundant flowers. To get the largest flowers from Grandifloras, prune them severely, as you do the Hybrid Teas. If, however, you are growing your Grandifloras as tall background plants, prune them only to the height you want.

Shrub Roses need pruning only to remove older wood and, if necessary, to keep them within their allotted space. You can cut them back severely like the Grandifloras if you wish.

For Miniatures, thin out twiggy growth and cut them back to the height you want. Cut flower stems back by half when deadheading.

Climbers and Ramblers, whether single or repeat bloomers, are pruned when they are dormant, after they finish flowering. First, allow them to grow for several seasons so you have plenty of flowering canes (do remove dead canes). After two or three years, begin pruning. For Climbers, remove one-third of the canes, or cut back to two or three lateral buds. On single bloomers, cut back that season's blooming laterals by two-thirds. On repeat bloomers, deadhead laterals throughout the season by two-thirds. Ramblers bloom best on two-year-old wood, so cut this year's flowering canes to the ground after bloom; the new canes that then appear will produce next season's flowers. For those Ramblers that produce most of their new canes from old wood, you leave most of that old wood, pruning back only enough of it to stimulate new growth. This is most feasible for Ramblers that can truly ramble, rather than those trained on arches or trellises. Cutting out old canes to keep ramblers open and uncluttered is a big help in warding off the diseases and spider mites these plants are susceptible to.

Hybrid Musks grown as shrubs only need their old wood removed; for those trained as Climbers, prune back the laterals after their first growth spurt.

In tree roses, any growth along the trunk, below the upper bud union, must be removed. Prune the top back by about one-half, maintaining the desired form for the particular tree. Daryl Johnson prunes back to eight to twelve inches from the bud union.

ROUTINE CARE

Weeding Though most gardeners find it tedious, weeding is a critical aspect of gardening. Weeds compete with other plants for nutrients, water, and sunshine, all of which your roses want in abundance. Weeds are also unsightly and can greatly detract from the beauty—one of the principal joys—of a rose garden. The best technique is continual hand weeding; go through the beds

Suckers are canes that arise from the base of the plant. They compete with the rest of the bush and are not welcome. Remove all suckers regularly.

regularly and pull any weeds you see, soon after they emerge. This way, they're easy to pull out, and you get to them before they flower and go to seed and multiply by the hundreds. For larger areas, you can use a hoe or hand cultivator, preferably on a hot, sunny day when the weeds will wilt and die quickly after they're hoed up. Mulching helps prevent weeds.

Mulching Mulching is covering the soil with several inches of some sort of protective and sometimes decorative material to keep down weeds and conserve moisture in the soil by preventing evaporation of water into the air. Moist soil is cool, makes water available to roots, and allows better penetration of rain or irrigation water, all of which are highly beneficial to your roses. Organic mulches also add nutrients to the soil and improve soil structure as they decompose. Mulch can be almost anything, most often bark or wood chips, compost, grass, shredded leaves or paper, straw, pine needles, or rotted manure. Peat moss, however, forms a hard, thick crust, so don't use it as a mulch (although it is a good soil conditioner, worked in). Fresh wood chips and sawdust rob nitrogen from your soil as they decompose; if you use them as mulch, you must add small amounts of a nitrogen fertilizer to compensate for the loss. Gravel and marble chips make a fine mulch for a cool and shady garden, as they reflect light and heat; these same characteristics make them unsuitable for gardens in hot climates. Cultivate the soil so it is loose just before you apply a mulch. The best mulches are those that break down, like leaf mold or manure.

Irrigating Roses must have plenty of water—at least one inch per week all through the growing season. Hot, drying temperatures in midsummer during full bloom call for more frequent watering–an inch every two or three days. Because water is an increasingly precious resource, and watering restrictions are in place in many communities during at least part of the year, it's preferable to water only when necessary. Remember that water penetrates sandy soil more quickly than clay soil, but conversely, sandy soil dries out more quickly than clay. This means that sandy soil requires less water with each irrigation but needs more frequent watering.

A simple plastic rain gauge in your garden can tell you when natural rainfall has become inadequate for your roses. When you do water, do so thoroughly, soaking the soil to the depth of the roses' roots–fifteen to eighteen inches for most roses; light sprinkling wastes water and encourages the development of shallow root systems. Nelson Sterner of Old Westbury Gardens considers it time to water again when soil is thoroughly dry down to two inches below the surface; Clair Martin at Huntington waters when soil is dry to one inch; Daryl Johnson and William Radler never allow the soil to dry during the growing season or in September and October as they prepare for dormancy.

You can use any method that delivers the required amount of water to your roses–simple hand-held hoses or watering cans, driplines, soaker hoses, or a sprinkler system. Don't water in the middle of the day, when evaporation is greatest. You don't need to worry about getting rose foliage wet if you water early in the day; the leaves will have plenty of time to dry out before nightfall. Avoid late afternoon watering. An irrigation system that automatically waters at the right time and in the right amount saves a lot time and work.

Fertilizing Along with water, roses also need a lot of nutrients, which provide the building blocks for new growth and abundant bloom. You give your roses a steady supply of these nutrients by applying fertilizer. The choice of fertilizer and time of application(s) depends on your climate, soil conditions, and personal preference. Organic fertilizers include naturally occurring materials like well-rotted manure and compost; these have the advantage of being environmentally friendly, safe for plants, and providing microorganisms and organic matter as well as nutrients. Simply mulch your roses with these materials, or work them shallowly into the soil with a cultivator.

Inorganic, or chemical, fertilizers are usually balanced with the three essential nutrients–nitrogen, phosphorus, and potassium–listed in that order. For example a 5-10-5 fertilizer has 5 percent nitrogen, 10 percent phosphorus, and 5 percent potassium; a one-hundred pound bag of 5-10-5 fertilizer has five pounds (5% by weight) nitrogen, ten pounds phosphorus, and five pounds potassium). Work a handful of this type of fertilizer into the soil around each rose bush with a cultivator and water well. Be careful to keep chemical fertilizers away from stems and leaves to avoid burning; extra care is required when using granular fertilizers in gardens where concrete walks restrict the volume of soil for roses. You can also apply liquid seaweed, fish emulsion, or a liquid houseplant fertilizer directly to foliage, alone or combined with insecticides or fungicides; it will be rapidly absorbed.

Yellowed midribs on leaves sometimes indicate a deficiency in iron (it can also indicate winter damage for which there is no remedy). Water with chelated iron, or for a long-term solution, adjust the pH of your alkaline soil so it becomes slightly acid, thus making the iron in the soil available. Sometimes, adjusting the pH does not correct manganese deficiency. At Boerner Botanical Garden, chelated iron does not work, but manganese sulfate–just one teaspoon per plant–does.

In areas with a period of winter dormancy, fertilize at the end of that period (when new growth starts) and again after the first bloom. In warmer climates, fertilize again after the second bloom period. Feed everbloomers monthly. To promote exhibition-quality blooms, fertilize one month before the show date. For stronger roots, healthier canes, and greener foliage, work two tablespoons of Epsom salts into the soil around each bush after growth begins and again one month before frost. Or use dolomitic lime, which has magnesium in it to substitute for the Epsom salts. (This practice, though widely recommended, has not been proven through scientific experiments). To promote dormancy, fertilize with high phosphorus/potassium compound in the fall. Experiments have shown that year round fertilizing does not make a rose more susceptible to winter injury.

Deadheading Deadheading–removing spent flowers–is a form of pruning, and it promotes rebloom. It also improves the appearance of the individual plant and the garden as a whole; a fairly severe pruning during the season keeps the bushes uniform and balanced in the South where plants tend to become overly large. Cut the spent flowers back to just above an outward-facing five-leaflet leaf. Stop deadheading toward the end of the season, to stop the production of tender new growth that would only be damaged by freezing temperatures. Do not deadhead Species, Shrub, and Old Garden Roses that produce hips after flowering, and stop deadheading Climbers that produce hips in late summer or fall (earlier in the North); if you remove the flowers, the hips will not form.

Disbudding Disbudding is a type of pruning in which all flower buds below the top one are removed. The plant puts all its energy into the single flower, which thus grows much larger than it would otherwise. Disbudding is a necessity for producing show-quality Hybrid Teas and Grandifloras. Remove the secondary buds as soon as they appear, while they are still tiny. Another form of disbudding is to remove the dominant center bud of a cluster, which creates a more evenly balanced spray.

Suckering Suckers are growths from the rootstock of a budded rose. They are usually easy to recognize (unless the bud union is deeply buried), since they originate below the bud union, and their leaves are often quite different from the top growth. Prune all suckers off immediately and completely; if left to grow, they will eventually overwhelm the desirable top part of the plant.

Cutting Back and Cleaning Up When pruning, deadheading, disbudding, suckering, and weeding your rose garden, always remove the debris promptly. It can harbor and promote pests and diseases, many of which can overwinter. Keeping your garden clean, open, and uncluttered can go a long way toward keeping your roses strong, healthy, and disease- and pest-resistant. Disinfect pruners between cuts if any of your bushes are diseased.

Transplanting From time to time, you will want to transplant an established rose. Perhaps the site where it is now growing has gotten too shady, or you think its color would work better in another part of the garden. Transplanting should be done when the bush is dormant and temperatures are cool. Water the rose thoroughly the day before transplanting, to ease transplant shock. Prune growth back as you would for a final pruning, so the roots have less top growth to support while they are reestablishing themselves.

Prepare the planting hole as you would for a bare-root rose. Dig all around the plant about one foot from the crown. Lift the plant carefully from its present site with a garden fork or spade; if it's too large to lift this way, make a sling of burlap underneath the rootball and lift with this. Prune back any damaged roots, and replant as with a container-grown rose. If the plant is very large or old, root-prune a month or two before transplanting by cutting down all around the bush with a straight-edged spade, one-and-one-half to two feet from the base, thus making the rootball more compact and at the same time more dense with new growth.

Water the transplanted rose regularly for the first few weeks, until new growth begins. If you must transplant a rose during the summer, keep the plant shaded for a few days after replanting it to reduce moisture loss.

WINTER PROTECTION Different classes of roses, and different cultivars within classes, vary as to their degree of winter hardiness. See the discussions of the rose classes in Chapters 1 and 2, and the descriptions of individual roses in the Plant Selector, Chapter 2. The bottom line is that tender varieties of roses need winter protection in all areas where the ground is frozen for any length of time. In warmer areas, where the ground does not freeze, winter protection is often not needed at all. Roses need to be protected not so much from the cold itself as from drying sun and wind and from alternate freezing and thawing, which damages roots and can encourage new growth that is then killed back off. Alternate freezing and thawing can lessen a plant's ability to tolerate low temperatures.

You can take some practical steps to encourage winter survival. Choose varieties that other growers and nurseries in your area have found reliable. Select your site to avoid low pockets that will collect cold air and exceptionally exposed sites that will be raked by winter winds. Use protection measures that have been used reliably in your area. Some experts suggest encouraging deep dormancy by leaving flowers on plants and ending fertilizing in the fall, six to eight weeks before freezing weather arrives. Continue to water, however; withholding water will probably make plants more susceptible to winter injury.

When the soil surface starts to freeze, mound added soil mixed with coarse, noncompacting organic material (such as shredded leaves or salt hay) six inches high all around the base of the plant. This insulates the plant from the damaging alternate freezing and thawing. Remove gradually and carefully in the spring as the mound begins to thaw. Teas and Chinas don't need this much protection, but they do benefit from a loose application of salt hay.

Another approach is to cover the entire plant, after the ground is frozen, with a foam rose cone or a homemade newspaper cone; be sure the cones are well ventilated. Cold frames, too, will protect a whole bush; you must raise the lid to ventilate on warm days. Before applying any form of winter protection, remove all leaves, spent flowers, and dead and diseased canes.

At high altitudes and in areas with winter temperatures regularly below zero, protect Climbers by removing them from their support, tying the canes together with soft twine, laying the canes in a trench, and covering with soil and organic mulch. Add a heavy layer of organic mulch after the ground freezes, and leave the plant this way until early spring.

The very tender tree roses must be thoroughly covered during northern winters. Cover the plant completely with salt hay, and then wrap and tie burlap around the salt hay to keep it in place for the winter. Do not unwrap until all danger of frost is past. At Minnesota Landscape Arboretum, all tree roses are tipped and buried. See page 206 for more information.

PREPARING FOR WINTER AT OLD WESTBURY GARDENS

When initially considering site locations for your rose garden, avoid areas of high exposure. These areas will lead to severe winter damage, no matter what you do.

We fertilize in late September with Muriate of Potash to promote dormancy development. Deadheading is also curtailed in September and October to promote rose hip development and further signal dormancy to the plant. The fall brings a slowing of the top growth of the plant, but not the root system. Be sure to water your roses thoroughly going in to fall to provide moisture for root development and retention of moisture in the canes.

Prune back the plant to prevent whipping in the winter. Follow through in the early spring with a more thorough pruning. We use hedge trimmers to reduce the size of the plant in a quick and easy procedure. Spray your rose canes with wilt proof or another anti-desiccant to minimize cane dehydration in the winter. Mound your roses with compost, manure, or soil, thoroughly covering the graft and canes approximately one to one-and-one-half feet deep. Follow this with a blanket of oak leaves to thoroughly protect the plant. Pull back mulch in the spring and incorporate into the soil if you can.

Salt hay mounded on pruned rose bush will help protect it from winter.

PROPAGATION (This section was prepared by William Radler of Boerner Botanical Gardens)

When the subject is broken down into simple terms, rose propagation is easy to understand and fascinating to do. Think of the common household practice of rooting a few slips of houseplants in a jar of water on the kitchen windowsill. Often these slips simply sprout roots. Or think of seeds from a packet of flowers or vegetables which are planted in loosened soil in the yard. Usually these seeds simply sprout and develop into new baby plants. These methods of propagation are basic examples of how plants can be multiplied. And both methods relate well to roses.

PROPAGATING ROSES TO DUPLICATE PLANTS When you want more identical plants of a particular rose, there are various methods that can be used.

Growing roses from cuttings The simplest method is to place cuttings of rose stems with leaves in a jar of water on the kitchen windowsill. Rose slips or cuttings are often easily rooted this way. For best results choose a stem that has just become woody. A stem that is just about to bloom or has just bloomed is considered ideal. When allowed to get too old, or when picked too young, rose cuttings will be more difficult to root.

Roses also root from cuttings when placed in a soil substitute that is loose yet holds water. Soil substitutes that work well include sand, sphagnum peat moss, vermiculite, perlite, or a combination of any of these. Dipping the end of the cutting in a hormone rooting compound will aid the process. And to keep the humidity in the air high until the cutting develops roots, covering the cutting with a plastic bag or a glass jar will suffice. For difficult to root cuttings, the plant industry often uses elaborate water misting systems in greenhouses, but this is only essential for some difficult plants, and most roses are not in the difficult category.

To insure success with rooting rose cuttings, remember some simple rules.

• Rose cuttings need the maximum amount of light possible to develop roots, but the heat of the sun will dry out nonrooted cuttings. The bright light from the shade on the north side of a building is ideal.

• Rose cuttings are easier to root early in the season than later.

• If all the leaves are left on the cutting, it stands a greater chance of not successfully rooting.

• Cuttings should be about six inches long for standard varieties of roses with the top two sets of leaves remaining. Cuttings of Miniature and small rose varieties should be proportionally smaller.

• Cutting off the leaflet tips is often recommended to help prevent drying.

• When rooting roses which require winter protection, it is often best to grow the cutting to a larger size since very small cuttings will have difficulty making it through the winter. To make the plant larger over the winter, grow the plant inside as a window ledge houseplant or under fluorescent lights for the winter.

• After four to six weeks, most rose cuttings will start to develop roots from callus tissue on the cut surfaces, and sprouting of new stems and leaves will occur. At this time, remove the clear cover, slowly if possible, to acclimate the cutting to drier air. Then, in a week or two, transplant the rooted cutting into regular soil.

• Good soil from the garden has worked for me. I simply choose soil that has not grown roses recently.

Dividing plants Roses inherit the ability to sucker or not to sucker. Suckering is the ability to send out an underground stem to some distance from the main plant and then produce a new plant at the distant end. While this natural ability to sucker affords plants another ability to reproduce identical plants, it becomes a maintenance nuisance to remove unwanted new plants that threaten to take over the garden. Nevertheless, with plants that naturally sucker, digging up the suckers and replanting them is another means of reproducing such plants. Most plants developed from the China and Tea roses do not have the ability to sucker and roses used as rootstocks for grafted plants are usually chosen because they do not sucker.

Established nonsuckering roses can often be divided, especially when the crown of the plant was originally planted deep and many of the stems have developed roots through time. These plants can be dug up and split into sections, each with its own root system that will develop into individual plants.

Budgrafting While many roses are now commercially grown from cuttings (especially Miniatures and, more recently, Old Garden Roses), traditionally it has been commercially expedient to propagate roses through budgrafting. This amazing yet simple process joins two dissimilar roses together. To develop the technique, begin by experimenting on roses with long canes such as a Climber or a once-blooming Old Garden Rose.

Budgrafting is done in summer when plants are actively growing. The method is simply inserting a mere leaf bud into the stem of another rose. A leaf bud is the tissue produced at the joint in the stem where the leaf is attached. Leaf buds are responsible for producing new shoots in plants. Since a cutting can have several leaf buds, you can duplicate more roses from the same amount of cutting material though the process of budgrafting.

Begin by purchasing or developing rootstock plants. Rootstock plants can be any rose, but a hardy vigorous growing rose is best. Rather than using cutting-grown plants, it is best to start with seedlings which are naturally uninfected with virus disease. While many roses can be used on which to graft, both *Rosa multiflora inermis* and *Rose canina inermis* do not naturally sucker. (See source list; these are difficult to obtain.)

1. Start by preparing the rootstock for planting. Seedling plants that have been grown close together to produce a taproot are best. If more than one main root exists, cut off the others. Rub any fine side roots off the main root for a distance of two or more inches from just below the crown of the plant where the stem or stems emerge. This cleaned area will produce the root shank onto which the grafting will take place.

2. Plant the seedlings high with the cleaned shank above ground level. Soil may need to be hilled around the base to support the plants.

3. Occasionally check the cleaned root shank to make sure that it remains free of roots by rubbing off any that may have reformed. This is especially

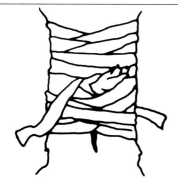

Three important steps in budgrafting: Cutting the bud from the stem, inserting it into the "T" cut, securing it with a budding band or plastic.

important to do about two weeks before the grafting is to occur. And at this time, tie together the top of the plant into a compact cylinder.

4. The rootstock should be well watered before actually performing budgrafting. With a clean cloth, rub off any fine roots and clean the surface of the root shank to be grafted. The root shank should be a minimum of one-quarter inch in diameter and a maximum of one-half inch to be best for budgrafting.

5. Near the base of the cleaned root shank, using a sharp curved bladed knife or one specially made for budgrafting, make a horizontal cut through the soft surface area of the root shank one-half inch from the top followed by a vertical cut started one-half inch above soil level. Where the cuts meet, expose the underlying wood by applying gentle pressure to the soft tissue. The "T" cut should open easily.

6. Choose the desired rose, using a stem that has just finished blooming. Thorns are easily removed with slight pressure from the side. Remove the leafy tissue at the base of each leaf and cut the leaf off leaving three-eighths on an inch of the leaf stalk for a handle.

7. From the bottom end of the leaf, cut the bud from the stem, trying to get the minimum amount of wood with the severed bud. Remove excess stem tissue without touching the cut surface.

8. Insert the bud, right side up, into the "T" cut on the rootstock, pushing it in gently but firmly to the bottom. Tie the "T" together with a special budding band, or a one-quarter inch strip of clear plastic. Leave the leaf bud barely showing so that as much as possible is covered but the leaf bud remains undamaged.

9. Within two weeks after budgrafting, it is usually possible to see whether the bud has accepted its new home. It should appear to be a part of the rose that it was grafted onto and not dried out. The budding band or plastic can then be removed.

10. Just before the soil freezes, hill soil at the base of the rootstock plants to protect the bud from winterkill.

11. The following spring, remove the hill of soil and just as the rootstock plant begins to leaf out, cut the top off the rootstock plant just above the grafted bud.

12. The bud will then start growing to become an exact copy of the desired rose.

PROPAGATING ROSES FROM SEED Another method of propagating roses is from seed. Seed is obtained from the fleshy fruit produced at the base of a flower. This fruit is called a hip. When ripe, the hip changes color, often to orange or red, but in a few wild roses it can turn to shiny black. As the color changes, the fruit may remain hard or get soft depending on the rose's inherent nature. The ripening will take two to four months depending on the rose. When ripe, the hip can be cut open to extract the very hard seed.

Special handling is required to get rose seed to germinate. It is important that the seed be kept moist at all times since it can lose its ability to germinate when stored dry. The easiest method to germinate the seed is to plant it outdoors when ripe. The seed should be covered with soil as deep as the seed is thick. After winter is over, the seed will germinate naturally when the right conditions exist. When spring weather is dry, a thin mulch will help keep the soil surface moist, a condition necessary for germination. A disadvantage to this method is that the seed and seedlings may be eaten by field mice, birds, and insects like caterpillars and cutworms.

It is also possible to propagate rose seed indoors. The secret to this method is knowing about stratification. Stratification is an after-ripening process needed by some seed to sprout. With roses, moist cold storage is necessary. Of the many methods which have succeeded in artificially inducing stratification in rose seed, one method stands out because of its simplicity, practicality, and efficiency. It combines Zip Lock sandwich bags, paper towels, tap water, and a household refrigerator. Fold the paper towel to fit snugly inside the plastic bag. Add about a scant one-quarter cup of tap water. Then add the seeds to one side of the wet towel, spacing the seeds evenly apart. Finally, seal the bag and place it seed side down in the refrigerator for a minimum of six to twelve weeks. As the seeds germinate in the bag, wait until the first round seed leaves show. Then, carefully remove each sprouted seed from the bag and plant each in a small two-inch pot of your favorite potting soil. The seedlings can be grown under fluorescent lights for a minimum of eighteen hours daily or on a windowsill for the duration of the winter. Do not let the soil become overly wet or completely dry or else the plant will die. Because the light from a south or west window can be very drying, a north windowsill is often best. The luxury of a greenhouse is even better.

When danger of frost is over in the spring, move the young plants outdoors. Acclimate the plants to the rigors of sun and wind by temporarily locating them in an open shade situation protected from the wind for a minimum of one week. A coldframe is ideal, but not necessary, for acclimation. Propagating roses from seed is done commercially to reproduce understock plants or wild rose species which are known to come true from seed. But most cultivated roses do not come true from seed. This is due to their complex background.

BREEDING ROSES The ultimate rose-growing satisfaction is reached by producing new rose varieties never before seen. The simplest method is to merely grow the seed from cultivated rose types. No two seedlings of such roses will be the same. And while it is possible to come up with a superior rose in this manner, most seedlings will, for the most part, resemble the seed parent. Most authorities prefer to further mix up the germplasm through cross-pollinating. This is done by taking the pollen cells from one rose and combining them with the egg cells of another rose. Through such a process, a whole new assortment of characterisitics can be expressed in the offspring.

There are several secrets to cross-pollinating roses. Few cultivated roses produce fertile egg cells while most cultivated roses produce fertile pollen. Therefore, it is vitally important that the rose used as the seed parent be capable of readily producing hips and that the seed has a high germination capability. Frequently, failure is met when hips do not set or seed does not sprout.

1. Choose the potential parents by selecting flowers that are almost fully open but whose inner petals are stil concealing the center of the flower. Remove petals cleanly by pulling them sideways.

2. With a small, sharp scissors, cut the anthers from the flower so that the flower is incapable of pollinating itself. The flower is now emasculated. The anthers can be saved to cross-pollinate another rose. The anthers will release their pollen in one day when stored in a glass container exposed to dry air at room temperature.

3. The pistils are the receptive organ of the flower for the pollen. To protect pistils from the elements and unwanted pollen, lightly cover the emasculated bloom with a three-and-one-half-inch square of aluminum foil shaped with your thumb into a little

4. The following day, temporarily remove the aluminum tent and with a clean fingertip lightly dab previously-saved pollen of your choice onto the pistils. Replace the tent.

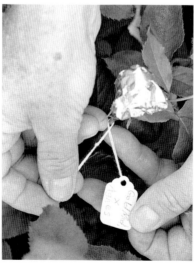

5. After the offspring are produced, it is often of interest to know which roses were responsible. To save this information, secure string tags to the flower stalk, listing seed parent first, the pollen parent second, separated by an "x" to indicate the combination. A pencil is the preferred writing instrument.

6. Starting two months later, peek under the tent on a weekly basis to see when the hip starts to turn color. Harvest the hip as soon as the color changes and then follow the instructions for "Propagating Roses from Seed" (page 196).

bility. Frequently, failure is met when hips do not set or seed does not sprout. Trial and error is the only way of knowing when the rose is a good seed parent. To save time and frustration, it may be best to start with a tried and true seed parent like 'Razzle Dazzle' (Floribunda), 'Country Dancer' (Shrub), 'Prairie Princess' (Shrub), 'Rise 'n' Shine' (Miniature), and 'Carefree Beauty' (Shrub).

When can you expect the first flower from a rose seedling? A sprouted seed, when grown under fluorescent lights at room temperature, can be expected to bloom within six to eight weeks.

DISEASES AND PESTS

As with hardiness, different classes and varieties of roses have differing resistance and susceptibility to diseases and pests. A clean, well-maintained garden with healthy plants is your first and best line of defense against pests and disease. Good air circulation and debris-free beds will cut down on disease as well as pests, and natural predators can also help you and your roses fight off pests.

Clear away prunings, dead leaves, and other debris promptly throughout the growing season. Thoroughly clean the garden at the end of the season to prevent diseases and pests from overwintering with your roses. Then spray with dormant oil in the later part of the roses' dormant period, to kill any disease, insects, or eggs that have survived the winter. A lime sulfur application will kill overwintering fungal spores. Remember that sprays will kill beneficial insects as well as destructive ones. Dormant oil does not kill diseases; lime sulfur does, and also kills insects and their eggs.

If you need to use chemical sprays to control pests or disease, contact your county extension service, local American Rose Society chapter, or local rose garden to see what works best in your area. Be sure to follow manufacturers' instructions for safe application of any chemicals.

DISEASES In general, Species and Shrub Roses, as well as many Albas and Damasks, are disease resistant. The Plant Selector, Chapter 2, mentions specific disease resistance or susceptibility of individual rose varieties. If a particular disease is prevalent in your area or a problem in your garden, choose a rose that is resistant to that disease.

A good general-purpose homemade treatment to prevent and treat foliar diseases is one tablespoon of baking soda dissolved in one gallon of water, with a pinch of Ivory soap flakes or horticultural oil (follow container instructions) added to aid spreading and sticking. Sprayed religiously every five days, this treatment is reportedly quite effective, but further studies are still being undertaken to find out if it is also safe. Sulfur is also sometimes used, but it will reduce pH level and will burn leaves when temperature is above 85° F.

RUST is a fungus disease that occurs in warm and damp climates; it's a cool-weather problem in Los Angeles. It appears as powdery bright orange spots on the underside of leaves near the ground. It can cause yellowing of leaves and defoliation. Remove and destroy affected leaves before they fall.

BLACKSPOT is the most common fungus disease that most frequently shows up in humid or wet weather. It starts as black spots on the leaves; yellowing soon forms around the spots, with the leaves turning progressively more yellow until they drop

VIEWPOINT

SPRAYING

We use a fungicide every ten days to avoid blackspot and mildew. It is important to rotate to avoid resistance. Organic methods such as baking soda and oil do seem effective if they are done often.
NELSON STERNER,
OLD WESTBURY GARDENS

The formal rose garden, where Hybrid Teas and Grandifloras are planted, is sprayed as needed based on the observations of the gardener in charge and the Integrated Pest Management person. This has meant less spraying than the seven-to-ten-day-no-matter-what cycle. The shrub and old rose garden is not sprayed on a regular basis; hopelessly disease prone plants are removed. Our IPM person is running trials for blackspot and mildew prevention using baking soda and horticultural oil.
NANCY ROSE, MINNESOTA
LANDSCAPE ARBORETUM

We use an IPM program. We do use a mildew spray, but only when needed.
CLAIR MARTIN, HUNTINGTON
BOTANICAL GARDENS

For fungus diseases such as blackspot, we spray regularly from leafbreak until frost and carefully remove all fallen leaves in fall to prevent the wintering over of fungus diseases. We never spray for insects unless they are affecting the quality of the plants. After pruning, we seal cuts with wood glue to prevent borers.
MIKE RUGGIERO, THE NEW YORK
BOTANICAL GARDEN

Plant selection helps control pests, but we do use pesticides.
DARYL JOHNSON

Good drainage, sufficient watering, and proper maintenance help us cut down the use of sprays significantly.
JIM BROWNE, MEMPHIS
BOTANIC GARDEN

From top to bottom: Blackspot, powdery mildew, rose mosaic, canker.

off prematurely. To avoid blackspot, water early in the day so leaves can dry out. Remove and destroy affected leaves and clean up debris. Jim Browne recommends weekly application of Ortho's fungicide to control blackspot.

POWDERY MILDEW, also a fungus disease, is a problem when days are warm and nights cool, especially when it is very humid. This disease thrives in foggy coastal areas. Leaves are covered with a whitish powder and may be curled and distorted. Mildew is an aesthetic problem and also adversely affects buds and the tips of young canes. To control, water plants early in the morning so they dry quickly, remove badly affected leaves, and increase air circulation. Choose resistant varieties.

BOTRYTIS BLIGHT, a fungus disease, affects large, many-petaled roses like the Centifolias. Flower buds turn off-color and fail to open; flowers rot from the inside, and outer petals turn brown and moldy. Cut away and destroy all affected parts, and deadhead promptly to maintain appearance.

CROWN GALL is a bacterial disease. It's a rounded, cauliflowerlike growth on the roots, stem, or bud union. Left unchecked, it will spread all around the affected portion; if it affects the bud union, it can kill the bush. Cut small crown galls out with a sharp knife and swab the cut and infected area with a mild chlorine bleach solution. (Note: a solution stronger than one part bleach to eight parts water will cause deformed growth.) To avoid, buy certified disease-free plants and keep them healthy.

ROSE MOSAIC is a viral disease that announces itself by leaves streaked, spotted, or mottled with yellow or light green. Leaves may become deformed and the plant stunted. The disease has no control or cure. A well-grown plant will often mask symptoms of rose mosaic. If the symptoms are apparent, you may want to destroy the plant, but don't worry about spreading the disease because it is only spread by using infected material in bud grafting.

CANKER, a fungal disease, causes discolored spots that enlarge to encircle and then kill canes. There are several forms of canker on roses; most attack in winter, though one occurs in summer and another occurs only on yellow roses. Remove and destroy infected canes. Canker usually occurs only on plants that have been under stress; avoiding stress is the key to avoiding canker. Prune out dead wood as it occurs and grow susceptible species on their own rootstock rather than as grafted plants; if you must grow grafted plants, plant them deeply.

PESTS You can make your own insecticidal soap by mixing one tablespoon of mild dishwashing liquid with one gallon of water; purchase it at a local nursery or garden center. When soap is added to water, the water becomes more fluid, and thus more easily flows into the air pores of the insects, drowning them. Remember that insecticidal soap will kill beneficial insects as well as predatory ones.

APHIDS are tiny, soft-bodied sucking insects that commonly cluster on tender new growth, especially flower buds, and suck out the sap. They cause stunted and deformed blooms, and their sweet secretions attract ants. Knock the aphids off with a strong spray of water, or pull the young shoot or bud through your fingers (gloved if you prefer!), squashing the aphids as you go along. Natural predators such as ladybugs enjoy a meal of aphids. Insecticidal soap is also effective against aphids.

JAPANESE BEETLES are iridescent, copper-green beetles that eat through leaves, flowers, and buds, leaving holes. They are very serious pests, capable of consuming entire flowers as well as foliage. The best way to get rid of Japanese beetles is to pick them off by hand and drop them into a bucket of water. Commercially available Japanese beetle traps use sex attractants (pheromones) and floral scent to attract and trap these destructive insects; Nelson Sterner finds they bring more pests to his garden. For longer-term control, treat the garden soil and lawn with milky spore, a bacterial disease that kills the grubs.

MIDGES are the larvae of small flies that lay their eggs on the plant; there are often two generations of bugs, in June and August. Midges are so tiny they're difficult to see, and their effects can appear suddenly. Signs of their presence are deformed, severely bent, and blackened leaves and buds. It's imperative to get rid of the midges before they drop off the plant into the soil, mature, and reproduce. Prune off and destroy all affected parts. To kill midges, you must treat plants and flower beds with an appropriate insecticide. Bill Radler claims that he never seen midge damage in forty years of rose growing, and suspects that it is being confused with leafhopper damage.

THRIPS are tiny insects, also difficult to see, most common in greenhouses and warmer climates; they most often affect light or white flowers. Affected flower buds are bent and discolored and may not open; flowers are streaked, spotted, and bumpy. Remove and destroy affected buds and flowers. It is usually only a problem in hot, humid weather. The systemic insecticide Isotox can be used as directed against thrips.

SPIDER MITES are tiny arachnids, most often red, found with their webbing on the underside of leaves. Signs of their presence are dull, russetted leaves. Spider mites are especially prevalent in hot, dry weather. Treat by spraying upward through the bush with cold water; do this regularly, as the mites can't tolerate moisture. Jim Browne recommends Ortho's Ortheintex, which contains Vendex, a miticide. He finds that spider mites have become immune to Malathion.

BORERS are the wormlike larvae of flying insects that tunnel in canes. There are several kinds; the least damaging and most abundant is the pith borer. The adult lays eggs on the cut surface of a cane; upon hatching, the larvae tunnels down through the pith. Damage is minor–although the plant becomes less vigorous, it is not apparent. A drop of white glue over the pith of newly cut canes will eliminate damage. Rose stem girdlers frequently affects roses that produce suckers, like *R. rugosa.* Evidence of rose stem girdler is spirals just under the bark of infected canes; the cane will sometimes break above the swelling. To control, prune out wood over three years old.

CATERPILLARS are the larvae of moths and butterflies; many feed on leaves. Symptoms of caterpillar infestation are holes or chewed-out parts of leaves; sometimes flower buds and young shoots are eaten as well. Caterpillars are usually easy to spot; hand-pick and destroy them, or spray with Bt (*Bacillus thuringiensis*), a bacterium that kills caterpillars but is otherwise harmless to living things.

LEAFHOPPERS cause wilting to tip growth, drying, and blackening of new buds and leaves, and yellowing or browning of leaf tips. The most common leafhopper in the Midwest is light green, one-quarter-inch long, and hops readily. Use insecticidal soaps to control; if infestation is severe, insecticides with longer residual control may be necessary.

NEMATODES are microscopic roundworms that live in the soil and affect the roots, causing them to become swollen and knobby. The plant is stunted and fails to grow. Remove and destroy badly affected plants and surrounding soil, and don't replant in the same area for several years. Nematodes are most often problematic in areas where the ground does not freeze; consider growing roses grafted onto resistant understock.

SCALE are small, round or oval insects with crusty shells of various colors. They gather on canes, shoots, and leaves, sucking the sap. Affected plants become stunted and off-color; leaves turn yellow and drop, and flowering ceases. To prevent scale, spray with dormant oil in early spring before plant growth begins. When noticed during the growing season, remove and destroy badly affected canes and spray plant with insecticidal soap (though it's only effective against the crawler population which occurs before the first bloom).

MICE, VOLES, RABBITS, DEER Large predators can cause even more damage than microscopic ones, and are becoming more prevalent in all areas of the country. Many repellents and mechanical devices are available to control them, but the problem continues.

Top: Japanese beetles. *Above:* The results of a cane borer.

EDIBLE ROSES

Since ancient times, roses have been used culinarily. The Romans introduced the concept of eating rose petals–candid, and in wines and puddings and other desserts. The ancient Greeks used rose petals medicinally, and medieval monks and later apothecaries continued the practice with preparations such as rose vinegars, rose conserves, and rose syrups. Rose petals were even touted as a cure for hangover.

Rose syrup can be made by bringing to a boil, then simmering, rose petals, water, and sugar in the proportions of one cup petals to one cup water to three cups sugar. Rose petals, sugar, honey, and lemon juice produce rose petal jam. Fresh or candied rose petals are a fine addition to salads and a tasty, attractive topping for desserts. An infusion of rose petals yields an appealing herbal tea.

USING ROSE HIPS

Rose hips–the seed-containing fruit of the rose–are better sources of vitamin C than citrus fruits, including oranges! During World War II, volunteers gathered rose hips from the hedgerows of Great Britain to provide the civilian population with the vitamin C they needed. To process, pick the hips–especially those of rugosa roses–when they turn bright orange or red, preferably after the first autumn frost. Remove stems and blossom ends and wash well.

To make a simple rose-hip jam, simmer one pound of rose hips in one cup of water until the hips are tender. Strain through a sieve to remove hips; Simmer pulp with sugar until thick, in the ratio of one pound pulp to one pound sugar.

ROSE CRAFTS

As pleasurable as roses are in the garden, for many people, their delight does not stop there. Roses are probably the most popular and appreciated cut flowers in the world (see page 125 for information on the best ways to cut and preserve flowers), whether singly or in elaborate arrangements. The art of arranging cut roses involves skill and talent and can result in amazing creations; even those less accomplished can produce a spot of beauty with a few blossoms in a simple container.

Cut roses rarely last more than a week. Several methods for preserving roses have been developed. By using one of these methods, you can use roses in crafts that find a permanent place in your home.

There are several methods for preserving roses. The simplest is air-drying; simply bundle the roses with twine and hang them upside down in a dry area that has good circulation for several weeks. Many craftspeople like to remove

lower leaves and spray the surface of the flower with hairspray. When bundling them, make sure the rose blossoms do not touch each other. Check the drying roses periodically; it will take one to six weeks for them to dry completely, depending on their moisture content when the process began. When they are crisp all over, remove and used in dried arrangements. Roses can also be air-dried in an upright position by placing them in a container with a small amount of water in the bottom in a cool, dry place for several weeks.

Another method of preservation involves the use of glycerine, which replaces moisture in the foliage and flowers. If stored carefully, these plants can last for years and do not have the dried, crinkly look of air-dried flowers. Mix the glycerine with almost-boiling water (one part glycerine to two parts water); place the roses in a container partly filled with glycerine so that they are standing in at least three inches of the solution. Check the plants periodically until the leaves have become brownish; add glycerine solution as necessary. When plants are ready, pat dry and hang upside down for a few days.

Roses also respond well to the desiccant method of drying, which preserves their brilliant color as well as their shape; this method provides the most lifelike results. See illustrations above.

All preserved flowers need to be stored and handled carefully. If they can be left hanging upside down in a cool, dry, dark place, that is ideal. They should always be kept away from heat, bright light and humidity unless on display. Do not store in plastic bags, and do not store glycerine-preserved flowers with other preserved flowers.

Air-dried flowers can be used in sachets or potpourris when mixed with a fixative such as orris root to enhance and prolong their fragrance. Simply crumble the petals and leaves (or use tiny rosebuds whole) and mix with fixative; essential oils also strengthen the fragrance. Experiment with different plant materials and containers for bouquets, plaques, and other dried arrangements.

Above far left: When preserving flowers using the desiccant (or any other method) inserting a wire into the base makes it easier to work with flower after if is dried. If using the desiccant method, cut stem to about one inch. *Above center:* To preserve a flower with desiccants, choose a somewhat dry blossom. Place it in a box with a heavy, airtight lid. The best desiccant is silica gel, available in hobby shops or drugstores. Place the flowers in a two-inch layer of silica gel. Press the wire stem into the silica gem so that it is upright; if you are preserving more than one flower in the container, make sure they are not touching. *Above:* Gently sprinkle additional silica gel over the flowers, making sure it gets between the petals. You may have to use a toothpick to do this. Shake the box very gently. Then cover the flowers completely with a layer of silica gel (about half an inch) and cover tightly. Check after two days; remove the smallest flower and if it is completely dry, remove the other flowers. If it is not completely dry, return it and reseal–it can take five or up to eight days for larger blossoms to dry. Remove flowers with a spoon, and brush off all silica gel with a soft brush. Check frequently; leaving them too long makes them brittle. The silica gel can be reused.

'Iceberg'.

GROWING ROSES IN THE MID-SOUTH

America's love affair with the rose is certainly warranted. With today's modern form, incredible fragrance, and everblooming qualities, the rose is a show-stopper in the sunny perennial bed.

However, in our humid climate, after the first year of marital bliss between the rose grower and the rose, troubles arise. One example is fungal blackspot which quickly takes hold in the garden, turning deep green foliage to shades of yellow. These leaves then fall to the ground, adding further frustration to the gardener. Sanitation of the garden in the dormant season with a horticultural oil and lime sulphur sprays are mandatory.

GARDEN LOCATION In our area, roses should be spaced three feet apart and away from wooden fences or building foundations to allow adequate air circulation. Rarely should companion planting be placed among roses since these plants will compete for available moisture and nutrients. I have noted, however, an exception to this rule: dwarf irises work very well with hybrid tea roses with little loss of vitality.

SOIL AMENDMENTS In our very heavy clay soils, organic material, i.e. compost, humus, ground bark, or as a last resort, peat moss, must be incorporated. When wet, our clay soil holds water like a sponge; when dry, it repels water. Organic matter enhances the heterogenous nature of the soil increasing water percolation and air movement. A small amount of coarse sand may be necessary as well. However, we often find that sand and our clayey soil produce a hard crusty surface over the rose bed. An application of crushed limestone or dolomitic limestone may be necessary. Before adding these soil amendments, have your soil pH checked!

Finally, because drainage is such a problem, elevated beds no wider than four feet are essential for best performance. If you install beds wider than four feet, the drainage in the middle of the bed is almost equivalent to no drainage.

GARDEN PESTS With proper drainage and adequate moisture, spider mites are usually not a problem. Miniature Roses, because of their dense growth habit, do display a greater tendency toward spider mites. Spider mites can usually be controlled by weekly spraying the rose bush with water. However, in more persistent situations, the use of a miticide is less time-consuming and perhaps more effective. I have seen some gardens where the roses are over-medicated with chemicals. A happy middle ground is ideal.

Aphids are usually not much of a problem. Using soapy water sprays effectively controls this garden pest.

Chewing insects like inchworms are easily held in check in the South with Dipel or Thuricide, both preparations with the bacterium *Bacillus thuringiensis*.

PLANTING ROSES Roses arrive bare root at most local nurseries in late February. Damaged roots are pruned off as these roses are potted for Sunday afternoon gardeners. These grade #1 roses are often dipped in a wilt-pruf type product to reduce dessication of the newly planted rose.

Planting of these new rose bushes should take place from March 1 to April 1.

Previous pages: The Memphis Botanic Garden rose garden.

Large paper grocery sacks should be placed upside down over the newly planted rose. This technique will help protect the canes from drying out while the root hairs redevelop on the rose. Over a period of two weeks gradually open the top (actually the bottom) of the sack, allowing an exchange of air. As the new growth breaks from the canes, increase the amount of light and air exchange until time to remove the sack.

This method is especially helpful if the new roses have arrived at your home bare root.

Without fail one cane on that very robust prepotted rose bush is destined to die. Why? In our area and the Atlanta area, the rose bush is labeled with a metal tag. This identification tag is wired to the healthiest cane on the rose bush with a thin metal filament, a perfect heat conductor. After one summer of the sun radiating on the nickel-sized ID tag with heat pulsing through the thin metal filament, and finally burning the tender epidermis of the cane, death of that cane is a certainty.

FERTILIZATION Once the rose is actively growing twice-monthly weekly feedings with mild water soluble fertilizers provides an abundance of bloom. Local rosarians may use alfalfa tea one time in combination with a water soluble products, while another time they may use a granular rose food. Magnesium sulfate (Epsom salts) is often applied in the spring and early fall to promote basal breaks.

JIM BROWNE, MEMPHIS BOTANIC GARDEN

RECOMMENDED ROSES FOR THE SOUTH
'Mr. Linclon'
'Fragrant Cloud'
'Double Delight'
'Dainty Bess'
'Tropicana'
'Shining Hour'
'Carefree Wonder'
'Apricot Nectar'
'Medallion'
'Iceberg'
'Garden Party'
'Century Two'

'Carefree Beauty', one of the hardy Dr. Buck Shrub Roses.

GROWING ROSES IN COLD CLIMATES

Most types of roses can be grown in Minnesota; some just require a lot more work than others. Of the Old Garden Roses, the Albas, Centifolias, Damasks, Gallicas, and Moss roses are sufficiently hardy to survive winter with minimal protection in the Minneapolis/St. Paul area (USDA Zone 4a, very close to 3b). The Chinas, Hybrid Perpetuals, Bourbons, and Noisettes are not hardy and require extensive protection to survive the winter. The modern Hybrid Teas, Grandifloras, and most Floribundas are not winter hardy and require protection to perform well here. Many, but not all, Species Roses grow well in Minnesota. The Shrub Roses are of particular interest here for their hardiness, and their popularity is growing. However, since Shrub Roses comprise a group of plants with many varied parentages, it is important to judge hardiness of individual cultivars rather than the entire group. Of the Shrub Roses, the Hybrid Rugosas, the Explorer and Parkland series from Canada, and many of the Dr. Buck roses from Iowa are good choices for winter hardiness.

Cold hardiness involves more than just the absolute minimum temperature at which a plant can survive. The processes of acclimation and deacclimation are also crucial. The acclimation process begins late in the growing season as the plant responds to shorter days and cooler temperatures. These factors cause plants to undergo certain chemical and physiological changes that allow the plant to tolerate colder temperatures. Plants reach a certain level of midwinter hardiness, based on their genetic background. In the spring, plants begin to deacclimate as days lengthen and temperatures rise. Early in the deacclimation process the plants retain the ability to reharden if cold weather returns. But later plant reach the point of no-return and are unable to reharden. The chance for cold injury to roses exists in each of these phases. If cold temperatures arrive too early, plants may not have hardened off sufficiently and may be injured at temperatures that could have tolerated if fully hardened. This seems to be the cause of much cold injury to roses in Minnesota. Roses such as Hybrid Teas, whose parentage includes rose species from regions with much longer growing seasons than ours, are particularly vulnerable, since they continue to produce tender, freeze-susceptible growth late in the season. In midwinter, temperatures below a plant's innate minimum hardiness level can cause damage. And in spring, severely fluctuating temperatures or late freezes can cause cold injury as the plant goes through deacclimation.

Thus, to grow the roses that are not winter hardy, extensive winter protection is needed. To discourage plants from continuing to produce new growth, we recommend stopping fertilization around the beginning of August. The most thorough protection that can be given to Hybrid Teas, Grandifloras, Floribundas, etc. is a procedure known as the "Minnesota Tip." Around the middle of October, the rose canes are tied together in a bundle. Then a trench as long as the canes is dug, extending from the base of the plant outward. The trench should be deep enough to accommodate the bundled plant. A spading fork is used to gently loosen the soil around the roots. Then the bundled plant is tipped over into the trench, taking great care that only the roots bend not the shank around the bud union (which could snap if bent). The rose plant is then covered with the soil removed from the trench, adding extra soil if needed to build up a mound. Then, in early to mid November, when the soil has started to freeze, a one- to two-foot-thick layer of leaves or straw is added. Low fencing such as chicken wire can be put around or on top of the mulch to keep it from blowing away. In early April, start removing the layers of mulch as they thaw. Roses are usually unburied and raised around April 15. Pruning is done late in the spring.

Less extreme methods of protection are also used in Minnesota, though with increased chance of damage on very tender rose varieties. Plants can be tipped over directly on the ground and covered as above, or plants can be mounded with eight to twelve inches of soil at the base, then covered with several feet of mulch. Polystyrene cones seem to be the most unsatisfactory protection method here, causing problems of overheating and excess moisture in the spring.

For information on winter protection in less extreme climates, see pages 192-193.

NANCY ROSE, MINNESOTA LANDSCAPE ARBORETUM

WINTER PROTECTION AT BOERNER BOTANICAL GARDENS

The Boerner Gardens uses the rose shelter method because of its reliability. This method, which involves the building of a portable coldframe with good ventilation and a light-transmitting roof, is more expensive and difficult than many home gardeners would like. A roof constructed of clear corrugated fiberglass is excellent. It should be constructed so that it can be easily opened when the temperature inside the shelter goes above 32° F. The roof should be closed only when there is danger of the outside temperature dropping to the low teens. Tree roses and climbers benefit from the tipping method in the shelter, which is unnecessary for other rose types.

Improper winter protection is often more harmful than no protection at all. Applying winter protection too early prevents roses from going dormant. In Zone 5, full dormancy is achieved at the end of November, and is delayed if the weather is warm. Follow the temperature and time of year in deciding when to protect, rather than the appearance of the plant—leaves often look healthy and do not indicate dormancy. All methods of protection have drawbacks and Boerner Botanical Gardens is constantly experimenting with new ones.

WILLIAM RADLER

Above: 'Sweet Chariot', a Miniature Rose. *Below:* Hybrid Teas and other annuals in a stone planter on a city street.

GROWING ROSES IN CONTAINERS AND INDOORS

Many roses are well adapted for growing in containers—Miniatures, Polyanthas, Foribundas, some Hybrid Teas, and small tree roses. The best containers for roses are made of wood or unglazed ceramic, because they can breathe. Impermeable materials like plastic or metal seal in heat and can bake the soil and a rose's roots. Be sure the pot is large enough to hold the roots comfortably as the plant establishes itself and grows. Drainage holes are crucial so the roots don't get soggy during the frequent waterings container-grown roses require. Best container sizes are: twelve to fourteen inches across and deep for Miniatures, Polyanthas, and smaller Floribundas; sixteen to eighteen inches across and deep for larger Floribundas and Hybrid Teas.

Roses grown in containers need some special care. Because their roots cannot move through the soil in search of water and nutrients, the gardener must watch carefully to make sure they are not dried out and that the soil is properly fertilized. Roses grown in containers need special winter protection because the soil in the container gets much colder than soil below ground level; the easiest method of winter protection is bringing the plant to a root cellar or other sheltered location. On the other hand, growing roses in containers gives the gardener the chance to provide them with the optimum conditions. If garden soil is poor or is not well-drained, containers are an ideal option: you can provide whatever soil you choose and perfect drainage in a container—which is essentially a raised bed. Containerized plants can be easily sheltered in the event of sudden, extreme weather.

Left: Miniature Roses flourish under good-quality light.

Growing Roses Indoors

Containerized roses that are brought indoors (whether or not they have been outdoors) become leggy and unhealthy unless supplemental light is provided. Miniature Roses are the only class truly suited to indoor growing, but many of them will do quite well if provided good-quality light. Fluorescent lights can be bought for this purpose, and the plants are usually placed eight to fifteen inches below the lights. A combination of cool white and warm white tubes provides light that closely mimics the sun's color spectrum. Lights sold specifically for plant growing are effective, but are much more expensive than standard fluorescent tubes and do not necessarily give better results.

Most lighting units are in use for fourteen to sixteen hours a day. Rotate plants regularly; experience with a plant's response to the placement will help refine your approach.

Plants need not only light, but they need darkness each night to rest and respire. Timers are helpful in regulating the hours of light a plant receives, especially when the gardener is away. Light fixtures should always have reflectors on top to direct light where it is most needed.

Light intensity and quality decline as the bulbs age. To continue to grow high-quality plants, replace the tubes after 5,100 hours of use (generally a year) and on a staggered schedule so that the change in light levels is not terribly abrupt. (Mark the date at the end of each tube to keep track of changes.) Bulbs that still have some life can be used to light garages and utility rooms. A small fan is useful to keep the air cool and circulating.

GROWING ROSES IN DRY CLIMATES

At the Huntington Botanical Garden, hardiness is not a question of whether a rose will survive winter cold, but whether it will tolerate our hot, dry summers. Our hot, intense summer sun and lack of rainfall puts stress on roses that prefer cooler, moister conditions. Although we are able to grow most roses without winter protection, we do need to choose carefully and take certain precautions unnecessary in other areas.

Spring and fall tend to be cooler and a bit wetter. A number of roses do well under these conditions. The early Tea and China roses seem to prefer our fall, and put on their best display at that time. The warm days and cool nights seem to intensify the colors of roses like 'Lady Hillingdon', 'Mrs. B. R. Cant', and 'Carmoisi Supérior'. Many white roses, like 'Iceberg' and 'French Lace' take on delicate shades of pink in cool weather.

Summer in the Southwest, with little or no rain from April through November, is the true test of a rose. Yet many roses are at their best under these conditions. 'Sun Flair', 'Touch of Class', and 'Olympiad' are all at their peak in our hot season. Some roses tend to be susceptible to leaf burn in hot, dry, weather and should be planted with some protection from the intense midday sun and drying winds. Some English Roses (David Austin Shrub Roses) are prone to foliage burn and benefit from some shade, particularly 'Heritage' and 'Sweet Juliet'.

Deep summer irrigation an a generous application of well-composted organic mulch worked into the upper surface of the soil gives roses a cool, moist root run and helps keep them flowering and growing through the summer. Salt buildup in the soil can be a problem in many soils west of the Rockies, so I avoid using steer manure as a mulch or soil amendment.

Pruning in the Southwest need not be as severe as in colder climates, where winter-damaged canes need to be cut back almost to the ground. Here, a light pruning is all that is needed. Tests done at The Huntington have shown that a light pruning results in more profuse bloom than severe pruning

Diseases like powdery mildew can be controlled by applying preventatives early in the spring before the problems arise. Blackspot is not prevalent in our dry summers. Regular summer irrigation and applications of water on the rose foliage is necessary to clean off air pollution and discourage red spider mites.

Rose cannot survive in the Southwest with natural rainfall. For those who wish to grow roses but are concerned about using water should try to group their roses in small areas rather than spreading them through the garden. Other water-thirsty plants can be grown with the roses, while the rest of the garden can be devoted to plants that do not need additional water. In that way, additional water can be applied only where it is needed, and use of water can be kept to a minimum

CLAIR MARTIN, THE HUNTINGTON BOTANICAL GARDENS

ORGANIC GARDENING

Few gardeners today are unaware of the devastating effect pesticides and other chemicals used in the past have had on our environment. Rachel Carson's searing exploration of the subject, *Silent Spring* (1962), exposed the "needless havoc" wrought by products designed to promote healthy plants. Not only were the chemicals poisoning our environment, they were also killing the natural predators of the pests we were seeking to destroy, making it impossible for nature to come to its own defense.

In the past few decades a vast and successful effort has been made to find new ways to garden without using harmful chemicals. The approach is directed at the soil and at the measures taken to control pests. Although most rose gardeners still resort to spraying of insecticides at some point, it is possible to greatly reduce using harmful chemicals most of the time.

The soil is built up through the addition of organic materials, especially compost. The addition of compost, homemade or store-bought, and other organic material such as peat moss, green cover crops, and bone meal makes the soil so fertile and productive that petrochemicals are not needed.

Pest problems are handled through a practice called Integrated Pest Management (IPM), developed by the Council on Environmental Quality. IPM is defined as "maximum use of naturally occurring pest controls, including weather, disease agents, predators, and parasitoids. In addition, IPM utilizes various biological, physical, chemical controls and habitat modification techniques. Artificial controls are imposed only as required to keep a pest from surpassing tolerable population as determined from accurate assessments of the pest damage potential and the ecological, sociological, and economic costs of the control measures." In other words, gardeners must make reasonable assessments of how much damage a particular pest will do. If the pest is just munching on foliage, let it be. If controls must be taken, nonharmful ones should be tried first. Only in extreme cases is chemical warfare waged—and then in the most nonharmful ways possible.

The weapons in the IPM arsenal include:

•Careful monitoring to identify problems before they become widespread.

•Beneficial insects, such as ladybugs, praying mantises, and some nematodes, which feed on garden pests. Some of these reside naturally in your garden; others can be bought and placed there.

•Bacteria such as Bt (*Bacillus thuringiensis*) that attack garden pests. These bacteria can be bought by the pound and dusted on the plants; strains have been discovered that breed and attack many common pests.

•Insecticides such as rotenone, pyrethrum, and sabadilla and insecticidal soaps, as well as non-chemical controls such as baking soda and horticultural oils which are being researched as blackspot controls.

•Pest-repellent plants such as marigolds, which repel bean beetles and nematodes, and garlic, which repels whitefly.

•Hand-picking pests off foliage wherever they are seen in small numbers.

See pages 199-201 for more information about pest control.

SOME SOURCES
American Horticultural
Therapy Association
 362A Christopher Avenue,
Gaithersburg, Maryland 20879
800-634-1603

Canadian Horticultural Therapy
Association
c/o Royal Botanical Garden
PO Box 399, Hamilton,
Ontario, Canada, L8N 3H8
416-529-7618

ENABLING GARDENS

Being forced to stop gardening is one of the worst fates that can befall a gardener, but the inability to get down on one's hands and knees owing to arthritis, a bad back, a heart problem, the need to use a wheelchair–or the normal aches, pains, and fatigues of advancing age–is no reason to stop gardening. By using a few different gardening techniques, modifying tools, following new criteria in plant selection, and tapping into the many resources for information and help, no one ever has to stop gardening.

Begin by thoroughly and frankly assessing your situation.
•How much time can you devote to gardening?
•Do you need crutches, a cane, or wheelchair to get around?
•Can you get up and down from the ground without assistance?
•How much sun or heat is wise for you?
•Can you bend at the waist easily?
•Is your coordination impaired? balance? vision? ability to hold tools?

Consult your doctor, occupational or physical therapist, and most importantly speak to a horticultural therapist.

Horticultural therapists are specially trained in applying horticulture in therapeutic programs for people with disabilities and older adults. They have developed specialized gardening tools and techniques that make gardening easier for every situation.

Once you've decided how much you can and want to do, the garden can be planned. For example, people with relatively severe mobility impairments should have firm, level surfaces an easy distance from the house and should use containers or raised beds to bring soil up to a comfortable working height–usually somewhere around two feet high with a maximum width of thirty inches if worked from one side and sixty inches if both sides of the container or bed are accessible. People with more mobility can work with easily worked, light soils mounded to eight to ten inches above grade and should use lightweight, long-handled tools. Smaller containers can be hung within easy reach on poles or fences, and an overhead structure can be used to support hanging baskets on ropes and pulleys so the baskets can be lowered for care and then replaced to an out-of-reach position.

Important considerations when planning the garden layout include:
•Start small: keep it manageable
•Use or create light, easily worked soils so less force is required to work them either by hand or with tools
•Keep all equipment and tools in accessible places
•Arrange for a nearby water source–soaker hose or drip irrigation, perhaps–to minimize the difficulties in watering
•Use mulches to cut down on weeding

Roses are a rewarding addition to the garden because the range of fragrance and color choice is vast. Select those that are relatively pest and disease free to minimize use of chemicals. Be sensitive to thorns in gardens used by people with visual impairments.

AARS: All-America Rose Selections, Inc., an association of commercial rose growers that tests and selects new rose varieties and selects winners annually.

ARS: The American Rose Society, a society devoted to the rose, located in Shreveport, Louisiana.

Acid soil: Soil with a pH level below 7

Alkaline soil: Soil with a pH level above 7

Annual: A plant whose life cycle comprises a single growing season

Anther: The part of a flower that bears pollen

Axil: The angle formed by a stem and a leaf stalk

Balled-and-burlapped: Describing a plant that is ready for transplanting, with a burlap-wrapped soil ball around its roots

Balling: A condition where outer petals stick together and fail to open, usually in damp weather.

Bare-root: Describing a plant that is ready for transplanting, with no protective soil or burlap covering around its roots

Bract: A modified leaf below a flower, often showy, as in dogwood

Bristle: A flexible, hairlike prickle.

Broad-leaved evergreen: A nonconiferous evergreen

Bud: An underdeveloped shoot that can develop into a shoot or flower.

Budded: Grown from a bud grafted onto a desirable understock.

Calyx: The outermost part of a flower, composed of five green sepals that support the bud.

Calcaceous: Containing calcium or calcium carbonate (lime), as soil

Cane: A long, often supple, woody stem

Capsule: A dry fruit having more than one cell

Chlorosis: A yellowing of the leaves, reflecting a deficiency of chlorophyll

Clay soil: A soil, usually heavy and poorly drained, containing a preponderance of fine particles

Climbers: Rose varieties that have long canes and can clamber up supports.

Compost: Decomposed organic matter, usually used to enrich the soil

Container-grown: Grown as a seedling in the container it is to be sold in

Creeping: Trailing along the ground

Cross-pollination: The transfer of pollen from one plant to another

Crown: The site on a plant where root joins stem

Cultivar: A variety of plant produced by selective hybridization

Cultivate: To work the soil in order to break it up and/or remove weeds

Cutting: A severed plant stem, usually used for the purposes of propagation

Deadhead: To remove spent blossoms

Deciduous: Losing its leaves at the end of the growing season; nonevergreen

Dieback: Death of part or all of the woody portion of a plant

Division: The removal of suckers from a parent plant, for the purposes of propagation

Double: In flowers, having an increased number of petals, produced at the expense of other organs

Dwarf: A shrub whose mature height is under three feet

Espalier: To train a plant to grow flat against a structure, usually in a decorative pattern

Evergreen: Retaining foliage year-round

Exfoliate: To self-peel, as bark

Family: A group of plants sharing common features and distinctive characteristics and comprising related genera; the biological category above genus and below order

Fertile: Having the capacity to generate seed

Friable: Ready for cultivation, easily cultivable, as soil

Genus: A group of related species

Germinate: To develop a young plant from seed; to produce a seedling

Glaucous: Blue-hued; covered with a bluish or grayish bloom

Graft: To insert a section of one plant, usually a shoot, into another so that they grow together into a single plant

Groundcover: A plant with a low-growing, spreading habit, grown specifically to cover the ground

Habit: A plant's characteristic form of growth

Harden off: To mature sufficiently to withstand winter temperatures

Hardpan: Soil sufficiently clogged with clay or other particles that draining is impossible

Hardwood cutting: Cutting taken from a mature woody stem for the purpose of propagation

Hardy: Able to withstand winter temperatures

Heel in: To store bare-root plants by burying them and keeping them moist until they can be planted.

Herbaceous: Without woody tissue support

Humus: Soil composed of decaying organic matter

Hybrid: A plant produced by crossing two unlike parents

Indumentum: A massing of fine hairs, glands, or prickles

Insecticidal soap: Soap formulated to kill, repel, or inhibit the growth of insect pests

Integrated pest management (IPM): A philosphy of pest management based on the idea of using escalating methods of pest control, beginning with the least damaging; incorporates the selection of resistant varieties, the use of biological and nontoxic controls, and the application of pesticides and herbicides only when absolutely necessary

Invasive: Tending to spread freely and wantonly; weedy

Lateral: Any cane growing from a main cane.

Layering: The development of roots on a stem while it is still attached to a parent plant, for the purposes of propagation

Leaf mold: A form of humus composed of decayed leaves, often used to enrich soil

Lime: Calcium carbonate, often added to the soil to reduce acidity

Loam: A generally fertile and well-drained soil, usually containing a significant amount of decomposed organic matter

Microclimate: Climate specific to a small area; may vary significantly from that of surrounding areas

Mulch: An organic or inorganic soil covering, used to maintain soil temperature and moisture and to discourage the growth of weeds

Named cultivar: A cultivar that has been given a recognized horticultural name

Naturalize: To "escape" from a garden setting and become established in the wild

Neutral soil: Soil having a pH of 7—neither acid nor alkaline

Node: On a plant, the site at which the leaf joins the stem; the area where most rooting activity takes place

Organic: Derived naturally, from living or once-living matter

Peat moss: Partially decomposed sphagnum moss, often added to soil to increase moisture retention

Peduncle: Flower stalk

Pegging: Securing the ends of canes to the ground so that the plant grows horizontally.

Perennial: A plant that lives for more than one growing season (usually at least three)

Perfect: Having stamens and pistils; bisexual, as a flower

Petal: Part of a flower's corolla, outside of the stamens and pistils, often vividly colored

Petiole: Leaf stalk

pH: An expression of soil alkalinity or acidity; the hydrogen ion content of soil

Pistil: A flower's female reproductive organ

Pollen: The spores of a seed-bearing plant

Prickle: Stiff or flexible, hooked or straight projections from the outer layers of a stem. This is the correct term for rose "thorns."

Procumbent: Trailing along the ground; prostrate

Propagate: To grow new plants from old under controlled conditions

Prune: To cut back, for the purposes of shaping a plant, encouraging new growth, or controlling size

Quartered: Flowers with central petals formed into a number of sections, usually four but sometimes three or five.

Raceme: An elongated flower cluster in which the flowers are held on small stalks radiating from a single, larger stalk

Ramble: To grow freely, often over another plant or structure

Reflexed: Curving back

Rejuvenation pruning: The practice of cutting all the main stems of a shrub back to within half-inch of the ground during winter dormancy; renewal pruning

Remontant: Able to rebloom one or more times during a single growing season

Renewal pruning: See *Rejuvenation pruning*

Root cutting: A cutting taken from the root of a parent plant for the purpose of propagation

Root pruning: The act of removing a portion of a plant's roots to keep top growth in check

Rootstock: The root of a grafted plant

Runner: A prostrate branch that roots at its joint

Semidouble: Having more than the usual number of petals but with at least some pollen-producing stamens

Semievergreen: Retaining its leaves for most of the winter, or in warm climates

Semihardwood cutting: A cutting taken from a stem that has just begun to develop woody tissue, for the purpose of propagation.

Sepal: The part of a flower that is circularly arranged outside the petals

Single: In flowers, having only one layer of petals

Softwood cutting: A cutting taken from a green, or immature, stem of a woody plant, for the purpose of propagation

Species: A subgroup of a genus, composed of reproductively similar plants or animals

Specimen: A plant deliberately set by itself to emphasize its ornamental properties

Sport: A branch or plant formed by a genetic mutation, often differing in appearance from the rest of the plant.

Spreading: Having a horizontally branching habit

Stamen: The male organ of a flower carrying the pollen-bearing anther

Staminoid: A pollenless stamen

Sterile: Unable to generate seed

Stolon: An underground shoot

Stratify: To help seeds overcome dormancy by cleaning and drying them, then maintaining them for a period of time under generally cool and moist conditions

Sucker: A shoot growing from the root or base of a woody plant

Tap root: A strong, vertical-growing, central root

Topiary: The art of trimming or training plants into decorative three-dimensional shapes

Truss: A flower cluster set at the top of a stem or branch

Understock: The stock or root plant onto which a shoot has been grafted to produce a new plant

Unisexual: Having either stamens or pistils

USDA hardiness zones: Planting zones established by the United States Department of Agriculture, defined by a number of factors, including minimum winter temperatures

Variegated: Characterized by striping, mottling, or other coloration in addition to the plant's general overall color

Very double: Roses with a great many petals.

Vine: A plant that trails, clings, or twines, and requires support to grow vertically

Winter kill: The dying back of a plant or part of a plant due to harsh winter conditions

Woody: Forming stems that mature to wood

Xeriscaping: Landscaping with the use of drought-tolerant plants, to eliminate the need for supplemental watering

NOTE: This list is presented for reference only. Inclusion of a source does not indicate recommendation, nor does absence from this list indicate that a particular source was found lacking.
There is a fee for some catalogs.

*entries marked with an asterisk are sources of Species and Old Garden Roses.

*The Antique Rose Emporium
Route 5, Box 143
Brenham, TX 77833
409-836-9051, 800-441-0002

*Blossoms and Bloomers
11415 East Krueger Lane
Spokane, WA 99207
509-922-1344

*Carroll Gardens
PO Box 310
Westminster, MD 21157
301-848-5422, 800-638-6334

Country Bloomers Nursery
RR 2
Udall, KS 67146
316-986-5518

Edmunds Rose
6235 S.W. Kahle Road
Wilsonville, OR 97070
503-682-1476

*Forestfarm
990 Tetherow Road
Williams, OR 97544
503-846-6963

*Forever Green Farm
70 Gloucester Road
North Yarmouth, ME 04021
207-829-5830

Gloria Dei Nursery
36 East Road
High Falls, NY 12440
914-687-9981

*Greenmantle Nursery
3010 Ettersberg Road
Garberville, CA 95440
707-986-7504

*Heirloom Old Garden Roses
24062 N.E. Riverside
St. Paul, OR 97137
503-538-1576

*Heritage Rose Gardens
16831 Mitchell Creek Road
Fort Bragg, CA 95437
707-984-6959

*High Country Rosarium
1717 Downing Street
Denver, CO 80209
303-832-4026

*Jackson & Perkins
1 Rose Lane
Medford, OR 97501
503-776-2000

Justice Miniature Roses
5947 S.W. Kahle Avenue
Wilsonville, OR 97070
503-682-2370

*Lowe's own-root Roses
6 Sheffield Road
Nashua, NH 03062
603-888-2214

McDaniel's Miniature Roses
7523 Zemco Street
Lemon Grove, CA 92045
619-469-4669

*Mileager's Gardens
4838 Douglas Ave
Racine, WI 53402
414-639-2371

*Rabbit Shadow Farm
2880 E. Highway 402
Loveland, CO 80538
303-667-5531

*Roses of Yesterday &Today
802 Brown's Valley Road
Watsonville, CA 95076-0398
408-724-3537

Sequoia Nursery–Moore Miniature Roses
2519 East Noble Avenue
Visalia, CA 93227
209-732-0190

Spring Hill Nursery
PO Box 1758
Peoria IL 61632
309-689-3849

Stanek's Garden Center
2929 East 27th Avenue
Spokane, WA 99223
509-535-2939

Thomasville Nurseries
PO Box 7
Thomasville, GA 31799
912-226-5568

Tiny Petals Nursery
489 Minot Avenue
Chula Vista, CA
619-422-0385

*Vintage Gardens
3003 Pleasant Hill Road
Sebastopol, CA 95472
707-829-5342

Wayside Gardens
1 Garden Lane
Hodges, SC 29695
800-845-1124

ROSE SOCIETIES

The American Rose Society
PO Box 30,000
Shreveport, LA 71130
Publishes *The American Rose,* a monthly magazine, and *Modern Roses,* an encyclopedic listing of roses.

The Canadian Rose Society
686 Pharmacy Avenue
Scarsborough, Ontario MIL 3H8

Heritage Rose Foundation
1512 Gorman Street
Raleigh, NC 27606

The Royal National Rose Society
Chiswell Green
St. Alban, Hertfordshire
England AL2 3NR

The Texas Rose Rustlers
9246 Kerrwood Lane
Houston, TX 77080
Publishes a newletter

CONTRIBUTORS

Main Gardens

William Radler
Boerner Botanical Gardens
5879 S. 92nd Street
Hales Corners, WI 53130
414-425-1131

Jim Browne
Memphis Botanic Garden
750 Cherry Road
Memphis, TN 38117
901-685-1566

Nelson Sterner
Old Westbury Gardens
PO Box 430
Old Westbury, NY 11568
516-333-0048

Contributing Gardens

David Sattizahn
Hershey Gardens
PO Box 416
Hershey, Pennsylvania 17033

Clair Martin
Huntington Botanical Gardens
1151 Oxford Road
San Marino, CA 91108

Nancy Rose
Minnesota Landscape Arboretum
3675 Arboretum Drive
Chanhassen, MN 55317

Daryl Johnson
Portland, Oregon

Michael Ruggiero
The New York Botanical Garden
Bronx, New York 10458

PHOTO CREDITS

All photograps © Albert Squillace with the following exceptions:

© Ian Adams: pages 136BR
© Ralph Antczyk, Crystal Studios: 10, 11, 15R, 23; 34TL, BL, 35, 36BR, 37, 40L, 41, 42TR, 45BR, 46BL, 47T, 48T, 49BR, BL, 51TL, BR, 54, 58, 59, 60, 63TR, BL, 66, 91, 92TL, 99TR, 101TR, 106, 107TR, 146, 147, 148, 149TL, BR, 150 TR, TL, BR, 160L, 164, 198, 208
© John Glover: 15L, 33B, 62BL, 67, 68TL, 68BL, 126, 136BL, 152-53, 159R, 160B, 161, 162, 165, 168
© Sylvia Martin: 172, 174
© Jerry Pavia: 71 BL, 80BL, 82TR, 124 BL, 127TL, 128BR, 130TL, 133TR, TL
© Photo/Nats,
©Peter Margosian, 105BR
©Ann Reilly, 80BL
©Albert Squillace: 62TL
©Virginia Twining Smith: 39TL, 99BR
© William Radler: 89
© Steve and Sylvia Sharnoff: 52T, 72
© Lori Stein: 32, 33T, 47B
© John Trager: 26-27
© Jimmy Wagner: 12B, 202-203
© Chani Yammer: 163

Illustrations on endpapers and on pages 20-21 by Delores Bego; illustration on page 29 courtesy of United States Department of Agriculture. All other illustrations by Eric Marshall.

T=Top; B=Bottom; R=Right; L=Left

LEAF SHAPES

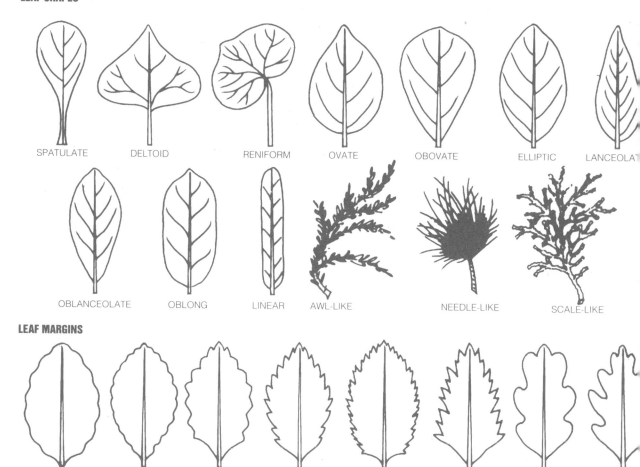

SPATULATE   DELTOID   RENIFORM   OVATE   OBOVATE   ELLIPTIC   LANCEOLATE

OBLANCEOLATE   OBLONG   LINEAR   AWL-LIKE   NEEDLE-LIKE   SCALE-LIKE

LEAF MARGINS

SINUATE   CRENATE   DENTATE   SERRATE   DOUBLY SERRATE   INCISED   LOBED   CLEFT

LEAF ARRANGEMENTS AND STRUCTURES

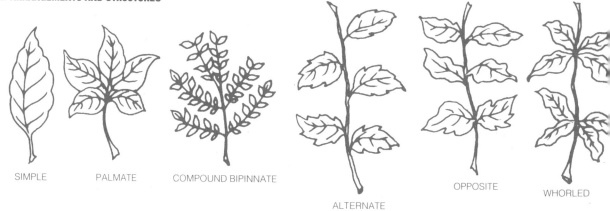

SIMPLE   PALMATE   COMPOUND BIPINNATE   ALTERNATE   OPPOSITE   WHORLED